AMERICAN LABOR UNIONS IN THE ELECTORAL ARENA

People, Passions, and Power
Social Movements, Interest Organizations, and the Political Process
Series Editor: John C. Green

This series explores the people, activities, and institutions that animate the political process. The series emphasizes recent changes in that process—new actors, new movements, new strategies, new successes (or failures) to enter the political mainstream or influence everyday politics—and places these changes in context with the past and the future. Books in the series combine high-quality scholarship with accessibility so that they may be used as core or supplementary texts in upper division political science, sociology, and communication studies courses. The series is consciously interdisciplinary and encourages cross-discipline collaboration and research.

Titles in the Series

After the Boom: The Politics of Generation X, edited by Stephen C. Craig and Stephen Earl Bennett

Multiparty Politics in America, edited by Paul S. Herrnson and John C. Green

The Social Movement Society: Contentious Politics for a New Century, edited by David S. Meyer and Sidney Tarrow

Social Movements and American Political Institutions, edited by Anne N. Costain and Andrew S. McFarland

Cyberpolitics: Citizen Activism in the Age of the Internet, by Kevin A. Hill and John E. Hughes

The State of the Parties: The Changing Role of Contemporary American Parties, Third Edition, edited by John C. Green and Daniel M. Shea

Citizen Democracy: Political Activists in a Cynical Age, by Stephen E. Frantzich

Waves of Protest: Social Movements Since the Sixties, edited by Jo Freeman and Victoria Johnson

Gaia's Wager: Environmental Movements and the Challenge of Sustainability, by Gary C. Bryner

American Labor Unions in the Electoral Arena, Herbert B. Asher, Eric S. Heberlig, Randall B. Ripley, and Karen Snyder

Forthcoming

The Art and Craft of Lobbying: Political Engagement in American Politics, by Ronald G. Shaiko

Leftist Movements in the United States, edited by John C. Berg

AMERICAN LABOR UNIONS IN THE ELECTORAL ARENA

HERBERT B. ASHER
ERIC S. HEBERLIG
RANDALL B. RIPLEY
KAREN SNYDER

ROWMAN & LITTLEFIELD PUBLISHERS, INC.
Lanham • Boulder • New York • Oxford

ROWMAN & LITTLEFIELD PUBLISHERS, INC.

Published in the United States of America
by Rowman & Littlefield Publishers, Inc.
4720 Boston Way, Lanham, Maryland 20706
www.rowmanlittlefield.com

12 Hid's Copse Road, Cumnor Hill, Oxford OX2 9JJ, England

British Cataloging in Publication Information Available

Library of Congress Cataloging-in-Publication Data

American labor unions in the electoral arena / Herbert B. Asher . . . [et al.].
    p. cm.
  Includes bibliographical references and index.
  ISBN 0-8476-8865-8 (alk. paper) — ISBN 0-8476-8866-6 (pbk. : alk. paper)
    1. Labor unions—United States—Political activity—History. 2. Presidents—
United States—Election—History. 3. Elections—United States—History.
4. Politics, Practical—United States—History. I. Asher, Herbert B.

√HD6510 .A46 2001
322'.2'0973—dc21

                                                                    00-051762

Printed in the United States of America

⊗™ The paper used in this publication meets the minimum requirements of
American National Standard for Information Sciences—Permanence of Paper for
Printed Library Materials, ANSI/NISO Z.39.48-1992.

Contents

List of Figures   vii

List of Tables   ix

Preface   xi

1   American Labor Unions and Politics: An Introduction   1

2   The Changing Face of Labor Unions   23

3   Members' Attitudes toward Unions and Politics   47

4   Traditional Political Strategy   65

5   Political Strategy in the Sweeney Era   89

6   Union Political Activists   107

7   Election Day Outcomes   133

8   Challenges and Opportunities for Organized Labor   155

Appendix A: Research Design   177

Appendix B: The Ohio Union Surveys   179

Appendix C: Variable Measurements: Ohio Union Surveys   181

References   187

Index   197

About the Authors   207

Figures

2.1   Concentric Circles of Union Political Influence   25
2.2   Blue-Collar/White-Collar Shifts among Union Members   29
2.3   Gender of Union Members   30
2.4   The "Disappearing Housewife"   32
2.5   Education Attainment of Union Members   33
2.6   Suburbanization of the Union Workforce   36
2.7   Younger and Older Cohorts of Union Members   38
2.8   Middle-Class Identifications among All Respondents   41
2.9   Democratic Party Identification   42
4.1   Labor Union PAC Contributions to Congressional
      Candidates   77

Tables

2.1 Declining Union Membership as a Percent of the ANES
Sample   27

2.2 Blue-Collar/White-Collar Shifts among Union Members
by Gender   31

2.3 Shifts in Unionists' Educational Attainment by Occupation
Type   34

2.4 Union versus Nonunion Median Wages for 1999 by Gender
and Race   37

2.5 Average Thermometer Ratings of Labor-Salient Groups   44

2.6 Summary of Changes in Union Membership over Time   45

3.1 OLS Regression of a Member's Level of Union Commitment   51

3.2 Party Affiliation   54

3.3 Party Identification by Union   54

3.4 Ideology   55

3.5 Ideology by Union   56

3.6 Liberal Issue Positions   57

3.7 Opinions on Health Care   58

3.8 Are Union Political Activities Appropriate?   60

3.9 Regression on Belief in the Appropriateness of Union
Political Activities   61

6.1 Union Campaign Participation   111

6.2 Number of Opportunities to Participate in Union Political
Activities   111

6.3 Probit Estimates of Receiving a Request to Participate in a
Union Electoral Event   116

6.4 Union Members' Participation in Electoral Activities   123

6.5 Correlates of Electoral Participation   124

6.6   Union Member Response to Electoral Mobilization Appeals   125
6.7   Nationwide Campaign Participation in Presidential Years   127
7.1   Self-reported Turnout Rates among Registered Voters in
      Ohio   135
7.2   Self-reported National Turnout in General Elections   136
7.3   Percentage Support for Democratic Candidates in National
      Elections   142
7.4   Percentage of Votes Cast for Union-Endorsed Candidates
      and Democratic Candidates   147
7.5   Determinants of Support for Union-Endorsed and
      Democratic Candidates   149

Preface

We wrote this book because we find the topic important and interesting, and we also think that American academics, with a few notable exceptions, have been shortsighted in ignoring unions and politics in the scholarly literature of the last three or four decades. American labor unions, although diminished in membership, are still a major political force of which candidates, legislatures, executives, and elected judges at all levels of government have to take into account in a variety of ways. In this book, we systematically explore the impact of labor unions in the electoral arena. We also examine union strategies to achieve political importance in the context of changing leadership, membership, and external conditions in society. We have used a rich mix of national and state-level data, both quantitative and qualitative.

This project began in 1990 and was concluded with publication of this book. The four of us have had a thoroughly enjoyable professional relationship during the course of this work. We all played special individual roles, but we also all collaborated on every aspect of the work. Eventually, we settled on alphabetical order for the authors; all four of us were essential in producing the product you now hold.

Herbert Asher, Randall Ripley, and Karen Snyder began collecting original data on Ohio in 1990, both through interviews with union leaders in the state and through designing and analyzing surveys following the elections of 1990 and 1992. These surveys included a sample of union members and a separate sample of the general population. [See Appendix B for details on the four original surveys that provided data for this book.] Snyder also designed and conducted focus groups for union members.

Eric Heberlig joined the project in time to play a central role in designing, implementing, and analyzing the Ohio surveys we did after the 1994 and 1996 elections. He also played a major role in obtaining grants to continue the project and reported to the agency that gave the grants [see below]. In designing and executing his dissertation research, he did extensive interviewing of union leaders, both in Ohio and in Washington. These interviews were a vital source of qualitative data for the book. His dissertation research led directly to the analysis in chapter 6. Even more important, he went well beyond his dissertation with his major analytical and writing contributions to the other core empirical chapters. He kept the other three authors on track and on time and was the driving force in converting what began as a vague publishing strategy into a book project.

Our debts are many. Alas, we must follow the convention of thanking people without getting to blame them for any shortcomings in the book.

Funding for the project came from the State of Ohio through line item appropriations to the Center for Labor Research at Ohio State University. The Center, in turn, awarded us six separate grants over as many years through a competitive process inside the University. The grants totaled over $200,000. We are particularly grateful to the director of the Center, C. J. Slanicka, who not only supported our work financially, but also used his excellent ties to organized labor to facilitate our access to union leaders. Sandy Jordan, the assistant director of the Center, was also very helpful. In addition, Eric Heberlig received support for his trips to Washington to conduct interviews through the William Green Memorial Fellowship for Labor Research, administered by Ohio State.

Union leaders, in both Ohio and Washington, were extremely generous with their time. Both John Hodges, past president of the Ohio AFL-CIO, and Bill Burga, who is the current president, were very supportive of our work and helped us get access to union leaders throughout the state. They also helped in our successful effort to get membership lists of most unions in the state for the purposes of drawing our survey samples. Other exceptionally helpful union officials in Ohio who opened doors and provided data include Michael Billirakis, Dave Kolbe, Carol Pierce Mix, and Patty Tutoki.

We commissioned two organizations at Ohio State to conduct the surveys we designed. The Polimetrics Laboratory in the department of political science implemented the surveys in 1990, 1992, and 1994. We are grateful to Professor Aage Clausen, director of polimetrics at that time, and his colleagues for their high-quality work. By 1996 the College of Social and Behavioral Sciences had established the Center for Survey Research, which built on and subsumed the survey expertise of the Polimetrics Lab. That Center conducted the 1996 survey. We thank Paul Lavrakas, center director at that time, and his colleagues for their careful work on that survey.

Among our academic colleagues at Ohio State, one stands out as particularly helpful: Bill Form, a distinguished sociologist who has done fine work on unions for many decades, was a generous colleague in many ways. We are also grateful to John Green at the University of Akron, editor of the series in which this book appears, several anonymous reviewers of the manuscript for the publisher, and the professional staff at Rowman & Littlefield, especially Jennifer Knerr, for their helpful and insightful reviews of the manuscript and professional handling of it at all stages.

1

American Labor Unions and Politics: An Introduction

In 1995, two candidates squared off for the presidency of the American Federation of Labor–Congress of Industrial Organizations (AFL-CIO), the umbrella labor union organization in the United States. One of the candidates was Thomas R. Donahue. He had served from 1973 to 1979 as an executive assistant to long-time AFL-CIO president George Meany (1952–1979). He then served as the AFL-CIO secretary-treasurer from 1979 to 1995, during the entire presidency of Meany's successor, Lane Kirkland. The other candidate was John J. Sweeney, the president of the Service Employees International Union since 1980 and an important figure in the group of union leaders who had forced Kirkland to retire. Sweeney was viewed as very successful because during his presidency the membership of his union had doubled to 1.1 million members in a period in which the membership of many unions was plummeting.

As the 1995 campaign unfolded, Donahue came to be identified with the prospect of only moderate change in the way the AFL-CIO pursued its goals. Sweeney appeared to be the candidate most likely to make significant changes. His bottom-line assessment of organized labor was unsparing: "The problem with the American labor movement, the problem with unions, is that we are irrelevant to the vast majority of unorganized workers in our country. And I have deep suspicions that we are becoming irrelevant to many of our own members" (quoted in Victor 1995a). "I believe that unless we make some drastic changes, membership is going to continue to decline, and we are going to be less of a political force in this country" (quoted in Victor 1995b, 2523).

Sweeney also tried to rekindle the notion of organized labor as a social movement rather than just another interest group. As he expressed it in his 1996 book, "When we participate in politics, we shouldn't act as one more special interest group. We need to act as a social movement that represents working people throughout the society—union members and nonmembers alike" (106).

At the AFL-CIO convention in late October 1995, the delegates elected Sweeney to a two-year term. His internal coalition was based on public employee unions, the International Brotherhood of Teamsters (Teamsters), the Laborers International Union of North America (Laborers), and three former CIO industrial unions—the United Auto Workers (UAW), the United Steelworkers of America (USWA), and the United Mine Workers of America (UMWA) (Dark 1999, 178–84). (For Sweeney's own brief account of the campaign, see Sweeney [1996, 88–96].) He has since been reelected. During his presidency, he addressed head-on the problems of labor that he saw in the areas of organizing, lobbying, and electoral activity.

Over what were these two long-time labor leaders, both more than sixty years of age, fighting? Did they see some potential for reviving the labor movement and making it more powerful in both the economic and political realms? The answer is yes. During the campaign for the AFL-CIO presidency both of them talked about the future and put forth ideas about how to make it a brighter one for organized labor.

On the face of it, Sweeney accurately analyzed the status of organized labor. Labor unions had, indeed, fallen on hard times. As the twenty-first century begins, union leaders have not yet found a way to increase both their economic and political power and relevance, which also means, among other things, that they have not found a way to reverse a decline in membership. Yet, even as the unions strive to improve their fortunes, organized labor still has considerable impact on American economics and politics and potential for even more.

This book is about organized labor in American politics. More specifically, it focuses on the influence of organized labor in the electoral arena. Inevitably, the political power of labor unions is tied to their economic power, which in turn is highly correlated with the number of members and the strategic location of those members. We look at the national situation for the labor movement's political activities. We also focus in detail on those activities and their impact in one large state: Ohio (see appendix A).

In this book, we will explore in detail the dynamics between labor leaders and union members as the former seek specific political behavior from the latter. The possibility of political renewal and revitalization is dependent in part on those dynamics, although they are, inevitably, set in the context of the external reality of fundamental economic changes. The relationship between union leaders and members will be critical to organized labor's ability to adapt to economic and social change.

In order to set the context for the rest of the book, we deal with several broad questions in the following sections. First, should American labor unions be considered as a social movement or as a set of interest groups?

Second, since we conclude they are interest groups, where do they fit in the diverse and vast universe of interest groups active in American politics? What interests do they pursue? Where does politics fit as unions seek to achieve those goals?

Third, what are the most salient features of union organization? How has the involvement of unions in politics evolved organizationally?

Fourth, what is the general state of present union strengths, weaknesses, and resources as they pursue their interests and goals?

Fifth, as unions seek renewal of their economic and political power what questions need to be addressed?

LABOR UNIONS: INTEREST GROUPS OR SOCIAL MOVEMENT?

Are labor unions interest groups or a social movement? Organized labor is often referred to as "the labor movement." Sweeney suggests a dichotomous choice for organized labor: either it must function as a "social movement" or as a "special interest group" (1996). That dichotomy is, in fact, too simple (e.g., see Burstein 1998; Freeman 1999; and Lowi 1971).

According to Jo Freeman, it is

> useful to think of all of the many forms of social action as existing along a continuum. At one end are those forms marked by their contagious spontaneity and lack of structure, such as fads, trends, and crowds. At the other end are interest groups whose primary characteristic is a well-developed and stable organization often impervious to spontaneous demands from their members. In the middle are social movements that, however diverse they may be, exhibit noticeable spontaneity and a describable structure, even if a formal organization is lacking. (1999, 1)

There is no single definition of social movements on which all scholars agree. One definition by a leading sociologist, William Form, who has worked on organized labor for many years (Form 2000; see also Jenkins and Form 1999), suggests that genuine social movements begin outside of normal institutional channels, that they challenge the traditional social order, and that they are willing to use illegitimate, disruptive tactics. Interest groups exhibit opposite characteristics: they are institutionalized, part of the social order, and law abiding. Some social movements simply wither away. Those that are transformed into interest groups are likely to go through a period of transition in which they become social movement organizations that share some characteristics of genuine social movements along with emerging characteristics of interest groups.

American labor unions have, over time, evolved from social movement status through social movement organizations into interest groups.

Sweeney's comment suggests there is still some tension in various self-images. Scholars have made the same point. Don Clawson and Mary Ann Clawson capture the inner tension very well.

> The terms "union" and "labor movement" capture a contradiction. The "union" is an institution, a legally constituted collective bargaining agent that represents workers in complex economic and juridical relations with employer and government. The "labor movement" is a more fluid formation whose very existence depends on high-risk activism, mass solidarity, and collective experiences with transformational possibilities. . . .
>
> Many contemporary workers have no experience of labor militance; they understand the union primarily as a servicing institution rather than a vehicle for collective action. In response, labor movement reformers have called for a rejection of the "servicing model" in favor of an "internal organizing" or "union-building" approach to revitalize dormant locals. (1999, 109)

Form views American unions as interest groups that have developed from what was initially a social movement.

> In its early phases, the labor movement displayed the militant features of protest movements. Over time, the very success of movements encourages their institutionalization. Full-time administrators devise organizational solutions to recurrent problems. Rank-and-file members cede decision making to officers, cease attending meetings, and become detached from the organization. Officers devise ways to stay in office, defend their organizational practices, and stifle protests. (1995, 16)

In short, the history of organized labor displays a general trend in which aspects of social movement behavior have diminished and been replaced by a bureaucratic set of organizations. One persuasive analysis of the progress of organized labor along this path (Lowi 1971, 12–21) portrays this development as basically inevitable. But the same analysis also makes it clear that neither model of social organization is pure. Organized labor has, in fact, moved from fraternal origins to a bureaucratized set of organizations with very specific political alliances.

It is important to realize that union members engage in few spontaneous political or economic actions. They are members of a bureaucratized organization. Worker-led sit-down strikes are a thing of the past in the economic realm, as are wildcat (i.e., unauthorized) strikes. Economic job actions, including strikes, are thoroughly planned and systematically implemented. Similarly, members' political action occurs overwhelmingly in response to recruitment by union leaders. Chapter 6 explores this relationship in detail. The political activities in which unions involve their members—for example, get-out-the-vote drives, making campaign contributions, and writing or phoning voters—are all well within the traditional interest group repertoire. So is participation in broader coalitions.

Despite Sweeney's rhetoric and the aspirations of a few labor leaders, the genuine social movement characteristics of the labor movement are subordinate to the necessities that have created formalized bureaucracies. Thus, we will characterize organized labor as an interest group. But it is essential to realize that not all interest groups look the same. In the case of organized labor, it is important to note that it continues to play an important role in building coalitions on issues that go well beyond the immediate interests of its members. In comparative terms, organized labor should in no way be confused with the National Rifle Association or the National Abortion Rights League or the thousands of interest groups, great and small, that are single or special interest groups. Organized labor is, in breadth and scope, a permanent "peak association"—a large conglomerate made up of a variety of organizations, in this case, individual unions at a variety of geographical levels. Another example of a permanent peak association, although with a different membership structure, is the U.S. Chamber of Commerce. Peak associations, of course, attend to issues affecting their specific interests. But they also address a broad range of issues well beyond their immediate self-interest.

In sum, organized labor is an interest group—closely aligned with one political party—that is capable of being an important player in broad coalitions on major issues, and of speaking for nonunion members in the context of paying primary attention to the needs and wants of members.

LABOR UNIONS AS INTEREST GROUPS

Interest groups abound in American politics. They range from being exceptionally broad in their interests to exceptionally narrow (the single-issue group). Many groups have individuals as members. Others groups are collections of organizations and do not have individual members directly. Some have both individuals and other organizations as members. Groups also form coalitions—both informal and formal—that work to achieve shared objectives on specific issues. Interest groups enter the political arena in order to promote or protect their organizational interests and/or their members' interests in relation to government action or inaction. The interests of the organization and of the members are not always identical.

Most interest groups in the United States, including organized labor, engage in a variety of political activities as an integral part of their overall effort to further organizational goals and provide benefits for their members. Groups usually have a number of resources to support their political efforts. The leaders of a group can seek to mobilize their members to become politically active in support of the organization's goals. They can provide money for political activities, especially election campaigns.

They can provide organizational support for politicians, again especially in election campaigns.

The most visible political activities in which such groups engage fall broadly into two categories. The first category involves elections. Most of these are general elections and may involve any of the roughly fifteen thousand offices filled by election in the United States. Less frequently they involve primary elections for some of these offices. They may also involve referenda on policy questions—that is, elections on issues.

The second most visible broad category of political activity is lobbying: efforts to persuade a legislative body—Congress, state legislature, city council, or county commission—to pass or defeat specific legislative provisions. Lobbying also occurs with chief executives—president, governor, or mayor—to get them to recommend specific legislation, to sign or veto individual measures, or to issue or refrain from issuing specific executive orders or policy interpretations. Likewise, a great deal of less visible and less frequently reported lobbying is directed at bureaucratic agencies—federal, state, and local—that are responsible for interpreting laws and implementing them in concrete programs.

There is also a third category of more subtle interest group political activity that receives less attention but is, in fact, very important. This is the effort by groups with membership bases of individuals, not just other organizations, to educate in ongoing fashion those members about the organization's political goals. Such education can be an important prelude to mobilizing members to engage in political activities desired by the organization, most often electorally oriented and occasionally in support of lobbying efforts.

In the chapters that follow, we focus primarily on organized labor's political activities related to elections and secondarily on education as part of mobilization of members. Education of members is a particular challenge for organized labor because, unlike many other politically active groups, members join labor unions for reasons other than political agreement with the organization. Thus, the organization cannot take desired political behavior by members for granted, but must actively seek it. We do not, however, examine lobbying directly.

What issues do unions pursue through politics? Labor unions' core interests are economic: more jobs, better jobs, higher wages, improved benefits such as health care and pensions, and increased job safety. To pursue these interests they need to focus first on organizing groups of workers into unions. To a lesser extent they also need to be vigilant in countering scattered attempts to deunionize through decertification elections. Then, of course, the heart of achieving their goals on behalf of their members is to engage in collective bargaining that results in the kinds of contracts with companies and industries that produce the desired economic outcomes for their workers.

In order to maximize the concrete results of organizing and collective bargaining, unions also need to pay attention to creating a supportive legal framework. This puts unions squarely in the political arena. Basic federal law defining the tasks of and guidelines for the National Labor Relations Board, governing various kinds of picketing and boycotts, regulating wages and hours, and regulating union political contributions are all examples of substantive areas in which unions seek specific policy outcomes. States also make a variety of laws that are important for setting the political and legal context in which organized labor must pursue its economic goals. For example, states regulate workers' compensation systems, some aspects of strikes and other workplace job actions, and aspects of financial contributions to campaigns.

Creating laws that are favorable to organized labor is a powerful incentive for unions to seek to nominate and elect candidates who support their preferences, to mobilize their members and families to vote for endorsed candidates and influence others to do likewise, and to lobby successfully elected union-friendly candidates to pass favorable laws and block unfavorable ones. Rulings by state courts are also often very important to organized labor. This fact motivates unions to become heavily involved in elections for judgeships.

Studies of unions have addressed the linkage of union economic and political interests as the motivation for political activity by unions. John Thomas Delaney (1991) discusses the core motivations in terms of unions' need to affect laws regulating organizing and bargaining and to offset the well-funded efforts of competing groups, especially employers, to create laws unfavorable to organized labor. Karen Orren (1986) adds that unions also have a motivation to work for expansionary macroeconomic policies (e.g., public works, a large government payroll, and low interest rates) that are helpful in maintaining and increasing wages and benefits for members because as businesses become more profitable, unions have greater leverage in asking for more economic benefits during contract negotiations.

Both scholars and union officials are well aware of the close linkage between the economic and political interests of unions. Delaney and Marick F. Masters summarize the point well:

> [P]olitical action is a complement to bargaining; its objective is to maintain a legal environment that permits bargaining between employers and unions. But legislation and judicial decisions have limited union activities—for example, to bargain over nonmandatory issues, to picket, or to have access to employees who are the target of organizing—and, as a result, union political action has also sought to achieve outcomes that would not be possible through bargaining. In this sense, political activity is a substitute for bargaining. (1991, 340)

An officer of the United Food and Commercial Workers made the same point during an interview when he referred to organizing, collective bargaining, and political action as the "three legs of a stool":

> Each is necessary to support the others. Politics affects our ability to organize and to be successful in collective bargaining. For example, because of legal restrictions, it is difficult to organize. It takes three years to settle a dispute before the National Labor Relations Board, by which time the organizing drive is dead. And if we can't organize, it is harder to protect our members because a non-union competitor can move into town. Organizing and collective bargaining give us the membership strength to be effective in the political arena.

Other studies make the point that unions have to make a tradeoff when they allocate resources to organizing activity and to political activity (Delaney, Fiorito, and Masters 1988; P. Johnson 1991). Union leaders at all levels have to choose among a variety of political issues on which to lobby and political campaigns on which to work and the pursuit of basic economic goals. Neither their time, nor the time and attention of union members, nor the money necessary to facilitate the achievement of various economic and political goals is unlimited. The leaders have to make tradeoffs and decide on priorities.

Unions not only work for laws that are directly relevant to their collective bargaining mission—laws regulating in detail who can be on a picket line, for instance—they also work more broadly for what they consider to be progressive social legislation. For example, in the 1960s progressive unions, such as the United Auto Workers, were active in the civil rights movement. Many more conservative unions, such as the building trades, were not so engaged. Unions have been active in efforts to raise the minimum wage over the years although almost none of their members are directly affected. They have been supportive of national health care initiatives. Many issues with broad social ramifications also have some direct impact, actual or projected, on union members. Attempts to reduce tariffs and other forms of protection for American production of goods and services are good examples of such an issue.

THE DEVELOPMENT OF UNION ORGANIZATION

Current Structure

The membership base of organized labor is made up of the individual men and women who are members of union locals. International unions are federations of those locals. The AFL-CIO is a federation of international unions. At present, over sixteen million people belong to some type of a labor union. Almost thirteen million are members of unions affiliated with the AFL-CIO. There are about 250 individual national/international unions, 79 of which are affiliated with the AFL-CIO.

The federated structure of the AFL-CIO is complicated and is paralleled by a structure for political action. The AFL-CIO has to seek voluntary support from the international unions as well as from state AFL-CIOs and central labor councils (CLCs) in cities, counties, and clusters of counties.

As if the central structure were not complicated enough, there are other labor organizations beyond the locals, internationals, and AFL-CIO. Building trades councils exist in many localities. They undertake their own activities, including political activities. Several major international unions were not affiliated with the AFL-CIO at all for a number of years. The United Auto Workers left the AFL-CIO in 1968 and rejoined fifteen years later. The AFL-CIO expelled the Teamsters in 1957 for corruption. It rejoined the AFL-CIO thirty years later. The United Mine Workers left the CIO in 1942 and rejoined the AFL-CIO in 1989. Even though formally rejoining the federation, both the UAW and the Teamsters have remained even more independent than most of the other international unions in the federation.

There are also some other international unions not affiliated with the AFL-CIO. The membership of most of these unions is small. However, there is also one major international union—although it does not use the word "union"—that has remained apart from the AFL-CIO altogether. This is the National Education Association (NEA), which represents public school teachers and some college teachers and has close to 2.5 million members. It maintains its own political action operation and is, like the AFL-CIO, a federation, in this case of state education associations that retain a significant degree of autonomy. In fact, the state and local chapters are the most politically active since school board and state education decisions are the most salient for teachers. The leaders of the NEA and the leaders of the competing American Federation of Teachers (AFT, an AFL-CIO affiliate) negotiated a merger in the summer of 1998. AFT members voted to endorse the merger, while NEA members voted against it and, therefore, the merger did not take place.

All international unions have national, state (or multistate), and local levels. The AFL-CIO has a national office, state offices, and CLCs organized on a county or multicounty basis. As already mentioned, there is a variety of other organizations such as building trades councils, area committees of the American Federation of State, County, and Municipal Employees (AFSCME), and state education association political action committees (PACs).

Evolution of the Current Structure

The fragmented structure just outlined evolved through a series of developments and choices over the last 130 years during which American unions have developed (see Bok and Dunlop 1970; Greenstone 1969).

In the late nineteenth century, unions were primarily small craft unions whose members were skilled artisans and apprentices. These unions had a high degree of local autonomy in all of their economic and political activity. The first federation of labor unions, the Federation of Organized Trades and Labor Unions (FOTLU), was formed in 1881. It was rapidly replaced by the American Federation of Labor (AFL) in 1886. Local autonomy remained the rule. Each individual union wanted to expand its own membership and maximize its economic well being regardless of FOTLU priorities. The FOTLU could seek unified action through persuasion, but it had no sanctions to enforce such action with the unions that belonged to it. This model put organized labor on the path to becoming part of the accepted social order while pursuing its employment-related goals (Greenstone 1969, chapter 1). This general model was strongly espoused by Samuel Gompers, the dominant union leader for many decades through his presidency and working control of the AFL. His view was largely unchallenged for the first several decades of the twentieth century.

The growth of industrial unions in the 1930s that resulted in the split of the Congress of Industrial Organizations (CIO) from the AFL in 1936 briefly challenged Gompers's vision. The reunification of the AFL and CIO in 1955 solidified the institutionalization of organized labor. Some leaders and unions in the new AFL-CIO retained genuine concern for broad social issues, such as minimum wage increases (which had virtually no impact on union members), health care, and civil rights. Others focused exclusively on the immediate economic interests of their members. Until Sweeney became president of the AFL-CIO in 1995, however, union leadership had become generally inward-looking and cautious.

The Organization of Labor for Political Action

Both the AFL and its predecessor federation took political positions on behalf of organized labor. But they largely avoided involvement in electoral politics and explicitly rejected forming a labor-based political party in line with what was becoming a common model in Europe. Gompers insisted that organized labor should remain nonpartisan, at least formally, and should also rely on "voluntarism" in seeking social ends, a philosophy that often led the AFL to be conservative in assessing proposals for increased governmental economic activity.

The AFL developed a Labor Representation Committee (later renamed the Nonpartisan Campaign Committee) that functioned from 1906 to 1922 to provide campaign literature to affiliates and political information directly to members through a newsletter, to send union officers on speaking tours, and to hold political rallies.

The next central union political organization, the Nonpartisan League, was formed in 1937 by the Congress of Industrial Organizations (CIO), after the AFL expelled CIO unions. CIO unions were industrially based (e.g., automobile workers or steelworkers) rather than craft based (e.g., carpenters or bakers). The CIO began with a more centralized organization. It also emphasized the class basis of union action in order to unite industrial workers with different skills and of different ethnicities who worked on assembly lines (J. R. Wilson 1973). Members of unions affiliated with the AFL were more similar both in skill level and in ethnicity. AFL unions tended to be much less interested than CIO unions in broad social and political matters.

The AFL reinvigorated its Nonpartisan League in 1943. That same year, the CIO formed its own political action committee (CIO-PAC). The key motivation for the creation of these organizations was to protect the legislative gains for organized labor that had been made during the New Deal years of the 1930s. These gains were now under threat as southern Democrats in Congress became increasingly conservative and alienated from northern Democrats (Sinclair 1982). Simple arithmetic made it clear that if the growing number of Republicans in Congress and a large proportion of southern Democrats agreed, they could gut union-friendly legislation.

The fears of organized labor were well founded. After the Republicans captured the majority of the House and Senate in the 1946 election, they and the conservative southern Democrats quickly passed the Taft-Hartley Act in 1947. This legislation gave the president of the United States the power to break strikes, gave states the right to ban "closed shops"—that is, mandatory union membership—by passing "right-to-work" laws, and restricted a number of union organizing practices and internal operations. The AFL responded by establishing the Labor's League for Political Education (LLPE), its first PAC. When the AFL and CIO merged in 1955 to form the AFL-CIO, the LLPE and the CIO–PAC merged to become the Committee on Political Education (COPE).

COPE was grafted onto the general union structure. Since the international unions affiliated with the AFL-CIO have considerable autonomy, this means that the political operations of the international unions also retained considerable autonomy. Through their own PACs, internationals choose whether to offer the same candidate endorsements as COPE, how much money to donate to COPE, and whether to coordinate political activities with COPE, undertake their own activities, or simply be politically inactive. COPE maintains substantial control over affiliates' financial contributions by assessing the internationals' PACs in line with the membership size of those internationals (Wilcox 1994, 22).

Some labor unions, particularly after the formation of the CIO in 1935, have been highly visible and vocal advocates of the disadvantaged classes. Other unions—especially those coming from the AFL tradition—have been reluctant to go beyond narrow economic issues. To the extent that the Democratic Party in national politics spoke for the less advantaged classes, that role was buttressed and even demanded by activist unions that developed a close affiliation with the Democrats. In many cities and states, organized labor provided the backbone of the Democratic Party organization. Nationally, from the late 1930s and early 1940s until the 1970s, organized labor also provided a significant part of the organizational muscle for the national Democratic Party (see Greenstone 1969).

The closeness of organized labor to the national leadership of the Democratic Party was diminished abruptly in 1972 when the AFL-CIO had little to do with nominating Senator George McGovern, the Democratic candidate for president, and then refused to endorse him in the campaign. The rupture was partially repaired after 1972, although the closeness of the unions and the Democratic Party hierarchy never recovered fully. (For evidence on how the unions had again become close to the Democratic leadership in the House by the late 1980s, see Dark 1996; for an overview of the general relationship between the unions and the Democratic Party see Dark 1999.)

Eventually, unions regained some of their influence in Democratic presidential nominating politics and platform writing, although they dictated neither (Rapoport, Stone, and Abramowitz 1991; Rozell and Wilcox 1999). Union-sponsored PACs gave almost all of their contributions—about 95 percent in the 1990s—to the Democratic Party (for a useful summary for three elections in the 1990s, see Rozell and Wilcox 1999, 90). They also increased the amounts of their donations in the 1990s compared to the previous decades.

At the same time, however, the unions' impact in terms of getting specific legislation favorable to their interests as unions diminished. One particularly notable failure came in 1978, with a Democratic president and solid majorities in both the House and Senate, when a bill to strengthen collective bargaining rights that was very important to the unions could not be passed (Fink 1998).

As the Democratic Party moved to the political center on issues and as President Bill Clinton also moved to the center, albeit erratically in his first term, organized labor became the chief spokesperson for what remained of the American "left" in politics—never a dominant force and now weaker than it had been at any time since the 1920s. Organized labor also became visibly and consistently protectionist on questions of international trade. It retained its willingness to speak on a wide variety of issues. It remained a broad-gauged, multi-issue interest group.

As some unions led the way in speaking on a broad range of issues well beyond their own immediate concerns with wages, hours, benefits, and collective bargaining agreements, they became visible spokespersons on those broader issues. In some cases, the members of the activist unions were not totally in support of union positions on issues that went beyond the provisions of collective bargaining contracts. In other cases, a sizeable portion of the membership was in disagreement with, or even hostile to, policy positions taken publicly by national union leaders. For example, as some unions led the effort to guarantee civil rights and equal rights for all Americans, some white union members become very edgy about perceived economic threats from minorities and some male members became wary of women's increasing importance in their industries and unions.

Significant changes have occurred in the range of interests articulated and the degree of agreement among union leaders on those interests in the last several decades. After the AFL-CIO merger, the differences in outlook between the two sets of unions gradually began to dwindle. Several decades of evolution resulted in a union movement by the 1990s for which the image of uniformly highly conservative, purely contract-oriented leadership no longer corresponded to reality. Leaders of a wider variety of unions became more interested in taking positions on issues that went well beyond narrowly defined interests of organized labor. More leaders were willing to speak up about social issues of broader interest. Part of this change stemmed from the replacement of older labor leaders with younger ones. Part of it grew, perhaps, from the realization by some labor leaders that they needed to be engaged with broader issues in order to have an observable impact on public policy. Labor needed to be part of larger coalitions on broader issues in order to succeed. Focusing on fairly narrow issues involving only union interests was not producing the desired results. Unions alone had very low legislative success rates.

UNION STRENGTHS, WEAKNESSES, AND RESOURCES

The Changing Status of American Unions

Membership: An Overview

The number of union members in the labor force peaked in the mid-1970s with slightly more than twenty-two million members. In terms of "density" of union membership—the percentage of the nonagricultural workforce who are union members—the postwar peak came earlier, in the mid-1950s. At that time, almost 35 percent of the workforce was unionized.

Density is almost as low now as it was in 1935–1936, just before the Wagner Act of 1935 took effect. That law established collective bargaining in its modern form and created the National Labor Relations Board to enforce fair labor practices and protect collective bargaining. The absolute number of members has fallen steadily since 1975 and is now about what it was in the early 1950s. Membership in the AFL-CIO is currently just short of thirteen million, about the same size as in 1955, the year the AFL and CIO merged. However, some unions now in the AFL-CIO were still independent in 1955, most notably the United Mine Workers.

Profound changes in the distribution of American workers by type of employment have also affected the distribution of union members. Manufacturing employment has shrunk in relative terms and service industries have grown. At the same time, unions have also been relatively successful in organizing public workers, another growing employment sector. These simultaneous changes are reflected in the composition of union membership.

In all likelihood, the traditional industrial unions will continue to shrink in size. Three major industrial unions—the United Auto Workers, the International Association of Machinists (IAM), and the United Steelworkers—announced their intent to merge into a single union. These three unions were three of the five largest unions in the nation in 1960. Four decades of changes in the nature of the American economy radically altered their size and importance. Other mergers of smaller unions have also occurred with regularity over the last several decades.

The relative strength of unionized private- and public-sector workers is also changing. In 1964, 92 percent of all union members were in the private sector and the rest were in the public sector. By 1996, only 58 percent of all union members worked in the private sector and the rest were in the public sector.

A different way of making the same point is to compare the density of unionization in the public and private sectors separately. In 1964, union density in the private sector was 34 percent; it was only 15 percent in the public sector. By 1976, union density was higher in the public sector than in the private sector (25 percent compared to 21 percent). By 1998, private-sector density had fallen to 9.5 percent. Public-sector density was at 37.5 percent (Swoboda 1999b).

In their basic economic realm, unions have succeeded in keeping the wages and benefits of the members they represent higher than wages and benefits for nonunion workers. How much of that differential is the result of union success at the bargaining table compared to simply organizing in higher-paying occupations is not clear. One recent study, which controls for the age and educational level of workers, finds that between 1974 and 1996 the advantage of union workers over nonunion workers is substantial and has, in fact, increased steadily (Johnston 1997, citing the work of Donald R. Deere). But this relative success has not been translated into success in organizing or retaining members. In fact, as union membership has declined and recruitment of new union members has faltered, the better paid, older workers have, at least in some unions, become a larger proportion of the membership. This fact helps explain the nominal success of unions in "producing" better wages and benefits.

Reasons for Shrinkage

The decline of organized labor in terms of membership size and density in the workforce—particularly in the private sector—over the last four decades has been explained in a number of ways (for two analyses that differ significantly, see Goldfield 1987, and Craver 1993).

It is undeniably true that employment has declined significantly in many of the industries in which unions were most successful in organizing workers in the late 1930s, 1940s, and 1950s. We make less steel. Railroads now employ less than 10 percent of the number of employees that they employed in the 1920s in what was, of course, a much smaller total labor force. Examples could proliferate. Thus, membership of unions in such industries, heavily unionized at their peak, is bound to fall. However, those losses could, in principle, be offset by gains in expanding industries. Aggressive unions in the service and governmental areas, for example, have grown substantially in recent decades. But, in fact, many unions have not been aggressive in seeking to organize workers in newly prospering companies and industries. Many of the traditional unions have simply focused on their historical membership base, which, by definition, puts them into decline.

For a complex set of reasons, the American electorate has become generally more conservative on economic and government management issues since World War II, with some temporary movement in a more liberal direction in the 1960s (Page and Shapiro 1992; Stimson 1991; Stimson, MacKuen, and Erikson 1995). But with that exception both parties have moved rightward—Democrats to a much more moderate stance on most issues and Republicans to a very conservative position. This helps explain the general trend toward labor legislation that is unfavorable to unions. It also means that unions have a harder set of policy "sells" to make to the president and Congress and their counterparts in the states.

Coupled with the uneven aggressiveness of unions in organizing new workers is the fact that national elections have produced Congresses that have, beginning with the passage of the Taft-Hartley Act in 1947, made the legal climate for unions progressively less favorable, even though most of those Congresses have had a majority of Democrats. There have been periods of little change in basic labor law, but when change has come it has usually been weighted in an antiunion direction. In 1959, even in a heavily Democratic majority, Congress added the Landrum-Griffin Act that created a number of new administrative and financial reporting requirements for unions. The rationale was to eliminate corruption in unions, although organized labor found the provisions of the act onerous.

No doubt, most employers, encouraged both by the passivity of some unions and by the general tone of national labor law, have remained quite active in opposing unionization. The aggressiveness of antiunion employers was reinforced by the successful destruction of the Professional Air Traffic Controllers Organization by the Ronald Reagan administration in 1981. Some employers have also been helped by the globalization of the economy and of major corporations, which means that jobs can be shifted out of the United States if the cost and conditions of American labor are viewed as reducing profits.

In short, job shrinkage in heavily unionized industries, uneven union organizing efforts, a legal climate tilting toward nonunion outcomes, aggressively antiunion employers, and economic globalization have worked together to explain much of the decline in union membership.

There is disagreement on whether the movement of jobs to the Sunbelt states has made union organizing more difficult since those areas have traditionally been hostile to unions. But efforts to organize there have been met with some success. If the effort to organize is not made consistently, it is relatively easy to blame Sunbelt culture, perhaps inaccurately. To be sure, there are regional differences in union density, but these differences are not necessarily immutable. In 1996, the Northeast and Midwest had union density of about 20 percent, the West Coast about 17 percent, the border states 10 percent, the mountain and plains states just under 10 percent, and the South 7 percent (Hirsch and Macpherson 1997, 26–7).

Some claim that the changing nature of the economy—broadly speaking, from an industrial base to a service base—has doomed unions to decline because they first became strong in the industrial realm. This claim seems weak. Aggressive unions in the service and government areas have done quite well. And unionization in the traditional areas of union strength has often declined even more rapidly than the industry itself.

Some also claim that traditional domination of unions by white males has meant that unions do not know how to organize a changing workforce that involves much higher proportions of women and minorities. This claim also seems weak. Many unions have changed leaders and attitudes at least as rapidly as management in dealing with a more diverse workforce. And, if women and minorities are disproportionate in low-paying jobs, they might, in fact, be more susceptible to unionization than others—presumably predominantly white males—in high-paying jobs. As such, they have more to gain.

Public Confidence in Union Leaders

The level of public confidence in the leaders of organized labor has not been high, either in absolute terms or in relation to public confidence in the leaders of other major American institutions. When data from 1973 to 1996 on the public's confidence in the leaders of twelve major American institutions is examined, union leaders did very poorly (*Public Perspective* 1997a).

The operative question in each year was: "As far as the people running these institutions [each is listed separately] are concerned, would you say you have a great deal of confidence, only some confidence, or hardly any confidence at all in them?" Public confidence in the leaders of organized labor has been consistently low. In 1996, only 11 percent of those surveyed had a great deal of confidence in them and 30 percent had hardly any confidence. The only worse numbers—and that by only a little bit—were for the media, the executive branch, and Congress.

The relatively low level of public confidence in union leaders almost surely limits their effectiveness even with their own members as well as with the public in general.

General Public Opinion about Unions

National surveys conducted by the Gallup organization over a number of years show a relatively favorable position for unions in general (Cornfield 1999). Two series of questions provide an interesting picture. Beginning in 1936, Gallup asked a national sample every few years the question: "Do you approve or disapprove of labor unions?" In 1936, 72 percent approved and 20 percent disapproved. In subsequent years approval has fluctuated between a high of 75 percent (1953 and 1957) and a low of 55 percent (1979 and 1981). Disapproval has ranged from a high of 35 percent (1981) to a low of 14 percent (1957 and 1959). In August 1999, 65 percent approved of unions and 28 percent disapproved. Unions have enjoyed consistent support in the sense that those approving have always outnumbered those disapproving by between 20 percent and 61 percent. In 1999, the gap was 37 percent.

The second general question that Gallup has posed every few years since 1965 is: "In your opinion which of the following will be the biggest threat to the country in the future—big business, big labor, or big government?" Big government has always been viewed as the greatest threat, but labor was viewed as a greater threat than business from 1965 until

1978. Labor and business remained close, both overshadowed by government, through the 1985 survey. Gallup did not ask the question again until 1995. In the last three surveys (1995, 1998, and 1999), labor has almost vanished as "the biggest threat." In 1999, only 8 percent of the sample saw labor that way; 24 percent felt that big business was the biggest threat, and 65 percent named big government as the biggest threat. It may be that as unions have gotten weaker in society overall their perceived threat potential has diminished. And, as noted earlier, there is general public approval of them.

Political Resources

Despite the relative decline of organized labor in the economy, it is still very important politically. That importance is based on some tangible strengths.

First, the access of the leaders of organized labor to millions of individuals in order to air their views and preferences on politics—and other matters too—is great. The AFL-CIO, international unions, and locals all have newsletters and other means of communication to get those preferences to members quickly. AFL-CIO leaders—although not dictating to the internationals that are affiliated with the AFL-CIO—are taken seriously and their views are publicized down through the internationals to the locals. It is also relevant to note that almost 80 percent of all union members in the country belong to unions affiliated with the AFL-CIO. Naturally, all thirteen million AFL-CIO members will not react to all situations as one, vote as one, or view their union leaders in the same way. Nevertheless, the simple fact that the leaders can seek to persuade millions of people with a variety of special communications with relative ease and relatively quickly gives union leaders major potential for influencing members. The AFL-CIO has an active political education program. So do major individual unions, both those in the AFL-CIO and those not affiliated (especially the NEA).

Second, unions are generally more politically active than many other membership organizations (Baumgartner and Leech 1998, 225; Knoke 1990, 19; Verba, Schlozman, and Brady 1995, chapter 5). They also are more likely to seek to mobilize their members for political purposes than other organizations (Baumgartner and Leech 1998, 230; Kollman 1998; Schlozman and Tierney 1986).

Third, the union hierarchy that already exists can be used to organize political campaigns—including those for broadly conceived political education programs, registration drives aimed at increasing political participation, working for specific outcomes in referenda, and working for victories by specific candidates in both general elections and, less frequently, primary elections. And the union leaders committed to these political ends are in a position to seek volunteer labor from a large membership base as well as to seek votes. Much of the original data we analyze in subsequent chapters in this book deals with the relationship between leaders and members as the former seek specific kinds of political behavior from the latter.

Fourth, organized labor can contribute sizeable financial resources to political parties and candidates. Labor interests are outspent by business interests, but their spending is still considerable. Few people remember that the concept of the PAC was invented by the CIO for the benefit of Democrats in the 1944 campaign. The concept really caught hold several decades later (Sabato 1990).

Labor PACs are important. They are also significantly different from most PACs in several respects. A leading scholar of campaign finance, Frank J. Sorauf, argues that labor PACs are more centralized, have more resources, are more inclined to support nonincumbents, and are more directly aligned with a single political party (the Democrats) than other PACs (Sorauf 1992, 106–12). These characteristics give them considerable clout in electoral politics, although in recent years, at both the federal and state levels, Republicans have taken the lead in trying to add additional restrictions to the ability of unions both to collect money from their membership and to spend it on politics. Chapter 4 will analyze labor PACs in detail.

The type and volume of spending unions undertake is important as well. For example, the $35 million the AFL-CIO spent in 1996 on ads in closely contested races for Congress probably magnified the impact of that spending in comparison to using the money for contributions to the political parties more generally. As part of its overall strategy, the AFL-CIO, reacting to the Republican capture of Congress in the 1994 election, tried to focus on swing districts, not just "friends of labor," who might well come from safely Democratic seats. The strategy was to focus on races in which defeat of a Republican by a Democrat had a reasonable chance of success.

Gary C. Jacobson (1999) showed that labor's 1996 spending was highly effective in helping to defeat some targeted Republican freshmen in the House, but did not have the same impact on senior Republican incumbents. Of forty-four targeted Republican freshmen, twelve were defeated and Jacobson argues that labor's efforts made the difference in seven of those twelve races. Labor's activities and spending would have been even more effective had the Democratic Party been able to recruit a larger number of qualified challengers.

In 1998, organized labor refined its strategy to fit a different kind of election. In 1996, the strategy was to attack marginal Republican House members who had been swept into office during the Republican congressional landslide of 1994. The 1998 election occurred in the middle of the second term of a popular, although distrusted, president. The president's party in Congress almost always loses a significant number of seats in a midterm election in the sixth year of an incumbency. Labor's strategy was to aim at ousting only the weakest Republicans in order to focus resources on protecting incumbent Democrats and winning open seats that had been held by Democrats. Realistically, organized labor was willing to have the Congress in 1999–2000 look a great deal like the Congress in 1997–1998. "Independent" expenditures of $28 million—those focused on individual races—were targeted to 41 districts, compared to the 102 that had been targeted in 1996. The spending emphasized grassroots mobilization, the recruitment and training of volunteers, and get-out-the-vote drives rather than television advertisements, which eat up more money more quickly.

The 1996 election was a success for the Democrats. The party gained a few seats in the House and cut the Republican majority to six seats. Organized labor repeated this strategy in the 2000 election. The Democrats gained two seats in the House and four seats in the Senate, neither sufficient to take over majority control. It would be too simple to credit organized labor's strategy as the major cause of these gains, but it certainly helped. The voting participation of union households increased considerably as a share of the electorate in both years.

In early planning for the 2000 congressional campaign, the AFL-CIO, at its annual winter meeting in 1999, decided to spend $46 million during 1999–2000 to seek to return control of the House of Representatives to the Democrats. As of February 1999, the AFL-CIO indicated it would focus on forty to sixty districts spread over about twenty states. The federation also decided to keep its political operations in place rather than to follow their normal habit of disbanding the operation after each election and then recreating it before the next election after a hiatus (Swoboda 1999b).

At its winter meeting in 2000, the AFL-CIO reinforced its commitment to help the Democrats win both the White House and the House of Representatives in the elections in November 2000. The organization targeted seventy-one congressional districts on which to focus their efforts, on behalf of the Democrat in seventy cases and on behalf of the Republican in a single case. Unions had identified sixteen hundred individuals to coordinate election efforts in 2000. This was a fourfold increase from 1998 (Swoboda 2000a; Greenhouse 2000a).

RENEWAL?

What does the future hold for organized labor as it pursues its political agenda? As described in the opening pages of this chapter, Sweeney campaigned for the AFL-CIO presidency in 1995 on a platform of renewing the labor movement and making it more aggressive. After his victory, he quickly moved on both key fronts: seeking new members and seeking to be more influential politically. He increased the central AFL-CIO budget for organizing to $20 million annually from about $2.5 million a few years earlier. He also had the AFL-CIO make a major effort to affect the 1996 election by spending $35 million centrally in support of candidates perceived as prounion.

In analytic terms, Sweeney's overall strategy for increasing labor's political influence is an instance of moving from an increasingly unsuccessful "inside" strategy to an "outside" strategy (Heberlig 2000). An inside strategy focuses on getting favorable policy actions by direct contact with public officials, whether elected, appointed, or in the career bureaucracy. An outside strategy focuses on getting favorable policy actions by mobilizing people outside the capital city to influence policymakers' perceptions of the intensity and direction of public opinion on an issue. Sweeney is leading the AFL-CIO in designing and implementing strategies for increasing membership, mobilizing union members for political action, and more closely coordinating lobbying on policy positions by targeting specific electoral results.

Whether Sweeney succeeds in revitalizing the influence of the AFL-CIO sufficiently—to increase membership, organize workers in additional companies and industries, and get more favorable election outcomes—remains to be seen. He is undeniably an activist and was president of his own union during a period of significant growth. But he and his colleagues face major challenges.

In this book, we will carefully analyze the opportunities beckoning and the constraints limiting union leaders as they seek desired political behavior from members. We also want to explain, on the basis of data, what the leaders can deliver at present in terms of mobilizing members for political action and also in terms of influencing their electoral behavior.

In chapter 2, we present a detailed look at the changing nature of American unions. The nature of these changes helps set important limits to what unions can accomplish politically. They also create some opportunities.

In chapter 3, we focus on members' attitudes toward unions and politics. These attitudes create constraints for union leaders in terms of what they can achieve and the strategies they use to mobilize those members for political activity. Union leaders have developed political strategies that account for the diversity of union membership and the range of members' political beliefs.

In chapter 4, we discuss how the strategies attempt to strike a balance between the need for the members' consent and the need for the leaders to act according to their perception of the long-term interest of organized labor.

Chapter 5 details the changes in unions' political strategies in the Sweeney era. When he became AFL-CIO president, he faced a new Republican majority in both houses of Congress and in many state legislatures. Labor's political strategy changed dramatically to adapt to this new political environment. The new strategy relied much more extensively on aggressive organizing, media advertising, and the political mobilization of members.

In chapter 6, we evaluate the potential for effective grassroots political mobilization by organized labor. We examine the strategies used by local officers to recruit political activists from the rank and file and limitations of these strategies. We also use our survey data of Ohio union members to analyze which members are targeted by leaders for political mobilization and which members respond positively to mobilization appeals from union leaders.

Chapter 7 focuses on the outcomes of unions' political mobilization—that is, turnout and vote choice. We examine the extent to which unions are able to get their members to the polls and the extent to which members vote for candidates endorsed by the union. We rely on data from both the national level (the American National Election Studies) and the state level (our Ohio union surveys in 1990, 1992, 1994, and 1996) to address these issues.

Chapter 8 draws broader conclusions about the importance of organized labor in American elections, both through directly seeking specific electoral outcomes and through broader mobilization of members for political purposes.

We do not claim to explain all that unions are, have been, and can be. But we do seek to offer a very clear picture of their political importance—both actual and potential—as the twenty-first century opens. More important, we explain, on the basis of data analysis, the dynamics of the interactions of leaders and members as the former seek specific political behavior, including voting choices, from the latter. In doing so, we add to the understanding of the internal functioning of interest groups in general as well as the specific functioning of labor unions in the political process.

2

The Changing Face of Labor Unions

As the economy has shifted from a manufacturing base to a service and information base in the latter half of the twentieth century, membership in unions not only has declined but the very nature of that membership has changed as well. The typical union member of four or five decades ago is not the typical union member of today. For decades, the prototypical labor union member has been the less educated, urban, white, male, blue-collar industrial worker who had a stay-at-home wife, an image that was justified by the demographics of union members in the 1950s. Today's unionized workforce is different as well as diverse, and logic says that those changes may have dramatic consequences for the power of the unions. Demography may not be destiny, but it certainly plays an important role. Who we are, where we live, what we do—these factors affect how we think and behave, and union members are susceptible to these forces as much as anyone else. In this chapter, using national survey data, we explore salient demographic and attitudinal changes among the union membership over time as well as some of the implications they have for labor's ability to be an economic and political force in the early decades of the twenty-first century. How will labor's revised strategies fare? Will Sweeney and his successors be able to achieve the political clout unions need to be a vital force in the American political arena between now and the year 2010? Or will labor union members continue to decline as a percentage of the workforce? If so, will that decreasing density be accompanied by a decrease in the influence of unions in the American political arena? Certainly, labor's ability to deliver votes is inextricably linked to its ability to persuade its members to behave in accordance with its interests: to register to vote; to take part in persuasive political activities; to give money to labor-related causes and candidates; and, most importantly, to vote the union-endorsed ticket, all of it. However, a critical mass of members must be present to begin with. Hence, sheer numbers of union members are important.

To gauge the unions' potential for successful member recruitment and political mobilization requires understanding the nature of union membership. As we reviewed briefly in chapter 1, the membership of organized labor has changed dramatically over the past few decades, both in number and in nature. The changes have been caused by forces beyond the control of any interest group or organization, with many but not all of the changes being driven by economic and occupational forces. Other forces responsible for changes include technological developments, changes in housing patterns, shifts in political attitudes and behaviors, and rising levels of education. This chapter focuses on the effect these changes have had on the faces and minds of America's union members.

The most comprehensive data on union members' changing demographics, attitudes, beliefs, and political behavior come from the American National Election Study (ANES), which has been conducted biennially since 1952 by the Center for Political Studies at the University of Michigan. We cite data from this source extensively in this chapter, focusing on data from the presidential years for simplicity's sake, except where otherwise noted. The data for the 1998 ANES are usually included to make the longitudinal data as current as possible. Though it is not cited, data from the General Social Survey, conducted regularly over the same time period by the National Opinion Research Center at the University of Chicago, have also been extensively reviewed and these data also support the conclusions drawn from the ANES data. Both of these databases are national in scope, utilize large sample sizes, and, most importantly for our purposes, ask questions of respondents regarding their membership in a labor union as well as the union membership of others in each respondent's household, thereby allowing examination of major demographic, attitudinal, and behavioral differences over time by union status. We first look at what these data tell us about the changing face of union members over time. Then, we examine changes in attitudes. We focus on those changes that have political consequences, especially at the polls.

Where appropriate, we compare each of these changes among union members with similar changes in one or two other groups—nonunion survey respondents who live in households with union members (we call these "union households") and nonunion respondents who live in households where no union members are to be found (we refer to these as "nonunion households").

- Union member: survey respondent identifies him/herself as currently a member of a labor union.
- Union household: survey respondent identifies him/herself as *not* currently a member of a labor union, but indicates that he/she resides in a household that includes at least one union member.

- Nonunion household: survey respondent identifies him/herself as *not* currently a member of a labor union and indicates that he/she does *not* reside with any union members.

Why do we look at respondents who live with a union member but are not union members themselves? We do this because the political influence of unions has traditionally been visualized as concentric circles: the closer one's position is to the center of the circle (see fig. 2.1), the more likely one may be to behave and think in accordance with the attitudes of union leaders, who occupy the center of the circle. The chain of influence can be thought of as moving outward from union leaders, who set policy, strategies, and tactics, next affecting union members, who then may influence other members of their households as well as their friends and neighbors, with the union influence weakening as one moves from the center toward the general public. For years, in fact, union leaders have had the following political strategy among the electorate: to influence union members directly and to encourage union members to influence family members and friends so that the union endorsement has a "multiplier" effect in elections.

FIGURE 2.1
Concentric Circles of Union Political Influence

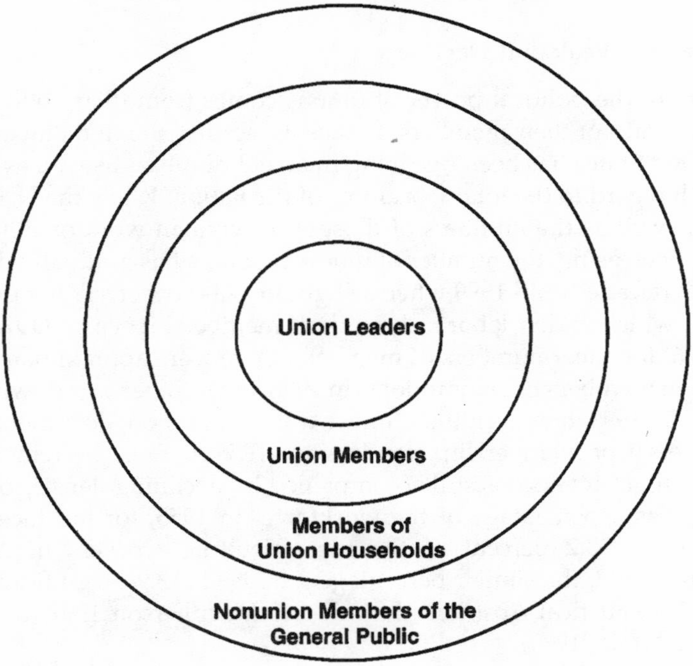

Union Leaders

Union Members

Members of
Union Households

Nonunion Members of the
General Public

With this model, one would expect union members, more so than those who occupy outlying circles, to display behaviors and attitudes that are more closely in alignment with those of union leaders. One might also expect the union influence to weaken with members of union households and weaken even further with members of nonunion households. Union leaders may also have a direct effect on those occupying any of the concentric circles through media. The concentric circles represent personal influence, as well as susceptibility to other union influences. The cumulative effect of the union movement among members of all of these circles may be perceived as determining union effectiveness with the citizenry in general, and can have considerable influence on the unions' effect on political leaders as well, especially as union leaders shift to an "outside strategy," as discussed briefly in chapter 1 and elaborated on in subsequent chapters.

A critical factor with such a model is sheer numbers of union members. The union's influence is greatest when its membership numbers are high in proportion to the rest of the population, and vice versa. For this reason, we begin our look at the changing face of the unions with a discussion of membership itself.

CHANGES IN UNION DEMOGRAPHICS FROM 1952 TO 1999

Membership Peak and Decline

The core of the political power of unions comes from their ability to deliver the votes of their members. In recent decades, union membership in the United States has been declining in actual numbers as well as in density with regard to the total workforce of the nation. While the U.S. population as well as the numbers of those in its civilian workforce has been steadily increasing, the number of union members has gradually declined in recent decades until 1999 when a slight increase occurred. For example, in 1976, which ended labor's three peak membership years (1974, 1975, and 1976) for sheer numbers of members, there were approximately 21 to 22 million members of labor unions; in 1996, the number was down to 16.3 million. By 1999, however, the number was 16.5 million, documenting the first reversal of membership trends since 1976. It must be remembered that this slight reversal is still accompanied by declining density of union members as a percentage of the workforce. In 1955, for instance, about one-third or 33.2 percent of the nonagriculture workers in America were unionized; the similar percentage for 1999 is 13.9—significantly less than half (Statistical Abstracts; Hirsch and Macpherson 1997; Bureau of National Affairs 1999).

Since the source of most of the data in this chapter is from ANES, it is useful to see how those data also document the decline in union membership, not as a percent of the total workforce but as a percent of the total survey sample, which was drawn randomly from the noninstitutionalized adult population of the United States. Because of the ANES sample design, we can infer within a small margin of error from the sample population to the U.S. adult population. As shown in table 2.1, the density of union members as a proportion of the U.S. adult population has declined by approximately 8 percent from 1952 to 1998. The decline in number of union households has been even greater—approximately 12 percent over the same time interval. The greater decline in union households as compared to union membership is undoubtedly a result of the declining size of U.S. households over the same time period. Not only are there fewer union members in proportion to the general population to be influenced by and supportive of union policies and leaders, there are also fewer union households to be influenced by their resident union member, and where a union household exists, there are fewer members in each union household to be influenced by the "chain reaction" of union influence. Some of the reasons for these declines have been mentioned in chapter 1, but they are worth repeating here. They include some reasons within labor's control, but more reasons outside of it: job shrinkage in heavily unionized industries that traditionally comprised union's membership base, uneven union organizing efforts, a legal climate tilting away from

TABLE 2.1
Declining Union Membership as a Percent
of the ANES Sample

Year	Union Members as Percent of Sample	Union Households as Percent of Sample
1952	17	27
1956	14	27
1960	15	27
1964	13	24
1968	15	25
1972	15	25
1976	12	23
1980	15	25
1984	13	21
1988	12	19
1992	11	16
1996	12	17
1998	9	15

Source: American National Election Studies (ANES), 1951–1998.

union interests, antiunion employers, and economic globalization. Referring again to our concentric circles of figure 2.1, we can visualize this change thus: the circles representing union members and union households are shrinking, while the circle representing nonunion members of the general public is expanding. Politically, this is indicative of less union influence in the political arena, as far as that influence is transmitted through union members to union households and the votes of both groups.

Occupational Shifts among Union Members

The changes in unions are not limited to changes in membership numbers, but go deeper to types of members. Since their inception in the 1930s, American labor unions have been associated with blue-collar workers: burly men in work clothes, shod in steel-toed boots, who carry lunch boxes, wear hard hats, and work in factories. The profound changes that have affected the entire American workforce over the last half of the twentieth century have also affected labor unions. As the economy of the industrialized world has seen a decline in manufacturing and a concomitant rise in occupations related to government, service industries, and technology, so have labor unions seen a related shift in the occupations of their membership. In 1952, the vast majority of union members (more than 81 percent) performed skilled or semiskilled labor in occupations that could be characterized as "blue collar," while fewer than 19 percent of union members could be classified as "white-collar" workers—a category that includes professionals (teachers and so on), managers, and those engaged in sales or clerical work. By 1998, labor's organizing success among white-collar workers had become very apparent. As shown by ANES data in figure 2.2, white-collar union respondents gained majority status (55 percent) over blue-collar ones. The shift has been slow but steady over the decades, until the lines for the two occupational types crossed in 1996, forming an X pattern that is becoming a norm when graphing changes that concern union trends. Looked at another way, unionized private-sector workers, which are composed primarily of blue-collar workers represented by traditional industrial unions such as the United Auto Workers, International Brotherhood of Electrical Workers, and the United Steelworkers, became a minority in 1994, while those in the public sector, composed primarily of white-collar workers represented by unions such as the National Education Association (NEA), the American Federation of Teachers, and the American Federation of State, County, and Municipal Workers, achieved majority status among unionists. To illustrate, in 1952 nine of the ten largest unions from a membership

FIGURE 2.2

Blue-Collar/White-Collar Shifts among Union Members

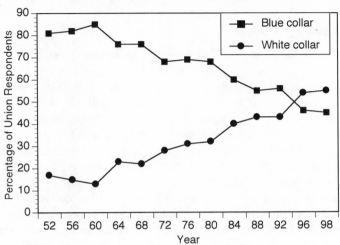

perspective were industrial, manufacturing, or crafts oriented. In 1993, five of the ten largest unions were composed of professionals such as educators or government or service workers (Bureau of Labor Statistics, as published in the *Public Perspective* 1997b). We label this trend the "white collarization" of the American unions. Sweeney's election to the presidency of the AFL-CIO was further evidence of the implications this shift may have for unions in general. White-collar unionists and their leaders may be the new dominant force in the union movement. The critical political question is: Will white-collar union members support the causes, issues, and candidates with which union leaders and blue-collar members have traditionally aligned, and do it with the same fervor? Or will their political agenda be different?

One white-collar sector in which unions are not successfully organizing is the technology sector. Indeed, many would describe this not as a white-collar sector, but as a "knit-collar" or "no-collar" sector, reflective of the casual dress style of golf shirts and tee shirts commonly worn by employees. Unions have not made headway in this fastest-growing sector of the economy, and may not be able to. Even though they frequently work extremely long hours, employees in this highly competitive sector are typically paid well, have very good benefits, and are unlikely to be open to union appeals (*Greenhouse* 1999g). What may be the fastest-growing sector of the new economy may be closed to unions.

The demographic differences between this new cadre of white-collar unionists and the traditional industrial unionists go far beyond occupational category, however. Other significant changes have occurred and are still occurring. These include changes in gender, educational attainment, place of residence, race, and age.

Gender Convergence

In 1952, when the first ANES survey was performed, only 14 percent of union respondents were female, while the overwhelming majority (86 percent) were male. As shown in figure 2.3, the shift over time has been slow and steady, with females having increased to 44 percent of the unionized labor force by 1998, while males dropped to 56 percent. The shifts are so dramatic when graphed that they form a *V* pattern over the years as the data for males and females converge. This demographic shift occurred almost imperceptibly over time, however. Within any five-year period, the change may have been unnoticeable (with the exception of the most recent five-year period), especially within blue-collar unions, as females increased on average less than one percentage point a year. The slowness of the shifts may have prevented union leaders from perceiving them as dramatic and thus requiring adjustment on the part of leaders' strategies and tactics in mobilizing members.

Are females ousting males from the traditional union jobs, or is there another dynamic at work? This brings us to the next consideration. Where are females most evident—in the traditional blue-collar jobs or in the white-collar union jobs of the service and professional sectors? Using the same ANES data again (see table 2.2) for type of occupation (i.e., blue

FIGURE 2.3
Gender of Union Members

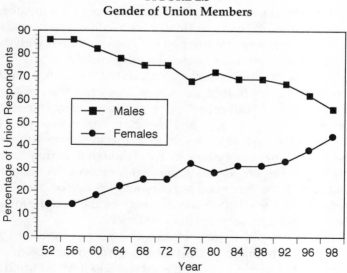

TABLE 2.2
Blue-Collar/White-Collar Shifts among Union Members by Gender

Year	Males		Females	
	% Blue Collar	% White Collar	% Blue Collar	% White Collar
1952	85	14	56	32
1956	85	14	67	22
1960	90	10	56	31
1964	80	20	60	33
1968	80	20	63	31
1972	77	22	41	45
1976	81	19	44	54
1980	76	23	46	55
1984	74	26	29	71
1988	63	35	38	59
1992	69	30	30	69
1996	62	38	21	80
1998	64	36	24	76

Source: ANES.

collar versus white collar—but separating males from females), we find that female union members are overwhelmingly more likely to be in white-collar occupations as compared to blue-collar ones. In 1956, female blue-collar unionists, though relatively few, outnumbered their white-collar counterparts, and increased in relative numbers until 1968. At that point, however, white-collar females began their climb to dominance, which occurred in about 1974. Males have always been more likely to be found in blue-collar unions, which is still true, but white-collar workers are increasing in their ranks as well.

The white collarization of the union workforce is likely to continue. In 1999, government workers were four times as likely to be union members as were their private sector counterparts, and local government workers, a group that includes police officers and firefighters, had the highest unionization rate in the public sector.

In fact, "In 1999, government workers continued to have a substantially higher unionization rate (37.3%) than workers in the private sector (9.4%). Within the public sector, local government workers had the highest unionization rate, at 42.9%. . . . The unionization rate in manufacturing continued to decline in 1999" (Bureau of Labor Statistics 1999).

If women are swelling the ranks of white-collar unionists, from whence have they come? They have left their households and gone to work, just as have many nonunion women. In 1947, women accounted for 28 percent of the civilian labor force and males accounted for 72

Chapter 2

percent (Bureau of Labor Statistics 1999). By 1999, women accounted for 46 percent of the civilian labor force in the United States, while males accounted for 54 percent. The gender gap is closing in union as well as in nonunion jobs.

Among the homes the women have left as they have sought employment are the union homes of yesteryear, a phenomenon we refer to as the "disappearing housewife," as shown in figure 2.4. ANES survey respondents are always asked to describe their occupations and, as this figure indicates, about 72 percent of the women considered themselves to be housewives in 1952, reflecting what is perceived as the prototypical union family of the mid-twentieth century: a working husband and a stay-at-home wife. In that same year, only 38 percent of female respondents living in nonunion households listed housewife as their occupation. In 1998, the figures were 8 percent and 12 percent, respectively, for union and nonunion households, with union households for the first time being *less* likely than nonunion households to include a housewife within their walls. Not only does the disappearance of yesteryear's housewife affect the nature of the workforce, it may affect the relationship between the typical union member and his or her union. There may be less time and freedom for extracurricular activities relating to the union, as both working men and women transport children to soccer games in the evening and

FIGURE 2.4

The "Disappearing Housewife": Percent of Female Respondents Reporting Their Occupation as "Housewife"

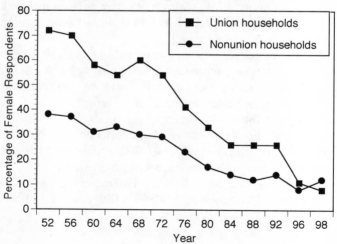

Note: If the respondent is a union member, then the category "housewife" is irrelevant, as the respondent is obviously employed; that is why we compare union households with the general population and exclude union members.

rush on weekends to perform household chores that, back in the 1940s, were performed by housewives as part of their weekday routines. As will be discussed later (see table 2.4 and the accompanying text), all things being equal, females seem to benefit financially from unionization. In 1999, unionized females earned over $8,600 more than females who were not members of labor unions.

The Educated Workforce

The typical union factory worker of the early 1950s was not formally educated beyond high school; indeed, 45 percent of them had only a grade school education in 1952, while barely 2 percent reported having a college education in that same year. Nonunion respondents were slightly more educated in the 1950s (though not by much). While education levels have risen steadily throughout the U.S. population over the past five decades, by 1996 union members had begun to pass the general population with regard to level of education. According to 1996 figures, 2 percent of union members had only a grade school education, while for nonunion respondents the figure was 5 percent. In 1996, 25 percent of both union and nonunion respondents were college graduates. The graph depicting the changing levels of education for union members depicts the familiar X pattern: college graduates among unionists began to outnumber those with no high school degree in the mid to late 1970s, as shown in figure 2.5.

FIGURE 2.5
Educational Attainment of Union Members

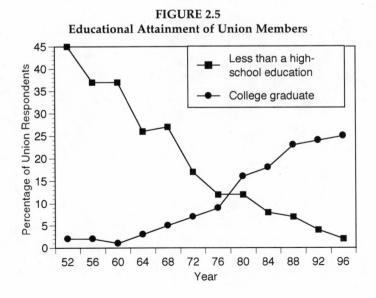

Educational achievement among union members is now the same as among members of the general population, if all union members are taken as a whole. A major reason for this, as has been discussed, is the changing nature of labor unions themselves: labor has successfully unionized groups of employees likely to have higher levels of education—teachers and other white-collar government employees. By 1996, 75 percent of union members in white-collar occupations were college graduates; for those in blue-collar occupations, the comparable figure is 27 percent, as shown in table 2.3. Thus, increasing levels of education among unionists are more reflective of the unionization of white-collar occupations than they are of educational attainment among traditional blue-collar union- ists, though both forces have been at work over the past five decades.

This trend can be both a boon and an albatross to union leaders as they at- tempt to mobilize their members for political action. More educated citizens may not rely on voting cues from their unions (or other interest groups, for that matter) to the extent that less-educated citizens do, perhaps limiting the unions' influence on their political behavior. On the other hand, more edu- cated citizens are much more likely to be political activists, turn out to vote, and complete their ballots while at the polls (see a variety of sources, includ- ing Verba, Schlozman, and Brady 1995; Nie, Junn, and Stehlik-Barry 1996).

Residential Suburbanization of Union Members

To return to the prototype of the union member of the New Deal era, im- ages of the auto workers of Detroit and the steelworkers of Pittsburgh

TABLE 2.3
Shifts in Unionists' Educational Attainment by Occupation Type

Year	Blue Collar		White Collar	
	% High School or Less	*% Some College or College Graduate*	*% High School or Less*	*% Some College or College Graduate*
1952	95	5	84	16
1956	95	5	68	32
1960	93	7	68	32
1964	92	8	76	24
1968	88	12	60	40
1972	85	15	65	36
1976	80	20	48	52
1980	85	16	33	67
1984	73	27	32	68
1988	73	27	24	76
1992	61	39	28	72
1996	73	27	24	75

come to mind. A typical union member was likely to live in the industrialized urban center of a major metropolitan area, close to the factory where he worked. Among his neighbors were fellow union members, many of whom were coworkers in the same factory. They attended the same churches, their children attended the same schools, their stay-at-home wives exchanged recipes and baby-sitting favors, and they socialized together at neighborhood diners and bars. And their local union hall was a short distance from both their home and place of work. It was the site of frequent meetings, wedding receptions, weekend dances, and summertime potlucks. Factory, family, union, and neighbors were intertwined. In 1952, the stereotype still held. Almost half of union members lived in major urban areas, with the remainder divided among the suburbs and rural areas.

As with the rest of the American population, the shift from America's inner cities has been slow but steady until, by 1996, union members were more likely to be found in the suburbs than in urban and rural areas. When we look at shifts in residence among both union members and union households, what we call the suburbanization of labor unions becomes even more dramatic. Because union members and union families are now scattered throughout our nation's cities, no longer living in homogeneous, prolabor neighborhood and community environments, the dissemination and reinforcement of prolabor attitudes and values may be problematic. For certain, a dispersed membership is more difficult to gather together for collective activities. Many individual members will be less inclined to commute back and forth to the workplace or the union hall in the evening to take part in meetings or candidates' nights. Geographical dispersion has occurred not only as a result of union members relocating to the suburbs from the inner city, but also by the unionization of typical suburban residents such as teachers and government workers. The steady suburbanization of the unionized workforce over time is displayed in figure 2.6.

Racial Diversity

The growing diversity of the unionized workforce is also evident in its racial composition. As the nation has become increasingly diverse, so have the unions, albeit more slowly. In 1952, 90 percent of union respondents were white; by 1998, that percentage had shrunk to about 80 percent. Increasing over the same time period was the percentage of nonwhites, accounted for mostly by blacks in the union force. In the past two decades, from about 1980 to the present, Hispanics have begun to account for a noticeable portion of the nonwhite union population (note that Hispanics can be classified as either white or black, depending on their

FIGURE 2.6
Suburbanization of the Union Workforce

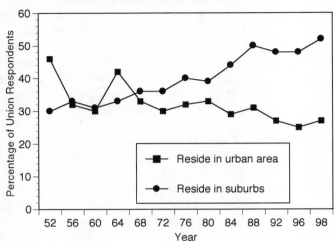

Note: Numbers reflect percentages of union members living in suburban or urban areas. During the same time period, generally 24–35 percent of union members lived in rural areas.

family origin). As the twenty-first century progresses, Hispanics are predicted to become the new minority in America, outnumbering blacks by approximately 2010 if the current trend continues. There are predicted to be 41,139,000 Hispanics in that year and 40,109,000 blacks. Whites are predicted to remain in the majority throughout the United States until at least 2100, with the exception of border states that receive large influxes of Hispanics, such as California and Texas, where non-Hispanic whites may be a majority even today (U.S. Census Bureau 1999). We should expect to see these trends eventually appear among unionists as well, as minorities reach adulthood and move into the workforce. The central questions for our purposes are: Are unions preparing for these changes? And what are the implications for the political power of unions?

Are members of these swelling minority populations likely to be attracted to unions? Current earnings data indicate that, everything else being equal, minorities may have a lot to gain financially by being unionized. Referring to table 2.4, black male union members earn almost $9,000 more per year than their nonunion counterparts, while black female union members earn almost $8,400 more annually than their nonunionized counterparts. These data disregard the type of occupation and whether or not it is in the public or private sector, and there are many factors at work in determining median incomes. Nevertheless, they make a compelling case for unionization. While Hispanics generally earn less on average than either blacks or whites (data not shown), Hispanic men

TABLE 2.4
Union versus Nonunion Median Wages for 1999 by Gender and Race

	Weekly Median Wage of Union Members	Weekly Median Wage of Nonunion Workers	Annual Wage Difference between Union and Nonunion
All Males	$699	$573	$6,552
All Females	$596	$430	$8,632
Both Males and Females	$672	$516	$8,112
Black Males	$597	$424	$8,996
Black Females	$537	$376	$8,372
All Blacks	$578	$398	$9,360

Source: Bureau of Labor Statistics 1999.

stand to gain the most by being unionized. The average Hispanic male union member earns over $11,000 more annually than his nonunion counterpart. For Hispanic females, the gain is less, but substantial: a differential of over $8,000 per year.

Many black men are reaping the advantages of higher union wages. In 1999, "[a] little over one fifth of employed black men were members in unions—the highest unionization rate across the major demographic groups." In fact, "Blacks in general have higher unionization rates (17.2%) than Whites (13.5%) and Hispanics (11.9%). Among the major worker groups, black men continued to have the highest union membership rate (20.5%), while white and Hispanic women continued to have the lowest rates (10.9 and 10.4% respectively)" (Bureau of Labor Statistics 1999).

Graying of the Union Workforce

To remain vital, all organizations must constantly attract new, younger members to replace older, long-time members as they inevitably retire or die. In fact, a worrisome sign in any organization is a rising average age of its membership over time. As shown in figure 2.7, when taken as a whole, the unions had a larger proportion of younger members among their ranks in 1952 than in 1999. The respective percentages for the two years are 19 percent and 7 percent, a net loss of 12 percent among the younger members during that interval. Just the reverse is happening among the older union members, who accounted for only 11 percent of unionists in 1952, and accounted for 26 percent in 1999, a gain of 15 percent over the same interval. There was an increase of younger members in the ranks of unionists during the 1970s when the sheer numbers of unionists reached between twenty-one million and twenty-two million in the

FIGURE 2.7
Younger and Older Cohorts of Union Members

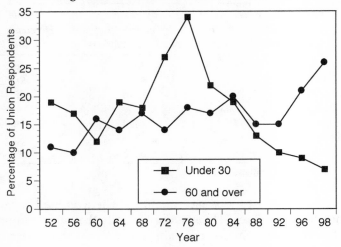

United States. Since that time, however, older union members have been outnumbering their younger counterparts. The aging problem may be affecting blue-collar unions disproportionately, as these are the unions that are losing their "market share" of members. This situation causes several problems for industrial-based unions. If generational replacement remains insufficient, the members' average age will continue to rise. As older members retire, the membership of blue-collar unions will shrink even faster due to the dual effects of fewer younger members joining and increasing numbers of older members leaving.

IS DEMOGRAPHY DESTINY?

As the foregoing discussion about the size, occupations, gender, educational levels, residential patterns, race, and age of the union workforce has made clear, the demographic characteristics of union members have changed dramatically in the last five decades. The 1952 portrait of the typical union member is no more. Today's typical union member, on average, is more likely to be college educated, to live in the suburbs, to be older, and to be female and of a minority race than the 1952 counterpart (though we must remember, especially with regard to race, that 80 percent of unionists are still white). If our 1999 unionist works in a blue-collar occupation, is male, and has a wife, the probability is great that the wife will work outside the home. Housewives are rapidly disappearing from blue-collar union households (and all other households, too, for that matter).

While blue-collar unionists still number in the millions, they are now in the minority among their fellow unionists. They have been surpassed in sheer numbers by a new cadre of workers who wear the union label: white-collar workers. These new unionists are more educated than the general population and much more likely to be female. Minorities are making headway in their ranks, too, though their numbers are still relatively small. Remember Sweeney's unsparing bottom-line assessment of the status of organized labor cited in chapter 1? He said it was "irrelevant not only to unorganized labor, but also to organized labor" (quoted in Victor 1995a, 1852). This assessment makes more sense now, as we know how dramatically union membership has changed. Mobilization of a homogeneous group of union members with similar demographics is one thing. But how do union leaders effectively mobilize union members who differ so much from one another, especially if the demographic heterogeneity is indicative of heterogeneity with regard to political attitudes, behaviors, and goals? Before addressing that question, we will look at attitudinal changes among union members over the same years in question.

Dramatic demographic changes, logic tells us, are accompanied by related changes in lifestyle. A male union member, whether employed in a white-collar or a blue-collar occupation, may have more demands on his time outside work than his counterpart had in the 1950s. Today's unionist commutes further to work. If married, he has a working wife, which means he may be assuming more childcare and household responsibilities out of necessity. He, too, is subject to the multimedia and hi-tech blitz of information that has taken place in American society since the 1950s, receiving cues from multiple sources, in particular his television set and the Internet, which require little energy and no travel to utilize, making them very attractive sources of information in his world. The female union member has a similar set of lifestyle constraints and opportunities, most of which were nonexistent in the 1950s.

How do union leaders connect with the new, more diverse rank and file? This is the challenge union leaders face in the twenty-first century. For labor to be successful, it must be focused. But how does it focus on what may be multiple targets, as represented by a more diverse labor workforce? Ultimately, in this book we must consider if the increased demographic diversity of unionists results in increased political diversity with regard to political participation, especially with regard to labor's power at the polls.

ATTITUDINAL CHANGES AMONG UNION MEMBERS
FROM 1952 TO 1999

Is demography destiny? Does the new union force think differently from that of the heyday of the union movement? Does it behave differently as well? Whereas in 1952 union members were fairly distinct demographically, at the turn of the twenty-first century they are more similar than different from their nonunion counterparts. The union force is more diverse, more educated, more integrated in many ways into the fabric of American life.

In this section, we examine how attitudes among unionists have changed between 1952 and 1999 by focusing on those attitudes that traditionally have had major political implications. We examine social class, party identification, and attitudes toward various groups with political importance. We do not examine voting behavior, per se, as that topic is covered in depth in chapter 7. Rather, we continue our examination of voting behavior's correlates and causes.

Social Class Identification

Historically, the labor union has been the champion of the working class as well as the disadvantaged. To protect and assist those groups economically was labor's raison d'être. Since the time of Franklin D. Roosevelt's presidency and New Deal politics in the 1930s and 1940s, unions have been identified with the Democratic Party and a politically liberal agenda as well. For decades, union leaders and members have considered themselves, if not adversaries of big business, at least involved in a dynamic tension with business management. Labor unions were of, by, and for the working class, and working-class identification in particular was an integral part of the labor movement. But that was then. What is it now?

For decades, ANES survey respondents were asked if they considered themselves members of the working class or the middle class. In 1952, more than 81 percent of union members described themselves as working class while fewer than 19 percent described themselves as middle class. By 1988, however, the number of union members describing themselves as middle class had more than doubled to 42 percent, approaching the percentage of respondents in nonunion households for the same survey question. As differences in social-class perceptions disappeared, so did the question itself. With class no longer a useful distinction among Americans, ANES dropped the question from the survey in the mid 1990s. Shifts in social-class perceptions have been minor among the nonunion survey respondents, in which 56 percent saw themselves as working class in 1952 and 44 percent identified with the middle class. By 1992, those perceptions had barely shifted. These data are displayed in figure 2.8 for all three groups of respondents. Once again, convergence occurs over time. Will this make the old class-based politics of the Great Depression and World War II–era unions irrelevant in the twenty-first century?

FIGURE 2.8

Middle-Class Identifications among All Respondents

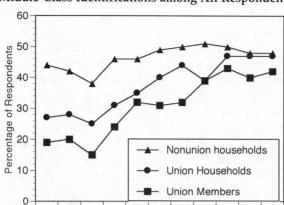

Party Identification

With regard to political behavior, party identification is the ultimate variable. As decades of research by political scientists have shown, one's party identification or lack thereof as well as the strength of the party attachment is a powerful predictor of political behavior, especially vote choice. (See Campbell et al. 1960, as well as the immense body of literature that builds on it. See also chapter 7, which focuses on vote choice.) This section looks at trends in party identification over time among union members, union households, and nonunion households, again using the longitudinal ANES data.

During each of the ANES survey years, respondents were asked if, generally speaking, they thought of themselves as being Republican, Democrat, or Independent. Those who identified with either the Republican or Democratic Party were asked if they thought of themselves as being a strong or not very strong Republican or Democrat, while those who claimed to be Independent or did not identify with any party were asked which way they leaned. For our purposes, we classified those who chose either the Republican or Democratic Party on the first round of questions as partisans, whether their affiliation was strong or not very strong, while most of the others were classified as Independents.

The unions' alliance with the Democratic Party became firmly established during the 1930s and Roosevelt's New Deal administration, and has remained in effect ever since. The question we address is: Are the changing demographics and attitudes of union members reflected in their party identification? If so, what are the implications for labor's ability to mobilize its members to support Democratic candidates and related issues?

As shown in figure 2.9, which displays the Democratic Party identification of our three subgroups, union members have been consistently more likely over time to label themselves Democrats than are members of union households or nonunion respondents. Those who live in households with union members are more Democratic than nonunion members, but less so than their union family members. The identification with the Democratic Party tends to be strongest among two demographic groups: those living in urban areas and those who are forty-five or older (not shown). Urban residents are labor's as well as the Democratic Party's traditional base; older members still display the traditional attitudes of labor. But another trend becomes obvious in these data: The graphed lines for all three groups slope downward over time and there is some convergence occurring. The Republican Party is not the big winner, however, as there is little evidence of "realignment." In fact, from 1990 to 1998, the percentage of union members claiming to be Republican actually declined from 19 percent to 15 percent. Where have they gone? In a phenomenon called "dealignment," they now claim to be Independent, the ranks of which went from 29 percent of unionists in 1990 to 41 percent in 1998. Thus, at the turn of the century, unionists were almost as likely to label themselves Independent (41 percent) as Democrat (44 percent). This could have important implications for union leaders trying to persuade members to vote for labor's endorsees. While the union ranks are losing members who affiliate with the Democrats, they are not gaining Republicans, who may be very difficult to persuade to support the union ticket. Rather, they are gaining Independents, who may be more persuadable than Republicans, but less so than Democrats. Later chapters explore this issue further.

FIGURE 2.9
Democratic Party Identification

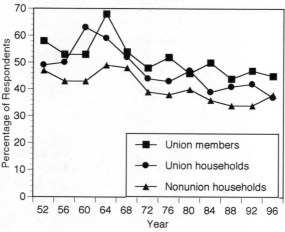

Feeling Thermometers

Consider again the history of labor unions. They were formed to represent workers collectively in negotiations with employers—that is, to gain better compensation, more reasonable working hours, better working conditions, and other benefits in an age when many workers were frequently exploited by their employers. The term "employers" meant "management," and "big business," and "Republicans." Unions, therefore, were a result of tensions between labor and management, tensions that led to a relationship between the two groups that were often adversarial, with conflicts frequently being resolved by seeing who could wield the bigger hammer or hold out longer when workers went on strike. Who could negotiate more effectively for a larger share of the profits: the company or the workers? It was perceived as a "zero sum" game, with only a certain amount of goods available, and the distribution of those goods was determined by negotiations. Winning, for business, meant more money for managers and more profits for owners. Winning, for labor, meant more benefits and compensation for workers. This dynamic tension created two opposing sides with labor unions, their members, and the core of the Democratic Party on one side and big business and the core of the Republican Party on the other. Given this tension, we would expect labor union members to feel warmer or be more friendly toward labor unions and the Democratic Party, their allies, and cooler or more hostile toward big business and the Republican Party, their adversaries. Why do we concern ourselves with how union members and others feel toward institutions such as labor unions and the like? We are interested because their affinity toward these groups can be a predictor of how open they may be to group persuasion on important political issues.

Beginning in 1964, ANES survey respondents were asked to rate their feelings toward a number of political candidates and groups using an imaginary "feeling thermometer," where ratings between 50 and 100 degrees indicate a favorable or warm feeling and ratings between 0 and 50 degrees indicate an unfavorable or cold feeling. As shown in table 2.5, which displays average ratings for union members and nonunion households, union members' feelings toward the Democratic Party and labor unions have "cooled" between 1964 and 1996, dropping fourteen points and twelve points, respectively. As evidence of the national political party dealignment discussed earlier, nonunion respondents also rated the Democratic Party "cooler" by twelve points. The largest drops in ratings, however, occurred among union members in their ratings of both the Democratic Party and labor unions, which are indicative of loosening ties between members and those two institutions. Drops in ratings for big business and the Republican Party are small in comparison. The changing faces of union members may

TABLE 2.5
Average Thermometer Ratings of Labor-Salient Groups

Year	Democratic Party		Labor Unions		Big Business		Republican Party	
	Union Members	Nonunion Households	Union Members	Nonunion Households	Union Members	Nonunion Households	Union Members	Nonunion Households
1964	78	70	79	51	57	61	52	61
1968	68	67	72	52	59	60	59	62
1972	68	66	66	52	50	54	60	64
1976	64	62	61	43	45	49	52	58
1980	65	64	65	51	51	53	56	60
1984	60	57	65	52	46	54	53	60
1988	65	60	72	52	52	56	54	60
1992	64	58	67	52	51	56	47	52
1996	64	58	67	52	52	58	49	54
Change: 1964–1996	–14	–12	–12	+1	–5	–3	–3	–7

be indicative of changing minds as well. Members are not as attached to their labor unions as they used to be. This makes political mobilization of members more difficult for leaders. Regarding agreement on issues and ideology, there are other problems, too, between unionists and union leaders, which will be discussed in later chapters.

CONCLUSION

From 1952 to the present, there have been dramatic shifts among labor union members in demographic composition. Unionists are now almost as likely to be female as male, to be college educated, to live in the suburbs rather than in the traditional urban setting, to be older, and to earn considerably more per year than their nonunion counterparts in the workforce. Regarding occupation, the majority of unionists are now white-collar workers, as compared to blue-collar workers. In addition, union members no longer think as warmly of their traditional allies—the Democratic Party and labor unions in general— as they did in the past. Many of these changes are summarized in table 2.6.

TABLE 2.6
Summary of Changes in Union Membership over Time

	1952	1999*	% Change
Education			
No High School Degree	45	2	−43
Some College or More	6	53	+47
Type of Occupation			
Blue Collar	81	45	−36
White Collar	19	55	+36
Gender			
Male	86	56	−30
Female	14	44	+30
Perceived Social Class			
Middle Class	19	42	+23
Residence Location			
Urban	46	27	−19
Suburban	30	52	+22
Age			
Under 30	19	7	−12
60 and Over	11	26	+15
Party Identification			
Democratic Party	58	45	−13
Race			
White	90	80	−10
Nonwhite	10	20	+10

*End-year data may be for 1992, 1996, 1998, or 1999, depending on availability.
Note: Figures are percent of union respondents in each category.

Unionists may also not feel all that warmly toward each other. Anecdotal data indicates that there may be a perceived hierarchy among unionists regarding which unions are *real* unions and which are not. Blue-collar unionists use the language of family when describing their fellow unionists, referring to them as *brothers* and *sisters*; white-collar unionists do not. There is a feeling in their ranks that they, the blue-collar workers, are the legitimate unionists. Civil service members, most of whom are white-collar workers, say that teachers' unions such as the NEA are not "real" unions. Rather, they view them as associations of college-educated people.[1] These feelings may be intensified if ongoing attempts to unionize college professors on campuses and physicians in hospitals across the nation are successful. Additionally, there have been long-standing feelings of antagonism toward both females and minorities among some blue-collar unionists, as well as feelings of distance between the political agendas of union leaders and union members. Some of these differences will be addressed in more detail in later chapters. In general, however, the union movement is not as united as leaders would like it to be. Can Sweeney and his successors bring together such diversity for any single political cause, whether issue or candidate?

In the next chapter, we focus on the relationship between union members and their unions, particularly considering what members want from their unions and what makes them committed to the organizations. We also consider the following: Are the demographic and attitudinal changes that have occurred and are still occurring among union members affecting their commitment and, hence, the union's ability to present a united front with regard to a political agenda that supports the union movement?

NOTE

1. In the fall of 1992, Karen Snyder and Randall Ripley facilitated focus groups with members and officers of union locals affiliated with the AFL-CIO. The focus groups were conducted in Columbus, Ohio. The purpose of the focus groups was to have unionists articulate how and why loyalty to the union and to their coworkers is developed.

3

Members' Attitudes toward Unions
and Politics

To understand the challenges of union political mobilization, we must not only understand how union membership has changed over time, but also the specific political demands of union members. Membership in a union or any other organization is not necessarily based on the congruence of one's political beliefs with the positions of the organization. Like many other interest groups, labor unions' primary purpose is not to advocate public policy positions or to assist in the election of candidates (Olson 1965; Salisbury 1984). Unions exist to represent their members before management on workplace issues. Members mostly join for this reason.

But, as described in chapter 1, the ability of unions to organize, bargain collectively, and deliver economic benefits and workplace protections successfully depends on government policies. The decisions made by agencies, especially the National Labor Relations Board, and the courts have a critical effect on the ability of unions to succeed in their primary mission (Waltenberg 2001). Unions are likely to be more successful in attaining these policy benefits to the extent that members support union political involvement, are supportive of its goals, and are willing to engage in political activities that help to produce these benefits.

This chapter starts to explore the challenges of representation and political mobilization by analyzing the beliefs of union members. Using surveys of Ohio union members, we evaluate members' support for their unions and their support for union political action. We also analyze members' political beliefs as well as their perceptions of union leaders' beliefs in order to determine areas of agreement and disagreement. By understanding members' political demands, we will then be in a position to understand the political strategies of union officers and the potential and limitations of those strategies.

47

THE BELIEFS OF UNION MEMBERS

At the core of collective action is the individual who must make contributions for the goals, which may not be achieved, to attain benefits which, if produced, must be shared with others in the group. There are a number of barriers that prevent individuals from making contributions to collective goals. The individual may calculate that his or her contribution would not make a difference in the achievement of the collective good or that costs of participation far outweigh the benefits to be obtained (Olson 1965). The individual may not be informed of the collective action taken by the group, may disagree with some of the goals being pursued, or may disagree with the strategy and tactics used to pursue goals that they do support. To engage in effective collective action, leaders must overcome these challenges.

UNION COMMITMENT

The strength of a member's relationship with the group is likely to be critical to his or her willingness to engage in collective action. Members who believe in the goals of the group and value membership are more likely to engage in behaviors that support the group, while those who are indifferent to membership or antagonistic to group goals will not.

Organizational psychologists have developed the concept of organizational commitment to explain individuals' retaining membership in the organization and helping the group attain collective goals (Mowday, Porter, and Steers 1982).[1] As applied to unions, commitment usually is defined based on four factors developed by Michael E. Gordon and colleagues (1980): (1) union loyalty (sense of pride and awareness of benefits); (2) responsibility to the union (acceptance of union expectations of member support); (3) willingness to work (willingness to serve the union "beyond the call of duty"); and (4) belief in unionism (support for the concept of unionism in general). Subsequent research has focused on the first dimension, loyalty, as the potential cause of the other behaviorally oriented dimensions (Kelloway and Barling 1993; O'Reilly and Chatman 1986). We focus on the loyalty dimension as well.

Commitment may provide a link between individual and group concerns (Kelly 1993). The member focuses on his responsibility to the group or on doing her "fair" share, rather than on taking advantage of others by letting others do the work while collecting the joint benefits. Commitment has been found to predict corporate employees' assistance of others beyond their job responsibilities (Kirchmeyer 1992; O'Reilly and Chatman 1986; Schaubroeck and Ganster 1991) and union members' participation in union activities (Fullagar and Barling 1989; Gordon et al. 1980; Kelloway and Barling 1993; Thacker, Fields, and Barclay 1990). Later, we will demonstrate the centrality of a member's commitment to the union to explain a number of prounion political behaviors, including supporting unions' involvement in politics, participation in union political activities (chapter 6), willingness to look for union endorsements, and voting for union-endorsed candidates (chapter 7).

Our Ohio union surveys find that members have a number of attitudes that are supportive of their unions (see appendix B for details of the surveys). We average members' responses among 1990, 1992, 1994, and 1996 in order to simplify presentation since the results do not vary greatly from year to year. For many, union membership is personally important: 56 percent claim it is very important. Not surprisingly, rates are higher for members of traditional AFL-CIO unions (64 percent) than for members of the National Education Association (NEA) (44 percent). Members also voice support for the union movement as a whole: 41 percent believe strongly in the movement. AFL-CIO members are also more supportive of the labor movement than NEA members, 48 percent to 26 percent, respectively. When asked how effective unions are in representing them, 38 percent of the union members replied that their union was very effective. If those who answered their union is "somewhat" effective are included, 85 percent of the members think their union represents them effectively. NEA members are slightly more likely to believe their union is *very* effective than AFL-CIO members, 44 percent to 39 percent, respectively. Finally, we asked members whether they thought their coworkers support the union; 69 percent replied affirmatively. There was no difference between AFL-CIO and NEA members on this question.

At this point, we will explore why members are committed to their union. There is extensive literature on union commitment and it is not our intention to review it here (for a thorough overview, see Barling, Fullagar, and Kelloway 1992, chapter 4). Instead, we will use our survey data from Ohio union members to describe members' characteristics that are associated with high levels of commitment. This will help us understand why union members behave as they do politically and the role of the union in promoting these behaviors.

We measure commitment with an index composed of three survey questions: (1) "How strongly do you agree with the following statement: 'I believe in the union movement and what it has done for workers in America.'"; (2) "In general, how important is your labor union membership to you?"; and (3) the difference between the member's feeling thermometer ratings toward labor and big business (see appendix C for details on index construction). Our measure emphasizes the loyalty dimension of commitment by measuring the respondents' belief in the union movement and the importance of union membership to the members themselves. We also want to capture some sense of liking one's own group (the union) and disliking the out-group (big business).[2] Thus, because of the historic tension between unions and big business, the difference in feeling thermometer ratings given to unions and big business by the member became a component of our commitment index. Certainly, respondents who believe that unions are important to themselves and to their fellow workers and who rate unions more favorably than big business will be more likely to support union-blessed political behavior.

Focus groups that we conducted with union members as part of our research suggests that a number of conditions promote union commitment. Certainly, the belief that the union enhances the economic conditions of its members is critical. Likewise, union intervention with management on a particular grievance of a member also enhances support. A few older participants in our focus groups who came from union families had a sense of history of the union movement and its struggles, which served to foster commitment to the union. Overall, however, support for the union movement rested more on the contemporary performance of the union in improving the lives of its members than on any historical sense of class conflict or union/management strife.

We propose that three different sets of variables are related to higher levels of commitment to the union: the member's relationship with his or her union, the member's political attitudes, and his or her social networks. We use regression analysis to separate the independent effects of each variable on commitment. Table 3.1 displays beta coefficients in order to facilitate comparisons of the magnitude of each independent variable's effect on the member's level of commitment. In order to simplify presentation, we include only those relationships that manifest statistical significance.

The evidence presented in table 3.1 provides considerable support for our expectations. First, the nature of the member's relationship with his or her union is related to commitment. This relationship rests mainly upon the union's ability to fulfill the economic needs of the member. Unions came into being to deliver material benefits to their members: better wages and benefits, and better working conditions. Not surprisingly, union members judge their union based on how it delivers on these promises. A member's belief that the union effectively represents his or her interests and that wages and benefits are an important reason for membership are the variables with the largest coefficients. Unions are also social groups, and the perceived levels of support for unions among the member's friends and coworkers are significantly associated with the member's own level of commitment. Prounion socialization by growing up in

TABLE 3.1
OLS Regression of a Member's Level of Union Commitment

	1990	1992	1994	1996
Union Variables				
Tenure				.09*
Voluntary Membership				
Union Family	.06		.10*	
Effective Representation	NA	.15**	.28**	.15**
Helps with Wages and Benefits	.41**	.13**	.24**	.28**
Friends Support Union	NA	.09*	.07	
Coworkers Support Union	.20**	.26**	.08*	.19**
Political Attitudes				
Liberal Ideology				.12**
Democratic Party Identification	.23**	.23**	.25**	.18**
Demographic Characteristics				
Race				
Gender (Male)		.11**		
Income				
Working Class		−.09*	−.08*	
Education	−.09*	−.17**	−.16**	−.25**
Constant	8.1**	4.6**	5.8**	6.3**
Adjusted R²	.39	.43	.45	.47
N	527	500	434	425

Source: Ohio union surveys.
Note: Only variables significant at $p < .10$ are displayed; *$p < .05$; **$p < .01$ two-tailed test. Beta coefficients are presented in order to facilitate size comparisons.

a union family is related to commitment in two of the four surveys only. Length of membership and joining the union voluntarily for the most part are unrelated to levels of commitment.

The second set of variables related to commitment revolves around the extent to which the member and the organization share a common world view. Part of this world view is likely to be political, as unions for many years have sought to improve the economic status of their members and workers more generally by pursuing public policies consistent with these ends. Even in the United States, although more so in other developed countries, this has meant strong ideological liberalism by union leaders and close affiliations with the more liberal political party (e.g., the Democrats in the United States). Members who share these political beliefs are likely to be more committed to an organization that promotes them. In fact, liberal members and Democrats are more committed to their union. The association between Democratic Party affiliation and commitment is particularly strong, which is not surprising given labor's historic ties to the party (Greenstone 1977). The liability, however, is that many conservative or Republican members feel less committed to the union.

Finally, several sociodemographic characteristics of the member are likely to be related to his or her level of commitment to the union. Traditionally, unions have advocated economic assistance primarily for the working class. Thus, it is not surprising that members with lower levels of education are more committed to the union. But it is surprising that members who perceive themselves as working class are less committed to the union than those who perceive themselves as middle class in two of the four surveys. Similarly, a member's level of income is unrelated to commitment, perhaps suggesting that some members credit the union with helping them achieve higher wages.

Given the trends toward greater diversity in union membership, it is important to examine the relationship among race, gender, and commitment. Traditionally, union members are more likely to have been white and male and this may affect an individual's level of comfort in the organization. Our data show that race and gender are largely unrelated to a member's level of commitment.

Several points are worth highlighting in summation. First, members' satisfaction with the union's economic representation and performance are consistently and highly related to members' level of commitment. This finding emphasizes members' stress on the core purposes of the union. In exchange for performance in delivering economic benefits and workplace protections, members express their loyalty to unions. Second, party identification is consistently related to commitment and the coefficients are similar in size to those of the economic variables. This shows that many members are loyal to their union and to the Democratic Party, and other Republican-leaning members are less supportive of their union. Finally, members with lower levels of education are more committed to the union. They have fewer skills than highly educated workers to obtain higher-paying jobs elsewhere and are loyal to the union for its training and protections. Unions provide assistance and a living wage to workers whom otherwise have limited leverage in the workplace. This demonstrates that unions retain their traditional appeal to workers of lesser social status.

The changing nature of union membership discussed in chapter 2 presents some challenges to union leaders in maintaining high levels of commitment among their members. Clearly, maintaining wages, benefits, and effective representation are core goals regardless of the specific demographic composition of membership. However, to the extent that union membership is more likely to include highly educated teachers and civil servants than in the past, these members are less likely to be committed to unions. To the degree that the nature of work is changing away from lifelong employment in manufacturing to short-term employment with many different employers, members may have less tenure in the union and thus less time to build commitment. If members are less likely to affiliate with the Democratic Party, unions must find ways of building commitment among the growing numbers of politically independent members. Thus, commitment may provide a critical resource that leaders can tap for political mobilization, but it must constantly be regenerated.

PARTY IDENTIFICATION

Although unions are foremost economic organizations, politics are clearly a central concern as well. However, in contrast to many other highly political organizations, members are unlikely to join the union to support its political agenda. People may join the National Rifle Association, the Sierra Club, or the National Organization for Women to show their political preferences, but union members are joining almost entirely for work-related benefits. Because of organized labor's long association with the Democratic Party and several other liberal causes, there may be a gap between members' political beliefs and unions' political agendas, especially with the shifting demographics of membership. This has the potential to cause considerable tension between union leaders and members and makes political mobilization more difficult.

We will discuss the extent of this problem by examining the perceived differences between members' and union leaders' political party affiliations, political ideologies, and issue positions. (There is extensive literature that documents these differences historically. For a review, see Masters and Delaney 1987b.) Data to do this come from the Ohio union surveys. We will then examine the extent to which members support union involvement in politics and the reasons why members support or decline to support such involvement.

In table 3.2, we present the party identification of Ohio union members and their perceptions of union leaders' party identifications. The first column shows the percentage of members who place themselves in each of the party categories (averaged across the four years of surveys). The second column shows the percentage of members who classified their union leaders in each of the party categories. The final column subtracts the difference between members' own party identification and their perception of leaders' party identifications.

A plurality of Ohio union members call themselves Democrat, consistent with the national results presented in chapter 2. Across the four years of our surveys, an average of 47 percent are Democrats (there is

TABLE 3.2
Party Affiliation (average % over 1990–1996 Ohio union surveys)

	Member's Self-identification	Member's Perception of Leaders	Difference
Democrat	47	66	19
Independent	21	10	11
Republican	24	5	19
Other	<1	<1	0
No Preference/Both	6	10	4
Don't Know	1	7	6

Source: Ohio union surveys.

little year-by-year variation). An average of 21 percent classify themselves as Independents, while 24 percent are Republicans.

Members are even more likely to classify union leaders as Democrats; on average, 66 percent of members say their leaders are Democrats (see table 3.2). Only 10 percent of members claim leaders are Independents and 5 percent think union leaders are Republican. The differences between members' party identification and their classification of leaders are nearly 20 percentage points for Democrats and Republicans. Relatively few members (7 percent) claim to be unaware of their leader's party affiliation. At the least, this suggests members are aware of the traditional political leanings of organized labor. Thus, while members lean towards being Democratic, they perceive an even greater Democratic loyalty among their leadership. This is not surprising given the political history and contemporary practices of labor unions, but it demonstrates a meaningful gap between members' political orientations and that of their unions.

A second aspect of union members' party identifications deserves mention: the differences across unions. This is particularly relevant as labor membership has shifted from the industrial and manufacturing to the public sectors of the economy. In table 3.3, we present the average party identification across our four Ohio union surveys of members of the AFL-CIO, the Ohio Civil Service Employees Association (OCSEA), and the

TABLE 3.3
Party Identification by Union (average %)

	Ohio AFL–CIO	OCSEA	OEA	Nonmember
Democrat	56	50	40	36
Independent	24	22	22	25
Republican	21	28	39	39

Source: Ohio union surveys.

Ohio Education Association (OEA). We also include the party identifications of nonunion members from a random sample of Ohioans for comparative purposes. Table 3.3 shows meaningful variation across Ohio unions. Members of the Ohio AFL-CIO are the most likely to identify with the Democratic Party. In fact, they do so at rates 20 percent higher than nonunion Ohioans. Members of the OCSEA and OEA are also more likely than nonunion members to be Democrats, though the difference is less dramatic particularly for OEA members. Differences across unions are also apparent in identification with the Republican Party. Teachers (members of the OEA) are much more likely than other union members to be Republicans. They are as likely to be Republicans as Democrats and are as likely as nonunion members to be Republicans. This may not be surprising given the traditional class and educational differences between teachers and industrial workers, but it does highlight the challenge to union leaders in political mobilization given union membership trends. Mobilization around party identification alone may be insufficient to produce members' support for Democratic candidates who tend to be the union endorsees.

IDEOLOGY

Table 3.4 presents members' descriptions of their own and their leaders' political ideologies. Generally, liberals favor a more activist government, especially on economic issues, while conservatives believe that the free market should be left to operate on its own as much as possible without government interference. Moderates believe in some government intervention, but not as much as liberals. And there are those who have different opinions on different issues, so they do not think of themselves as fitting into one of these overarching belief systems. The first column contains the percentage of members who place themselves into each of

TABLE 3.4
Ideology (average % over 1990–1996 Ohio union surveys)

	Member's Self-identification	Member's Perception of Leaders	Difference
Liberal	21	38	17
Moderate	27	18	9
Conservative	33	14	19
Don't Think in Those Terms	17	10	7
Don't Know	2	15	13

Source: Ohio union surveys.

the ideological categories. The second column lists the percentage of members who believe their union leaders fit each category. The final column is the difference between members' own ideological classification and their perception of their leaders for each category.

Members perceive themselves to be ideologically more conservative than union leaders. A plurality of members (33 percent) label themselves conservative, but members are rather evenly distributed across the ideological spectrum. A clear plurality of members believe union leaders are liberal and many fewer members believe their leaders are moderate or conservative. There is almost a 20 percentage point difference between members' self-classification and their classification of leaders in the liberal and the conservative categories. It is important to highlight that, as with party identification, there is a considerable gap between how members perceive themselves and how they perceive their leaders ideologically.

Also, like party identification, there are interesting differences in ideological identification across unions. Table 3.5 distinguishes members of the Ohio AFL-CIO, OCSEA (civil servants), OEA (teachers), and nonunion Ohioans. If Democrats are generally considered the more liberal party, and AFL-CIO members are more likely to be Democrats, one might expect members of the AFL-CIO to be more liberal than members of other unions and nonunion members. This is not the case. AFL-CIO members are slightly less likely to identify themselves as liberals than even nonunion members. They are more likely than others to identify themselves as moderates. Civil servants are more likely than others to be liberal and are least likely to be conservative. An activist government provides them employment and, if tax revenues correspond to the size and activism of government, higher salaries. Teachers are more conservative than other union members, but are in between OCSEA and AFL-CIO members in liberal identification.

These ideological distinctions are important because of the way they diverge from party identification. AFL-CIO members are more Democratic and ideologically moderate than others. Where AFL-CIO members are most likely to be persuaded by partisan appeals, they are least likely to be persuaded by ideological appeals. Appeals to liberalism may be some-

TABLE 3.5
Ideology by Union (average valid %)

	Ohio AFL–CIO	OCSEA	OEA	Nonmember
Liberal	23	36	28	24
Moderate	37	30	30	35
Conservative	39	34	41	42

Source: Ohio union surveys.

what more effective with civil servants. Teachers are both more conservative and more Republican than other union members, but are also more polarized ideologically than nonunion members. Their relatively even distribution across the partisan and ideological spectrums makes traditional electoral appeals with a unified message rather difficult.

ISSUE AGREEMENT

Union leaders may ask members to communicate their issue positions on legislation to public officials or may use issues as a way of explaining to members why members should support endorsed candidates. To gauge the extent of agreement between union members and leaders, we asked members their positions on several salient issues and their perception of union leaders' positions on these same issues in the Ohio union surveys. The percentage of members, averaged over the four surveys, who responded with the more liberal answer is presented in table 3.6.[3] As in earlier tables, we present members' own opinions, members' perceptions of leaders' opinions, and the difference between the percentage of members' and their perception of leaders' "liberal" opinions. We also present the percentage of members who claim that they do not know the opinion of their leaders on each of these issues.

Analysis of these data leads to several important observations. First, members consistently perceive the positions of union leaders to be more liberal than their own. On all four issues, a majority of members who responded perceive that union leaders take the liberal position. However, the difference between members' and leaders' positions varies across issues. The difference is smallest on the government's role in the economy

TABLE 3.6
Liberal Issue Positions (average % giving more liberal preference)

	Member's Opinion	Member's Perception of Leaders	Difference	Don't Know Leader's Position
Government's Role in Economy	50	57	7	38
Health Care	44	56	12	52
Help Blacks	16	50	34	55
Abortion	55	74	19	72

Note: Valid percentages are used to facilitate comparisons. That a higher percentage of members support the liberal position on abortion than on other issues exists because the only options on the abortion question were favor/oppose, others had an "in between" option.
Source: Ohio union surveys.

and on health care; the political issues that most closely parallel unions' core workplace concerns—wages and health benefits. Unions cannot decrease unemployment or create universal health care through collective bargaining and members are in accord with officers that these are worthwhile goals, necessary to enhance the monetary benefits of union membership.

An important qualification is that members have a low level of knowledge about union leaders' positions on these issues. On three of the four issues, a majority of members are unaware of the union position. This is intentional on some issues, such as abortion, on which unions typically do not take positions because the issue is divisive to their membership and unrelated to workplace concerns. Yet, even on the government's role in the economy, over one-third of members claim not to know the union position. These data indicate that unions have done an ineffective job of educating members about the union position, let alone taking the more difficult steps of persuading members of the merits of the union position and mobilizing them to take action.

The ineffectiveness of unions' issue education can be further demonstrated by examining members' support for a government health care plan in table 3.7. In 1990 and 1992, a slight majority of union members favored a government health plan, the traditional union goal, and larger majorities perceived union leaders holding the same position. However, union members' support for a government health care plan plummeted 20 percentage points in 1994 in the aftermath of the public debate over President Clinton's failed health care reform package. Support for the president's plan from the general public dropped dramatically in between the president's speech to a joint session of Congress in September 1993 and the plan's demise in Congress in September 1994 (Skocpol 1997, 74–5). This was due in part to a barrage of negative television ads from small business and the insurance industry (most famously the Harry and Louise ads by the Health Insurance Association of America). Although it may not be surprising that the trends in union members' opinions paralleled those of the general public, it shows that unions' mobilization in

TABLE 3.7
Opinions on Health Care (% favoring a government health plan)

	Member's Opinion	Member's Perception of Leaders	Difference
1990	52	58	6
1992	54	68	12
1994	34	54	20
1996	36	45	9

Source: Ohio union surveys.

favor of health care reform was clearly ineffective (Johnson and Broder 1996; Skocpol 1997). It is interesting to note that the gap between members' own positions and their perceptions of union leaders' positions is widest in 1994. This suggests that many members were aware of their unions' support for national health care reform, but were more persuaded, or overwhelmed, by the industry coalition opposing reform.

APPROPRIATENESS

If members are to engage in collective action politically on behalf of their union, they must believe that political action is an activity unions ought to be doing. To the extent that members are wary of union political action, political mobilization of the rank and file is much more difficult. Concerns regarding the propriety of organizational political involvement is more likely to be a problem in primarily economic organizations whose members have not joined to support its political positions, whereas in primarily political organizations, many members join to show support for the organization's political positions.[4]

Regardless of their agreement with union leaders on partisanship, ideology, or specific political issues, members differ on whether or not unions should be actively involved in politics. Some members mostly agree with union political positions, but may decry the involvement of "special interests" in politics. Other members disagree with union political positions, but believe that it is proper for unions, just as for any other interest group in the United States, to petition government for redress.

Polls of union officers and members in Ohio show considerable support for union political action. A 1982 survey of local officers in the Ohio AFL-CIO internationals found that 49 percent thought labor should spend more time on politics; only 11 percent thought labor spends too much time on politics (Clark 1982).

In the Ohio union surveys, we asked members whether it was "OK" for unions to participate in three distinct electoral activities: making endorsements, registering voters, and making campaign contributions. We asked whether it was "OK" for unions to lobby in 1996 only. We asked the same questions of nonunion Ohioans for comparative purposes. The percentage of union members responding that it was "OK" for unions to participate in each activity is presented in the first column of table 3.8, the percentage of nonunion members giving the same response is listed in the second column. The third column is the difference between union members' and the general publics' levels of support for each union political activity.

TABLE 3.8
Are Union Political Activities Appropriate? (average % approving)

	Union Member	Nonmember	Difference
Registering Voters	90	76	14
Making Endorsements	66	42	24
Lobbying	55	36	19
Making Campaign Contributions	48	45	3

Source: Ohio union surveys.
Note: Data on lobbying are from the 1996 survey only.

The extent of members' and the general publics' support for union political action varies across the specific activity, but in each case, the level of support is higher from union members than from nonmembers. Support for registering voters is extremely high; 90 percent of union members and 76 percent of nonmembers approve. Support is lower for a more partisan electoral activity of making candidate endorsements. The difference between union members and nonmembers is greatest on making endorsements—twenty-four percentage points. The gap between members and nonmembers is also rather large on support for lobbying. In contrast, support for making campaign contributions is comparatively low, with just under half of both populations approving and with very little difference between the two populations. This suggests general mistrust of the contemporary system of campaign finance rather than specific disapproval of union campaign contributions.

Some members are more likely than others to be supportive of union political activities. To explore this issue, we counted the number of electoral activities of which each member approves (making endorsements, registering voters, and making campaign contributions). The range of this scale is zero to three, as the member can support all three activities or may not support any of them.[5]

Three sets of variables are likely to be related to members' extent of approval of union political action. The first set of variables measures the members' relationship with his or her union. Those members with more positive relationships are more likely to be supportive. As shown in table 3.9, members' level of commitment to the union and the number of political activities that the member perceives his or her union to have undertaken are both related to their beliefs in the appropriateness of union political involvement. As previously discussed, commitment is an indicator of the member's overall attitude toward unions and his or her loyalty to the union. Thus, it is not surprising that committed members would be more supportive of activities that may benefit the organization. The relationship between the union's number of political activities and the mem-

TABLE 3.9
Regression on Belief in the Appropriateness of Union Political Activities (beta coefficients)

	1990	1992	1994	1996
Union Variables				
Commitment	.20**	.10**	.08**	.09**
Tenure	−.08			−.01*
Voluntary Membership		−.14		
Union Family				−.12
# of Union Political Activities	.31**	.11**	.09**	.13**
Political Attitudes				
Liberal Ideology		.04	.10*	
Democratic Party Affiliation	.08	.04		.09**
Political Interest	.09*			.08
Political Efficacy	NA	NA	.07*	
Demographic Characteristics				
Race				
Gender (Male)				.22*
Working Class		−.24**		
Education	.18**		.06	.13**
Constant	−.85*	.71*	.73**	.31
Adjusted R²	.25	.18	.15	.25
N	527	520	515	543

Source: Ohio union surveys.
Note: Only variables significant at $p < .10$ are displayed; *$p < .05$; **$p < .01$ two-tailed test. Beta coefficients are presented in order to facilitate size comparisons.

ber's belief in the propriety of those activities may be due to politically active unions educating their members on the need for union political involvement, or to unions becoming politically active only when they have support from their members. Alternatively, members who approve of union political action may be more likely to notice such activities as they are undertaken.

Members' political attitudes are also related to their evaluations of the appropriateness of union political activities. Specifically, Democrats and liberals are more likely to be supportive. Presumably, these members support union assistance of mostly liberal Democratic candidates. Members who are interested in politics tend to be significantly more supportive of union political action than members who are apolitical. Finally, members who are politically efficacious, that is, who believe that people like themselves can understand politics and can make a difference, are more likely to believe that union political activities are appropriate.

Members' sociodemographic characteristics are, for the most part, unrelated to their beliefs regarding the appropriateness of union political action. In particular, gender and race do not have a significant association (cf. Fields, Masters, and Thacker 1987). Social class and education manifest significant relationships only in selected years. Yet, it is noteworthy that middle class members and those with higher levels of education are more likely to believe that union political action is appropriate. These members, even if they do not necessarily support labor's specific political agenda, apparently are more supportive of a pluralistic interest group system, that is, the right of "special interests" to promote their agendas and defend themselves in a democratic society.

In all four surveys, the fact that only two variables are significantly related to beliefs in the appropriateness of union political involvement (the level of commitment and the perceived number of union political acts by the members' union) is worth highlighting. These results suggest one important effect of high levels of commitment to the union—committed members are also likely to be supportive of union political action.

There are, however, a number of impediments to union members' participation in collective political action. To the extent that they do not believe that union political activity is appropriate, they are less likely to participate. To the extent that they disagree with the political objectives they think unions are trying to achieve, they are less likely to participate. The variations in members' support for and agreement with the goals of union political action create challenges and opportunities for union leaders who attempt to mobilize politically. Leaders must develop strategies to recruit members who are sympathetic to the cause being pursued and who are potentially willing to participate. Their strategies must also attempt to persuade those who are indifferent to union political action or who have different predispositions from the union's.

CONCLUSION

To the extent that union members and officers are in agreement on major political issues, union lobbying, and political action accurately represents the views of members. Officers can act as the "delegates" of their members and speak for the positions of unions as to how both officers and members perceive them. To the extent that there are differences between officers' and members' political beliefs, officers must choose whether or not to act as "trustees" for members. In a trustee role, the leaders pursue the interests of the organization despite members' lack of information about policy issues, or they look beyond members' short-term self-interest to advocate policies that will have long-term or indirect benefits.[6] If there is substantial agreement between officers and members, collective action through political mobilization is less difficult. But to the extent this agreement is lacking, not only is rank-and-file mobilization more difficult, but public officials are also likely to be more distrustful of leaders' claims that their positions represent the interests of members.

This chapter finds varying levels of congruence between members' political beliefs and their perceptions of union officers' political beliefs. This is to be expected in an organization the primary purpose of which is not political and the members of which have not joined to signal their political beliefs to policymakers. Members vary in their levels of commitment to their union, their levels of support for union political action, their levels of knowledge about union political positions, and their levels of agreement with union leaders' political positions. Members have the highest levels of knowledge of and agreement with union leaders' positions on economic issues. These are the issues most related to unions' role in the workplace and their ability to deliver benefits from management. Members are supportive of union efforts to advocate government policies that expand general economic and health benefits beyond those that can be negotiated concretely in collective bargaining.

Members offer moderately high levels of support for their unions. Their levels of commitment to the union vary in predictable ways based on their evaluations of their union's success in delivering economic benefits, their coworkers' support for the union, their political beliefs, and their level of education. To the extent that union demography is changing, there is good news for union leaders in that race, gender, and class do not significantly affect commitment. The news is less positive, however, to the extent that the proportion of Democrats is declining and the proportion of more highly educated workers is increasing.

At the same time, members with higher levels of education are more likely to believe that union political action is appropriate. They are joined by committed members and those who share unions' political positions. Members who perceive that their union sponsored a number of political activities are also more likely to be supportive. This may suggest that union leaders who actively attempt to educate and involve members in political action can elicit, at the very least, supportive attitudes towards these activities.

The challenge for union leaders is to develop political strategies that can help them to deliver the benefits that members expect and to help their own organizations survive in potentially hostile economic and political environments. Full employment, a higher minimum wage, and national health care are the public policy versions of the same specific benefits for which unions negotiate with individual employers. The public versions, however, cannot be delivered through collective bargaining.

Changes in government policy are necessary for these goals to be achieved. This depends in part on which candidates are elected. Such policy changes may then facilitate greater union leverage at the bargaining table with individual employers. Officers must decide whether to invest organizational resources in educating and mobilizing members politically, or whether to speak on behalf of members' interests even if the members are unaware of the issue or are ambivalent in their level of support. Union political success may partially depend on how leaders address this strategic choice.

NOTES

1. "Commitment" is a term that has been used with slightly different meanings by others outside of organizational psychology. Paul A. Sabatier (1992) and Sabatier and Susan McLaughlin (1990) have used the term to mean ideological extremity. This usage differs from ours in the object to which one is committed: an ideology versus an organization.

The usage of commitment in the organization psychology and rational choice literatures differs along several dimensions (see Robertson and Tang 1995). Rational choice scholars seek to understand how individuals can make "credible commitments"—that is, how individuals can make and fulfill promises without reneging. Where organizational psychology focuses on commitment as an attitude or internal motivation, rational choice views commitment as a result of situational or external constraints that lead to collective action.

2. For the notion of "polar affect," see Arthur H. Miller and colleagues (1981).

3. For all issue tables, we present the percentage of members who gave a valid response and excluded those who responded that they did not know. This facilitates comparisons between members' own positions, which most respondents knew, and leaders' positions, which fewer knew. By focusing on the responses of those who were aware of leaders' positions, we can concentrate on perceived levels of agreement and disagreement between members and leaders and not on levels of knowledge. Where knowledge is relevant, we discuss separately the implications of the percentage of members who were not aware of union leaders' positions on issues.

4. Of course, many political organizations offer material and social benefits as well (J. Q. Wilson 1973; Salisbury 1969; Walker 1991).

5. We do not include lobbying in the scale for the dependent variable since we only asked this question in one year. Comparing regression equations with and without lobbying included in 1996 indicate that results do not differ substantially.

6. The delegate versus trustee distinction is common in the literature on legislative representation. Generally, the leader who follows a delegate role votes according to the expressed desires of his or her constituents. The trustee votes based on his or her independent judgment of what is in the best interest of his or her constituents or the nation over the long term. For classic discussions of the delegate and trustee roles, see John C. Wahlke and colleagues (1962) and Warren E. Miller and Donald E. Stokes (1963).

4

Traditional Political Strategy

What makes unions powerful, ultimately, is the power of members acting together, linking arms, figuratively or literally, taking a stand, and forcing their agenda on either their employer or political representatives. Thus, collective action or the threat of collective action—in the form of strikes, voting as a bloc, or contributing to charities—gives unions their power. The challenge for leaders is to promote collective action when individual unions or individual members have varying priorities.

Union officials pursue multiple goals. One is to procure benefits—wages, health care, job security, and favorable working conditions—for their rank-and-file members. Union officers can achieve this end through collective bargaining with employers and through affecting government economic and health policies. Many union leaders also seek to promote a broader, liberal policy agenda at the national and state levels, often in concert with the Democratic Party.

From the perspective of rank-and-file union members, direct workplace benefits are the most important reasons for belonging to the union. If the union can deliver on these issues, then the rank and file may be reasonably supportive of the union, even if they are not as supportive of the broader policy and political objectives of the leadership. Indeed, there is reason to expect that some members would be unhappy with leadership strategies that tie unions too closely to the Democratic Party.

From the perspective of the union leadership, the union will be more successful in achieving its broader policy objectives if the leadership is working with sympathetic public officials. As a result, the leadership strongly advocates participation of unions and their members in the electoral process. In addition, the leadership's political clout is enhanced if it can demonstrate that union political involvement affects election outcomes.

To achieve these political goals, the AFL-CIO faces two critical problems. One is to get affiliated unions to contribute to achieving the collective goals of the labor movement. As described in chapter 1, international unions who are members of the AFL-CIO have considerable independence in choosing the collective activities in which they wish to participate. The second is to get diverse members to mobilize on issues that may not affect them immediately and personally.

Traditionally, the AFL-CIO has solved these dilemmas in two ways. First, affiliates have substantial independence to advocate their own priority issues while the AFL-CIO coordinates on consensus issues. Second, the AFL-CIO has relied on officers, staff, and lobbyists to deliver messages through inside contacts to the legislative leadership of the Democratic Party, rather than consistently educating and mobilizing its rank-and-file members. Changes in the political environment, especially the Republican takeover of Congress and many state legislatures, have made this traditional political strategy untenable and have caused a new AFL-CIO leadership to devise new methods for unions to influence elections and public policy.

This chapter will explore the relationship between rank-and-file members and union leadership in the development of union political agendas and strategies. As we saw in the last chapter, members' beliefs differ from those of leaders on some issues. Here, we discuss the extent to which members' views are incorporated into unions' political agendas and the conditions under which members have an influence. We then discuss how union leaders attempt to create a unified political agenda, given the diversity of members' political beliefs, and how the strategy to implement this agenda has changed over time in response to changes in the political environment and within the union movement. After a general review of members' roles in organizational decision making, we detail areas in which members have considerable influence, such as over local candidate endorsements, as well as areas in which officers exert greater control, such as through electoral targeting, political action committee (PAC) contributions, and lobbying. Even in areas where members do not exert a direct influence, they can act as an important constraint on officers.

AGENDA SETTING AND DEMOCRATIC CONTROL

If members' political beliefs differ from union leaders, to what extent do they have any influence on the agenda and goals of their own organization? Alternatively, from the perspective of union leaders, if members have diverse beliefs and at times disagree with the union position, how can the union effectively influence elections and public policy? How can leadership attempt to mobilize members as a political resource when many are unaware of union political positions, disagree with those positions, or are opposed to union involvement in politics?

Most unions allow some level of democratic involvement in organizational decisions by rank-and-file members. Members are commonly involved in the approval of new programs, officers' salaries, strikes, and collective bargaining agreements (Bok and Dunlop 1970, 70–7; Schlozman and Tierney 1986, 137–9). Unions hold periodic conventions that are attended by local officers and elected delegates. These conventions may debate and vote on amendments to the union constitution, dues increases, major new programs, collective bargaining goals, public policy objectives, and candidate endorsements. Union leaders are often elected and contested elections are not unusual. Indeed, Kay Lehman Schlozman and John T. Tierney (1986, 139) find that unions are more likely than other interest groups to elect officers and have contested elections. The race between Sweeney and Donahue for the AFL-CIO presidency in 1995 is a highly salient example.

As is common even in democratic organizations, the leadership exerts greater control over organizational goals and activities than rank-and-file members (Michels 1915/1958). Officers have higher levels of information, the ability to control organizational resources, and the motivation to preserve their status in the organization. The average member rarely has the resources or desire to mount an effort to change the operations of the organization.

In unions, rank-and-file members are attracted by material benefits—wages, pensions, and health care plans—and to a lesser extent by the social benefits of fitting in with coworkers (see chapter 3; J. Q. Wilson 1973, chapter 7). Thus, they are likely to exert most of their control over economic issues that they care most about—especially local contracts, strikes, and dues (Moe 1980, 173–4). Political issues seem more peripheral to their membership in the union, so there is less incentive to become involved in setting union political goals. This allows officers and activists greater control over the agenda, but does not assure that members will support the leadership's agenda in elections or grassroots lobbying campaigns.

Staff, officers, and activists, however, are driven more by purposive incentives—their desire to achieve larger ideological goals—than rank-and-file members (for a review of this literature, see Moe 1980, 172–6). To the degree that activists devote their time and energy to the union movement in order to advance the economic and social status of working men and women, they may seek to achieve this goal through policy change that affects all workers and goes beyond negotiation with individual employers. Indeed, union leaders tend to be more cohesive in their economic liberalism and affiliation with the Democratic Party than leaders of other interest groups (Heinz et al. 1993, chapter 10). They are able to take advantage of their participation in decision-making bodies to advance their agendas. Similarly, leaders with strong personalities and policy preferences may dominate their union's decision making. Such leaders may influence the union's policy agenda beyond their tenure in office by surrounding themselves with like-minded lieutenants who become the next generation of officers. For example, Walter Reuther set a liberal political agenda for the United Auto Workers from the 1940s to 1970s, which has been followed by his successors (Mundo 1992, chapter 5). As a result, some argue that members' participation in organizational decision making is merely "ceremonial," that convention participants only approve decisions already made by union staff and executive boards (Heldman and Knight 1980; Moody 1988, 162). Still, John Thomas Delaney, Jack Fiorito, and Marick K. Masters (1988) find that unions with democratic structures are more politically active. They suggest that greater political involvement occurs when there is greater congruence between the interests of union leaders and members.

Nationally, leaders claim to act as trustees in the best interest of the "movement," rather than as delegates who merely reflect the opinions of a majority of rank-and-file members at any point in time. Officers justify this because they believe that members may not understand the connections between the benefits they desire in the workplace and the political and economic environment that allows leaders to deliver those benefits. Their duty is to articulate and act in the long-term, collective interest of the labor movement and to educate rank-and-file members regarding the proper course of action. This creates a situation in which there may be a tension between political preferences of national leadership and rank-and-file members that creates potential challenges for political mobilization.

ENDORSEMENT DECISIONS IN ORGANIZED LABOR

To explore the manner in which potential political disagreements between union members and officers are played out, we examine the process of making candidate endorsements. Union organization allows for significant influence by members, usually activists, on endorsement decisions for local races. Activists also have the ability to make, or at least to veto, endorsements for higher-level offices at union conventions. The complexity of union organizational structures and decision making, and the fact that unions are much more likely than other interest groups to make endorsements (Schlozman and Tierney 1986), gives members a variety of opportunities to influence unions electoral activities.

In the AFL-CIO, endorsements can be made by regional central labor councils (CLCs), by the state AFL-CIO executive boards, and by the Committee on Political Education (COPE), the federation's national PAC. Internationals and their locals also make endorsements. The local and central labor council endorsements focus on local races, including state legislative races; the state affiliate endorsements mostly focus on statewide races; and the COPE endorsements focus on federal offices, including the U.S. presidency. State affiliates make recommendations to COPE regarding endorsements for the House of Representatives and Senate. Officially, all nominations originate at the local level; internationals and locals can endorse candidates other than those endorsed by COPE, though endorsements usually are the same. In some unions, the National Education Association (NEA), for example, the emphasis on localism is even stronger: the national PAC can only endorse a candidate if state and local committees have as well.

AFL-CIO Center Labor Councils

CLCs are regional aggregations of AFL-CIO affiliates. They are usually organized on a countywide basis or multiple counties in rural areas. Locals do not have to join their CLC even if their international is affiliated with the AFL-CIO. Delegates from locals attend CLC meetings, debate and vote on collective issues, and pass information on to their members. Delegates are usually appointed; many are officers of the locals. Much of the business of CLCs is coordinating union political and community service (e.g., the United Way) activities. CLC officers are usually part-time, voluntary positions. Ohio is unusual in having six CLCs (Cincinnati, Cleveland, Columbus, Akron, Toledo, and Dayton) with full-time professional officers.

CLCs also make endorsements for candidates for local offices. The scanning committee screens the candidates.[1] The committee sends questionnaires to candidates and solicits comments from local unions. Incumbents have an advantage in the endorsement process: if they have not hurt unions, they are reendorsed. One CLC officer explains: "We recognize that while in office the person can't please labor one hundred percent of the time. So when we get reports from members that X office-holder has done Y to hurt union members—signed a nonunion garbage contract, violated prevailing wage on a contract, or maybe it's a judge that ruled against us—we investigate the claim to determine how serious it is and whether it's an isolated incident." Scanning committees usually do not offer endorsements in primary races for open-seat candidates and challengers unless there is an overwhelming favorite.

Once the committee has completed its review, a vote is held. Candidates must receive two-thirds of the vote to be recommended. The CLC executive board then considers this recommendation and must also approve it by a two-thirds majority. Voting in the CLC is weighted by union membership size, so larger unions can exert substantial influence. There is, however, some compensation for extremely small unions: all locals are guaranteed a minimum of two delegates and, at higher levels of membership, the representation ratio drops (e.g., from one delegate per three hundred members, to one delegate per five hundred members). Finally, the endorsement must be officially approved by two-thirds of the CLC delegates. Recommendations for state legislative and congressional races must also be ratified by two-thirds of the delegates of the state AFL-CIO convention. The state executive council then officially issues the endorsement. The Ohio AFL-CIO has recently instituted COPE voting scores for Ohio legislators in order to sway local evaluations of incumbents' responsiveness to union priorities. The multistage, supermajority process helps to ensure that endorsees are the overwhelming choice of union activists. CLC endorsements are not binding on local unions. Locals can make an endorsement if the CLC does not and can even endorse a different candidate than the CLC. However, candidates who do not receive an endorsement cannot use the AFL-CIO membership list for mailings or phone calls, which is an extremely valuable resource for making contact with potentially sympathetic voters.

LOCAL ENDORSEMENT PROCESS: THE NEA

In order to understand how endorsements are made, it is useful to examine an example of the local endorsement process in some detail. The NEA provides an interesting case of the role of rank-and-file members in the political process. The NEA considers itself a "bottom-up" organization and thus prides itself on facilitating members' involvement (for the Washington perspective on the "bottom-up" procedures of the NEA, see Baer and Bailey 1994).

Local unions handle endorsements for local government, including school board, but special screening committees are necessary for state legislative races. State legislative districts tend to encompass multiple school districts, especially in the suburban and rural areas organized by the Ohio Education Association (OEA). (The American Federation of Teachers organizes all cities in Ohio except Columbus and Youngstown.) Each local in the Ohio House of Representative's district has the right to at least one representative on the screening committee for each legislative district in which the school district lies. Each screening committee has five votes, so larger districts get more than one representative if necessary to fill the slots. Committee members are officially appointed by the local president, but they can also be elected by the local. The process for selecting school district representatives is left up to the local. Representatives must be NEA–PAC contributors (Educators' PAC [EPAC] in Ohio), but this requirement is not onerous, as explained by an OEA Executive Committee member: "Participants must be EPAC contributors, but there is no requirement on how much has to be contributed. So if somebody comes into the meeting and they haven't contributed, we'll hand them an [EPAC] envelope and ask them to put in a dollar."

The screening committee meets twice. The first time is for training and organizational purposes, the second is to conduct the screenings. The first meeting is held on the basis of Ohio Senate districts. When legislative districts are drawn in Ohio, senate districts are drawn first. Three house districts are then constructed in each senate district. So when the screening committees meet on a senate district basis, they first break up into the three house district committees. There must be five people present to elect a chair and the district's delegate to the EPAC convention. Once this is accomplished, the three house district committees get together to elect a chair and a senate district delegate to the EPAC convention. The senate screening committee itself is made up of only three individuals: the chairs of all three house districts. Each committee, in conjunction with an OEA labor relations consultant (LRC), decides at this time if a primary endorsement process is necessary.

Screening committee members are trained by LRCs regarding the procedures of the screening process and the criteria for endorsements. LRCs handle the organizational logistics for the screening committees and attend the meetings with candidates. They are present at the interviews in an advisory capacity to educate the members on how the process works. They are supposed to get the committee members to ask questions, rather than to ask questions themselves, although this happens only occasionally.

To start the screening process, the committee sends formal written questionnaires to candidates and invites them for interviews. The questionnaires are developed by the EPAC, so everyone in the state is making endorsements on the same basis. (The questionnaires are developed by the Governmental Services staff and are modified and approved by the EPAC executive council.) The questionnaire is modified somewhat after each election in order to keep the questions topical and to excise questions that failed to generate the expected information.

The candidate's formal interview is important because it allows for interaction between the screening committee members and the candidate. Though committee members have candidates' written responses, candidates' oral responses are usually more informative. Especially in primary contests, the questionnaires are received early in the campaign so candidates often are ill prepared. Thus, committee members start the interview by asking the exact questions from the written questionnaire. At the least, this assures that the candidate gives the same response (in case an aide filled out the form). Committee members can push the candidate for elaboration. If the candidate basically supports the NEA position, committee members try to get a commitment from the candidate to vote that way if the issue comes to a vote in the legislature. The endorsement process is viewed as a way of keeping representatives accountable to local members.

In addition to the candidate's oral and written responses, the committee also reviews the candidate's NEA voting scores if he or she is an incumbent. Incumbents with good records have an advantage over any challengers in receiving endorsements. Endorsement recommendations are made by a majority vote of the committee. The committee can also recommend whether or not the candidate should be given a PAC contribution.

Both the endorsement and contribution recommendations go to the state NEA–PAC convention for final approval. But whereas endorsement recommendations are almost always ratified, contribution decisions are really made by the state NEA–PAC executive council and staff rather than the local committees. The Governmental Services staff recommends spending levels and races to target based on their conversations with state party leaders. The local recommendation carries greater weight when local members know their representative well and have a close working relationship. The local committee's endorsement also constrains the executive council since contributions cannot be made to candidates who have not been endorsed. At times, however, the council believes it is necessary to give contributions to legislators with poor voting records but to whom lobbying access is needed. In this case, contributions can be made to the Ohio party's legislative caucus with a specification of how the money will be spent. The state NEA–PAC conventions give the final approval to contribution decisions.

ENDORSEMENTS FOR CANDIDATES IN STATEWIDE AND FEDERAL RACES

The state AFL-CIO executive board and conventions make the endorsements for statewide races and make recommendations to COPE for congressional races. (In the NEA, congressional contact teams, the local coordinators of grassroots lobbying, make recommendations to the NEA–PAC on congressional endorsements.) As in the CLCs, a scanning committee reviews the candidates and makes recommendations. Also like the CLCs, voting in the state federation is weighted by per capita contributions of each union, so larger unions have a larger say. COPE rarely overrides state endorsements, but it does review candidates' COPE voting scores and their willingness to work with lobbyists. Since Washington lobbyists and COPE officers select the issues for the COPE voting scores, the national federation can use this means to influence local perceptions of the "friendliness" of incumbents.

After the endorsements are made, the state federation office develops the strategic plans for the election, and as the campaign unfolds, it primarily coordinates political education among the internationals. The CLCs, internationals, and locals have direct contact with the rank-and-file members; they are primarily responsible for mobilizing and executing electoral events. State officers spend considerable time traveling around the state to meet with locals, urging them to implement union campaign plans.

INTERNATIONALS

Most internationals have a process parallel to the AFL-CIO's whereby a state or regional executive board and convention approve local endorsements and make statewide endorsements. Occasionally, convention delegates will overturn the recommendation of the screening committee. In the 1998 Ohio governor's race, the screening committee of the Fraternal Order of Police (FOP) voted six to five to endorse Democrat Lee Fisher. The FOP convention overturned the screening committee's recommendation and endorsed Republican Bob Taft by a vote of 198 to 129 (A. Johnson 1998).

Some internationals vary in the details of their process of endorsement. One variation is persons involved in making the endorsement decision: whether only executive boards decide, whether screening committees are used, whether only officers participate at conventions or rank-and-file members participate as well. One interesting variation is the presidential endorsement process of the American Federation of Government Employees (AFGE). Rank-and-file participation is encouraged by the inclusion of a ballot in the AFGE's quarterly newspaper. At the same time, voting is weighted towards activists: those who gave more than $100 to the PAC and/or those who participated in a political activist training program. These legislative activists get an extra ballot. The rank-and-file endorsement is ratified by a vote at the national conference followed by a vote of the PAC executive board.

Occasionally, internationals will make different endorsements from the federation's. This occurs when some internationals support particular

Republican legislators who, though they generally do not vote as unions would like, have supported a particular sector of unions on an important issue. For example, in 1996, the Ohio Building Trades Council broke with the AFL-CIO and endorsed and targeted Congressman Bob Ney and four-teen other Republicans in the Ohio General Assembly because of their efforts to protect prevailing wage requirements on government construction contracts.

TARGETING

Members have less influence over other strategic decisions in elections. COPE makes targeting decisions for federal candidates and the state executive board chooses targets for state races. Although COPE makes the decisions on targeting and resource allocation over the course of the election, it relies heavily on state and local activists for updated information. Thus, there is considerable state and local influence over national decisions (see Wilcox 1994).

Union political officials are well aware of the need to target limited resources toward races where those resources are most likely to make a difference. One AFL-CIO officer summarizes: "The bulk of our activities is spent on targeted districts; very little is spent on safe or lost districts." Ohio unions claim their first priority is helping incumbent "friends" in marginal districts. Polling and voter registration data are used to determine which races are close and need extra assistance. Thereafter, they will consider targeting open-seat races where a candidate has taken prounion positions. Of course, they will still help friends who are in little electoral danger, but these races are not targeted. Races in which prounion candidates have little chance of winning are ignored.

The COPE targeting list is divided into two sets of races that differ in their priority level. The "marginal" list is the highest priority. Candidates appear on this list when there is a consensus among members of COPE's marginal committee.[2] If there is not a consensus on a candidate, yet some committee members think the race could be competitive, the race is placed on the "watch" list and is made a secondary priority. As the campaign unfolds, a particular candidate can be moved to higher or lower priority levels as the race increases or decreases its competitiveness, respectively.

To determine the competitiveness of the race, unions do their own extensive polling of the district. One union political director explains: "We do our own so that we're not dependent on the candidate or the parties." They essentially ask the candidate to submit to a union inspection of his or her campaign. Union staff analyzes the candidate's polling data, campaign finance data, and campaign organization. Unions also work with party caucuses in evaluating campaigns at both the national and state levels. In the end, if the candidate cannot demonstrate that he or she will be able to run a professional, competitive campaign, the union directs fewer resources toward the race. Continued polling throughout the election allows the state AFL-CIO to tell if untargeted races become close unexpectedly and allows them to inform their locals in the district and to provide extra assistance.

AFL-CIO affiliates usually follow the targeting decisions made by COPE and the state executive board. Indeed, they are represented on the committees that made the decisions. In the rare instances in which different endorsements are made, internationals may target the same race—but support different candidates (as occurred in the Ney race in 1996). Many internationals will only target districts where they have membership strength and will rely on other unions to carry the burden in other districts.

The NEA-PAC attempts to target marginal incumbents who have been most helpful to the NEA while in office. Supporting challengers to antagonistic incumbents and supporting friendly candidates in open seats are second and third priorities, respectively (see also Baer and Bailey 1994). The director of governmental affairs of the OEA explains the logic of the OEA's targeting process:

> When candidates call for contributions, we want to see polling data. We want candidates to prove they're competitive. We won't throw money down a rat's hole. As an example, a local EPAC council in suburban Cincinnati was very excited about [a challenger to an OEA nemesis in the Ohio House]. I met with the candidate and was very impressed. But the district was safe, so money would be wasted. We didn't give him anything.

The state NEA-PAC council decides on targeted races at state level. The national committee makes decisions on congressional candidates based on the recommendations of and consultation with state NEA-PAC committees.

PACS AND ELECTORAL SPENDING

One of the major resources that can be targeted to a specific campaign is money. Traditionally, the main source of union contributions to political candidates has been the PAC. Labor unions pioneered the development of PACs to provide organizational structures to educate members regarding union endorsements and political positions, register members to vote, encourage turnout among members and their families, and collect campaign contributions from members.[3] Since the Federal Election Campaign Act of 1974, unions and other interest groups are prohibited from using members' dues or operating funds for contributions to candidates. In order to give money to candidates' campaigns in federal elections, they must establish PACs to solicit voluntary contributions from members.[4] Many states have passed similar laws governing contributions in state and local campaigns.

The fact that union PAC money must be contributed voluntarily by members gives the rank and file some influence over contributions. Activists who solicit contributions must convince their colleagues that the money is going for a worthwhile purpose; members who disagree with union political involvement or with the stances unions take are unlikely to contribute. To the extent that unions accurately represent their members on salient issues, contributions are likely to be more forthcoming and unions will have the ability to contribute more money to more campaigns.

COPE is the AFL-CIO's PAC. COPE maintains substantial control over affiliates' financial contributions by assessing their PACs according to the international's total membership (Wilcox 1994, 22). A percentage of each member's individual contribution is earmarked for COPE. Each union international may form its own PAC. International PACs raise money and make contribution decisions independently of COPE. In 1976, there were 224 PACs sponsored by labor unions, constituting 20 percent of the total number of PACs (Federal Election Commission 2000). By 1998, the number of labor PACs had risen to 353, but the number of business and ideological PACs increased even more rapidly and union PACs had fallen to only 8 percent of the total population.

Union PACs raise and contribute a significant amount of money in federal campaigns. Figure 4.1 shows the increase in labor PAC's contributions to congressional candidates over the past twenty years. In the 1977–1978 election cycle, they raised $18.6 million and contributed $10.2 million to candidates. By the 1997–1998 election cycle, union PACs raised $111 million and contributed $44.6 million (Federal Election Commission 2000). Although labor PAC contributions have increased, they have not increased as dramatically as contributions from business PACs. In the 1977–1978 election cycle, business PACs outspent labor PACs by $5.6 million (Sousa 1998); by the 1997–1998 cycle, the gap was $156 million in favor of business.[5]

Even though unions and other interest groups must raise voluntary contributions from members to contribute to candidates' campaigns, they may use dues to pay the overhead costs for their PAC, for lobbying activities, and for political communications with their own members.[6] Unions face one restriction in their political spending that other organized inter-

FIGURE 4.1
Labor Union PAC Contributions to Congressional Candidates

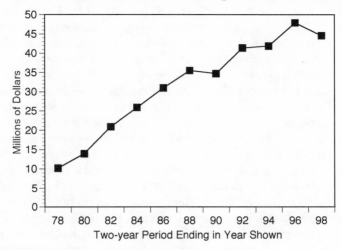

Source: Federal Election Commission 2000.

ests do not. In *Communication Workers of America (CWA) v. Beck* (487 U.S. 735 [1988]), the U.S. Supreme Court ruled that labor unions may not use "agency fees" for political purposes. Agency fees are paid by employees of companies in which the union represents all employees, yet not all employees wish to join the union. These employees objected to the use of their agency fees for political purposes, rather than for collective bargaining, contract administration, or grievance adjudication. The Court supported the nonmember employees and allowed them to request refunds of the portion of their agency fees that is spent on political activities (for more detailed discussions of legal restrictions on union political action, see Delaney 1991, and Wright 1982).

Republicans in Congress have attempted to pass the Paycheck Protection Act as part of campaign finance reform legislation. This act would have required unions to notify members every year that they could request refunds of any parts of their dues that are spent on political activities. More stringent versions would have prevented unions from spending any portion of a member's dues on political activities unless that member annually gave written permission. Republicans argued that this would facilitate members' ability to protect the rights guaranteed them in *CWA*. Union leaders countered that it was a thinly veiled attempt to inhibit unions' expressing their political voice, noting that no other organizations would be so restricted. Democrats rejected the act as a cynical attempt to undermine campaign finance reform by forcing Democrats to vote against broad reforms they favor in order to defeat provisions that harm labor unions.

In 1998, an initiative was placed on the ballot in California, called Proposition 226, that would have implemented the provisions of the Paycheck Protection Act in that state. In February, polls showed substantial support for the ballot measure, including among union members, 71 percent of whom claimed to favor it (Grossinger 1998). Unions strongly mobilized against the proposition, arguing that the measure was an attempt to silence the voices of working families and noting that similar restraints were not imposed on corporations or other organized interests. Unions educated their members on the subject through one-on-one personal contacts. By the vote in June, 71 percent of union members voted against the proposition, a turnaround of forty-five points in three months (1998). Apparently, members were persuaded that their union spoke for their political interests and were willing to forego annual invitations to get some of their dues back. In addition, unions reached out to Democrats and other liberal groups to persuade them that the proposition was a partisan attack attempting to cut off financial support for a progressive agenda. Ultimately, the unions' efforts were successful as Proposition 226 lost.

Another source of union electoral spending is "soft money" contributions to political parties. These contributions are made to political parties for "party-building" activities such as registration or get-out-the-vote drives or generic party advertising ("Vote Republican"), rather than to support the election of specific candidates. Soft money contributions are not regulated as tightly as hard money contributions, which go to candidates' campaigns. Unlike hard money, the amount of a soft money contribution is unlimited and may come from an organization's treasury or members' dues. Soft money contributions are hard to track, but indications are that unions route their contributions mainly through PACs. The Center for Responsive Politics (2000) found that fourteen out of fifty of the largest political contributors overall in the 1997–1998 election cycle were labor unions, but only two of the top fifty soft money contributors were unions. One estimate found that 91 percent of the dollar amount of soft money contributions came from businesses, and only 5 percent from unions (Sousa 1998).

Total spending on elections is heavily biased toward business. The Center for Responsive Politics (2000) added total PAC, soft money, and individual contributions in the 1997–1998 election cycle and found that business outspent labor twelve to one, a $421 million gap. This ratio is consistent with that found in prior elections. Out of a total of $559 million spent on the 1998 election, labor spent 7 percent.

Also consistent with past elections (Sabato 1990; Sorauf 1992; Wilcox 1994), labor unions contributed overwhelmingly to Democrats in the

1997–1998 election cycle—90 percent—while business spending was more evenly split, with 43 percent of their contributions going to Democratic candidates (Center for Responsive Politics 2000). Unions have long followed an electoral contribution strategy of supporting candidates closest to their ideological positions. These have overwhelmingly been Democrats. Business PACs often prioritize access to incumbents over ideological purity. During the 1980s, business interests gave heavily to Democrats to maintain an open door to the majority party despite their greater ideological affinity with Republicans. After the Republican takeover of Congress in the 1994 elections, many business PACs shifted their contributions to give more to their soul-mates in the majority Republican Party (Biersack, Herrnson, and Wilcox 1999; Rudolph 1999). Labor, however, did not follow an access-oriented strategy and continued to give heavily to Democrats.

Democratic congressional candidates have been very reliant on labor contributions. Union contributions ranged from a high of 50 percent of total contributions to Democrats in the 1977–1978 election cycle (Stanley and Niemi 1990, 167), to a low of 32 percent in the 1991–1992 cycle. Democrats' dependence on labor rebounded to 45 percent in the 1995–1996 election cycle (Stanley and Neimi 1998, 103) after Democrats lost their congressional majority and substantial contributions from business. Of the top contributors to the Democrats (both to the party and to the candidates) in the 1997–1998 election cycle, nine of the top ten, eighteen of the top twenty, and twenty-six of the top fifty were unions (Center for Responsive Politics 2000). In terms of soft money contributions, ten of the top fifty Democratic contributors were unions (2000).

Finally, union PACs are much more likely than other PACs to contribute to nonincumbent candidates (Sorauf 1992). Because challengers have a low probability of winning and, unlike incumbents, cannot offer contributors access, they traditionally have difficulty attracting PAC contributions. In elections that look promising for Democrats to pick up congressional seats, COPE contributed two-thirds of its funds to Democratic challengers or open-seat candidates.[7] In conditions when the Democrats were threatened or party competition was even, COPE still contributed about one-half of its funds to nonincumbent Democrats (Rozell and Wilcox 1999, 92–3; Wilcox 1994). Democratic challengers are extremely dependent on labor, as they receive about two-thirds of their PAC contributions from union PACs (Sousa 1998). This evidence shows that union PACs are more likely than others to respond to the opportunities presented by changes in the political context from election to election (Herrnson and Wilcox 1994).

In campaigns for the House of Representatives in 1996, 31 percent of labor PAC contributions went to "safe" incumbents, while 22 percent went to Democratic incumbents who were in close races (plus 3 percent to endangered incumbent Republicans), 25 percent to competitive Democratic challengers (none to Republicans), and 10 percent to competitive Democrats in open-seat races (none to Republicans). By contrast, corporate PACs gave 52 percent to safe incumbents, 36 percent to endangered incumbents, and only 9 percent to competitive challengers and open-seat candidates combined (Herrnson 1998a, 117). In Senate races, only 6 percent of labor PAC contributions went to safe incumbents, while 48 percent went to competitive candidates in open-seat races. Corporate PACs gave 15 percent of their contributions to safe Senate incumbents and 32 percent to competitive candidates for open seats (118).

Labor union PACs are critical to understanding labor's role in elections. Certainly, the amount of money they contribute is important, particularly to Democratic candidates, but their electoral spending is only a small part of the overall spending in federal campaigns. Labor PACs are important because, unlike most other PACs, they do more than raise and contribute money. They also attempt to educate and mobilize voters. Their goals are different from many other PACs'. They are less concerned with using contributions to "buy access" to incumbent members of Congress for their lobbyists. Rather, their ideological and nonincumbent emphases demonstrate their desire to change the partisan composition of Congress. Because these behaviors are similar to those of political parties, campaign finance scholar Frank J. Sorauf (1992, 111) concludes that labor PACs are the most "party-like" of PACs.

LOBBYING

Labor unions, especially the AFL-CIO and UAW, have long taken positions on a wide variety of issues well beyond those that directly affect collective bargaining (Greenstone 1977; G. Wilson 1979). In many cases, this means that unions have attempted to advocate positions that would assist all types of wage earners, not just their own members. Unions have taken a leadership role in raising the minimum wage, introducing family leave and national health care, and protecting social welfare programs and affirmative action. Such priorities create frequent alliances between unions and a variety of other liberal organizations, especially civil rights and women's organizations, advocates for consumers and the elderly, and welfare rights groups.

A union officer explained why many unions are involved in a variety of issues outside of the workplace context: "Issues that might not directly affect unions are also labor issues. For example, we're very involved in Medicare and Medicaid. They have an immediate effect on the families of our members, so they are labor issues too." When asked how he decided whether or not to get involved on an issue, one lobbyist replied with an expansive conception of his duties: "My rule of thumb is any issue that effects [*sic*] working families." Another union officer proudly showed a newspaper article that called him a "warrior for the middle class."

Internationals do not uniformly have such broad political agendas. They organize different sectors of the economy and organize members with very different skill levels, from hotel maintenance workers, to electricians, to college faculty. Thus, they have wide and varied interests to protect and different internationals have different priorities (Masters and Delaney 1987a). The heterogeneity of affiliates' interests means that the AFL-CIO sticks to common issues, such as the minimum wage or pension regulation, and lets internationals focus on concerns of their own members. The consequence is that internationals will not always assist each other or the AFL-CIO in lobbying, though rarely will internationals actively espouse positions contrary to the other unions or the AFL-CIO. In the development of labor policy, conflict is essentially dominated by two "peak organizations." Business groups and corporations align themselves with the U.S. Chamber of Commerce and the National Association of Manufacturers, as one peak organization. Unions align themselves with the AFL-CIO as the other (Heinz et al. 1993, chapter 10).

Interviews show that internationals vary in the extent to which they will mobilize on a wide variety of issues. Interviewees were asked about the type of issues on which their union has mobilized in recent legislative sessions. A majority said they mobilized on a wide variety of issues: the Ohio AFL-CIO central office, all six CLC officers, and ten international officers (four of whom said they mostly rely on the Ohio AFL-CIO and the CLCs for issue mobilizations). Five international officers replied that they engage in grassroots lobbying only on issues that directly affect their membership. Two international officers said they do not engage in grassroots lobbying mobilization often, but when they do, it is only on issues that directly affect their membership. One officer said his international had not engaged in grassroots lobbying mobilizations recently. The industrial unions of the old CIO tend to mobilize more broadly: all eight international officers from industrial unions who were interviewed mobilize on a variety of issues. Professional and construction unions tend to be more selective: 78 percent of interviewees (seven out of nine) only mobilize on issues affecting their members.

Internationals themselves may have substantial internal diversity. They may have members with different skill levels, perform very different job tasks, or work in different industries, which creates heterogeneity of interests among members. One sector that might expect to be politicized and united would be public employees who seek expanded government to increase their pay, job security, and job responsibilities. But here too, substantial heterogeneity exists according to a political director of AFSCME: "Public employees don't go into the workforce expecting to be public employees. They train as secretaries or whatever and end up with government as their employer. Therefore, there is a range of political attitudes. They don't necessarily see the connection between their job and source of income and their political attitudes."

Heterogeneity makes political mobilization more difficult because not all unions are willing to contribute to work collectively to advance the same goals. To do so allocates organizational resources in ways that do not directly help them service their members. And even if unions do clearly share a collective interest, the "free rider" problem serves as an additional barrier (Olson 1965). That is, when policy benefits affecting the labor movement as a whole are achieved, individual internationals can profit from the activities of the AFL-CIO or other internationals without using their own organizational resources to assist.

DIFFICULTIES OF EDUCATION AND MOBILIZATION

The collective action problem among union internationals occurs among rank-and-file union members as well. Traditionally, unions have attempted to use activism of their members to achieve political goals. Surveys of interest groups find that unions rely on their members as a political resource more extensively than other types of interest groups (Knoke 1990, 195–201; Kollman 1998, 52–6; Schlozman and Tierney 1986, 105). However, heterogeneity of members and their interests and the fact that many members do not share the political priorities and preferences of union leaders creates difficulties in political mobilization.

Although the AFL-CIO produces general mobilization messages and coordinates between unions, it often relies on the internationals themselves to motivate their members on issues of special concern to the union itself and to produce more targeted mobilization appeals. The fragmented structures of organized labor and the variety of interests of different unions make this possible, and probably necessary. Many interviewees stated that helping members make a connection to the core concerns of their own union was critical to getting members involved. One OEA activist explains:

> We get involved in educational or public employee issues, not other labor issues. Education and the rights of individual members are our primary concerns. Member issues include retirement and [teacher] certification. Education issues often concern funding. . . . NEA has gotten into other issues with

a more tenuous connection to education, but it makes an effort to explain the link to education to members. For example, the effort to restrict guns near schools was not explained as an issue of gun control, but as a matter of combating violence in schools.

A lobbyist for the state employees' union makes a similar point:

> Another part of the problem [of mobilizing members] is that many partisan and labor issues are not attractive to our members. So our members won't get involved with them, since they don't see how they are affected. For example, to get members involved in worker's comp[ensation], we had to approach the issue as: we, as state workers, are the ones who deliver the services, so we need to have input into how that service is delivered, not as a typical labor issue.

To make these connections to personal interest even more clear, mobilization is often targeted to certain segments of an international's membership. A United Auto Workers officer describes the union's attempts to target appeals to those most likely to respond: "We concentrate on our own members as do the other internationals of the federation. We focus on issues specific to the UAW. We use more specific messages for different groups when we can: retirees, unemployed members, active members, issues important in specific communities." Similarly, lobbyists for AFSCME and OCSEA claimed that almost all of their grassroots lobbying mobilization occurred with only a small segment of the membership: transportation workers mobilize on highway maintenance, corrections officers on prison issues, and so on. The major exception to this is the industrial unions that rely almost totally on the AFL-CIO and its CLCs for their lobbying and grassroots mobilization activities. Because they depend on the generalized federation issue information and strategy, little membership targeting seems to occur.

Many officers, particularly those from the industrial unions that mobilize on a broad variety of issues, noted that they often attempt to mobilize their members on issues that do not directly affect the industry they organize, but that do affect unions in other industries. Essentially, the officers are following a norm of reciprocity among unions: our members will help you out when you need it with the expectation that you will help us out when we need it. But members do not necessarily respond to calls to participate in activities that do not directly affect their own union. An officer of one union committed to this strategy complains: "It's tough enough to motivate members on our own issues, let alone on others'. Members don't want to help public employees because that will raise their taxes. They don't want to help the auto workers because that will raise the cost of their car. Others don't want to help us because it will raise their utility bills."

Achieving member mobilization on a broad liberal agenda is even more difficult. One officer, after discussing the wide variety of issues in which they are involved, notes they do not mobilize on all issues: "Affirmative action and equal pay for women are issues we lobby on but don't mobilize our members because the, well, white men on the factory floor probably wouldn't support these issues."

Interest groups use "outside strategies"—the mobilized opinions of the public and/or their members—because this strategy provides the group a way of influencing public officials through their constituents. Politicians may support the group's political agenda because they perceive that politically active constituents (i.e., voters) support these policies. If getting members to participate is difficult and costly in terms of time and effort, leaders have an incentive to use strategies that can provide greater political impact with less effort. "Inside" strategies involve the direct contact between group representatives (lobbyists). Groups obtain access to public officials and use the opportunity to provide information regarding the group's positions on public policy. In Washington and in many states where they have membership strength, unions traditionally have had this direct access to policymakers through the Democratic Party.

RELIANCE ON INSIDE LOBBYING STRATEGIES

Labor has long built its coalitions to pass favored legislation through the Democratic Party and used its contacts with liberal Democrats in key positions to block legislation that threatened its interests (Dark 1996; Greenstone 1977; G. Wilson 1979). Unions helped to mobilize the party behind major elements of Lyndon B. Johnson's Great Society: civil rights, Medicare, and the War on Poverty. In the 1980s, the Democratic leadership included labor priorities as party priorities in exchange for the help of labor lobbyists in passing the leadership agenda. Taylor E. Dark describes the daily informal contacts between former speaker James E. Wright's staff and labor lobbyists: "These contacts were so extensive that the community of labor lobbyists became, in effect, an arm of the Democratic leadership" (1996, 90).

Labor could get much of what was possible through inside access; it did not need to invest in creating and maintaining an active grassroots. Thus, members of Congress like Democrat Tony Hall continued to report scant grassroots contacts from union members despite a strong labor presence in his Dayton, Ohio, district: "I don't think labor does a very good job of educating the rank-and-file, so I get few letters from them" (quoted in Morehouse 1988, 1520).

The reliance on inside strategies was true in Ohio as well as Washington. When labor wanted something in the Ohio General Assembly, it went to House Speaker Verne Riffe (1974–1994). If Riffe agreed, labor got what it wanted; if Riffe did not agree, it did not matter what labor did. The president of one Ohio international explains the situation:

> Over the past ten to fifteen years, the labor leadership has been complacent in dealing with its own members. They could always rely on the House Democrats, even with a Republican governor and Republican Senate. There was no need for rallying to get members involved. They [labor] didn't necessarily have any gains, but they didn't have any losses either; there were no threats. So they had no system in place for when the day did come that they couldn't rely on the House Democrats anymore.

Others have noted the same phenomenon with other interest groups in the Democratic coalition in the late 1980s and early 1990s. Democratic pollster Stanley B. Greenberg comments: "Democrat-allied groups have atrophied because with Democratic control of Congress, they could achieve their goals by lobbying the right committees. 'Being effective' meant being effective in Washington, D.C., and membership became mainly a source of funds" (quoted in Kosterlitz 1996, 475).

In short, if persuading members of the correctness of the labor leadership's political positions and getting any member to participate politically is difficult, labor leaders took a less time-consuming path. They used PAC contributions, which were one-third of the average House Democrat's PAC donations (Abramson and Greenhouse 1997). They used the extensive network of lobbyists from union internationals to work with supporters in Congress and state legislatures. Many interviewees offered indictments of labor political strategy similar to this one of AFL-CIO president Sweeney:

> What's gone wrong with organized labor is similar to what's gone wrong with so many other organizations whose hearts are in the right place but whose minds have become complacent and whose muscles have gotten flabby. Too often, our idea of legislative influence and political action has degenerated into writing checks to political candidates and party organizations, lobbying entrenched members of Congress, and—shortly before Election Day—sending mailings to union members informing them of our endorsements. (1996, 104)

But with an "insider" strategy, unions' organizational resources could then be spent on providing the services members expected rather than political mobilization (P. Johnson 1991; Moody 1988).

CONCLUSION

The labor movement faces two collective action problems in political mobilization: how to get internationals and their locals to contribute to achieving a collective agenda, and how to get members to contribute to achieving a collective agenda. Collective action, the strike, is a core union economic strategy aimed at individual employers. The difficulty is to create the same willingness to sacrifice for collective public policy goods.

Unions have developed a number of organizational entities to make collective decisions. Some involve rank-and-file members directly at the local level, others involve activists at the county or regional level, yet others involve mainly union officers and staff. These serve the purpose of representing a variety of views within the labor movement. The consequences of union autonomy are that in politics, internationals that disagree with the federation can go their own way, locals that disagree with their international can decline to participate, and members who disagree with their union are free to work against the union position.

Traditionally, it has been costly and difficult to mobilize rank-and-file members whose beliefs differ from their unions' positions. It has been easiest to hand out fliers in the weeks before an election as the basis of a political education program. It has been easiest to let staff and officers choose targeted races, dole out PAC contributions to those campaigns, and if the candidate is elected, lobby the person once he or she is in office. By minimizing union resources spent on politics, resources devoted to servicing members' contract needs—uncontroversial among members—could be maximized. At the same time, unions could "succeed" politically, or at least protect themselves from losses, by working with Democrats in Congress and state legislatures. Under this system, officers could act as trustees on behalf of the movement and could dominate political action. Members were not necessary to be politically influential (Dark 1999).

This system was efficient and long-lasting. The political environment that sustained it, however, did not last forever. It changed suddenly and dramatically in the 1994 elections as the result of sweeping Republican victories. Labor no longer had the Democrats to protect them in Congress and state legislatures, and did not have the membership numbers in many districts or the believable threat of electoral retribution (based on past electoral mobilizations) to gain access to the new Republican majorities. Republicans could pass legislation favored by their corporate allies, and with President Clinton on the defensive in 1995, look forward to recapturing the presidency in the 1996 election to remove the protection the veto offered to labor. Unions now had an immediate incentive to rethink their traditional political strategy.

NOTES

1. Titles of the endorsement screening committees vary by international. The AFL-CIO COPEs are called scanning committees.

2. In the national federation, the marginal committee consists of thirty to thirty-five members who are heads of affiliate unions (Wilcox 1994, 23); smaller committees composed of state or regional affiliate heads make targeting and funding decisions at the state level.

3. The CIO formed the CIO-PAC in 1943. The AFL established the Labor's League for Political Education (LLPE), its first PAC, in 1947. When the AFL and CIO merged in 1955, the LLPE and CIO-PAC joined to form COPE (Bok and Dunlop 1970; Greenstone 1977).

4. The Smith-Connally Act of 1943 and the Taft-Hartley Act of 1947 had previously banned unions from making direct contributions to candidates.

5. David J. Sousa (1998) follows Edwin M. Epstein's method (Epstein 1980) of calculating business spending. This method entails adding all corporate spending plus one-half of all spending from trade/membership/health, corporations without stock, and cooperative PACs. This method understates business PAC spending as many of the organizations in these other categories are likely to be businesses. The Federal Election Commission's method of classifying PACs, however, does not make the distinctions clear.

6. Many unions have set up special "education accounts" that are used explicitly for political communication with members.

7. Contributions patterns show that the NEA-PAC is more incumbent-oriented than COPE, but still much less so than nonlabor PACs (Baer and Bailey 1994, 72–4).

5

Political Strategy in the Sweeney Era

A confluence of events transformed labor's political strategy in the 1990s. One was external to labor: the Republican Party's stunning electoral success in 1994. The second was internal to labor: the election of AFL-CIO president Sweeney in 1995. The Republican revolution swept away Democratic control of both the House and Senate in addition to many state legislatures, Ohio's included. Gone too was labor's ability to influence legislation through the Democratic Party leadership. The Republican agenda not only threatened unions directly, but also sought to end or curtail many of the social welfare programs labor had fought for over the years. Traditionally, it had been hard to reallocate resources within political activities or from other union activities to politics without a direct threat (P. Johnson 1991). After the 1994 election, there was a direct threat.

This chapter details organized labor's response to that threat, particularly through the new strategies of the AFL-CIO. In previous elections, labor seemed to have lost its ability to deliver its members. Now, it had to find a way to communicate effectively with its members and to persuade them to support endorsed candidates. The AFL-CIO's strategies are not "new," though there are some innovative wrinkles. Rather, they represent a simultaneous intensification of several traditional strategies. In particular, we will examine Sweeney's emphasis on organizing new members and mobilizing existing members in order to regain political influence.

TO REGAIN INFLUENCE

Sweeney set an aggressive agenda for organized labor. He called on labor to act as a social movement to emphasize the need for labor to reinvigorate itself at the grassroots level and to strengthen its alliances with other progressive organizations. He has argued:

> Revitalizing the labor movement is like weaving a seamless garment of activism—organizing campaigns, contract campaigns, and political campaigns. A revitalized labor movement can bridge the gap between working people whose living standards are stagnating and those who also work hard but have been shut out of middle class security. We can bring working people together, mobilize the potential power of their great numbers, and hold political leaders accountable to their concerns. We can prove that organized people can prevail over organized money. (1996, 99)

After his election in 1995, Sweeney quickly united the labor movement behind him. He was supported especially by the traditionally liberal United Auto Workers (UAW) and the United Steelworkers of America (USWA), the reformed Teamsters and Laborers unions led by relatively liberal officers, public employees unions whose incomes are dependent on growth in the public sector, and the growing service unions whose memberships are populated by low-income female and minority workers (Dark 1999). In interviews, staff and officers at the national, state, and local levels uniformly supported his more assertive political strategy:

> [Former AFL-CIO president] Kirkland paid lip service to politics and mobilization. . . . He never made us feel like we had to kick ass. Sweeney does, and I'm glad.
>
> The past twenty years of effort has been merely to maintain the status quo. We must be agents of change.
>
> We need to stop acting like we have power and start asking how we get power.
>
> We are reinvigorating grassroots involvement. We had a pattern of giving money and thinking we had influence because of it.
>
> We must rebuild our grassroots power. We can't deliver unless we rebuild our base.

For any interest group faced with the loss of access and political influence, there are several possible strategies for regaining them. Many of these are visible in the AFL-CIO's post-1995 mobilization strategy, which is detailed in the following list.

1. *Expand membership.* The group can attempt to increase the number of constituents affiliated with the group. The more voters in a district who share the group's goals, the more likely politicians will be responsive.
2. *Mobilize.* Numbers matter, but intensity does as well. Through mobilization, members show their willingness to devote time and effort to

support the group's goals. Active members demonstrate to politicians that the group's message should be taken seriously because, if members are willing to mobilize on the issue between elections, they may be willing to mobilize on the issue during an election (Wright 1996). At least in the short term, the shift to outside strategies demonstrates constituents' support for government programs and to protect those programs from repeal or budget cuts. Other interest groups that traditionally relied on access to the Democratic majority in Congress for political influence have also quickly emphasized greater use of outside strategies since the 1994 Republican takeover of Congress (Cook 1998; Gimpel 1998).

3. *Media.* Interest groups can demonstrate constituent support not only by mobilizing their own members through organizational structures, but also by attempting to mobilize the general public. Often, this means using the media to attempt to sway public opinion in a manner favorable to the group's political goals.

4. *Spend money.* Active members and supportive public opinion are important political resources, but in the memorable words of Jesse Unruh, the former California Assembly speaker: "Money is the mother's milk of politics." Unions are somewhat unique in the interest group universe in that they have access to significant financial resources, unlike many citizens' groups, and access to many individual members, unlike many economic groups (E. Gerber 1999). Groups make campaign contributions to candidates in order to help supporters win and/or to help the group achieve lobbying access after the election. The belief is that busy officeholders will be more willing, at a minimum, to give scarce time to hear the position of those who contributed to their election.

Labor has long used its political action committees (PACs) to raise voluntary contributions from members to donate to endorsed candidates, as detailed in chapter 4. To avoid the $5,000 cap on PAC contributions, interest groups have increasingly made unlimited soft money contributions to political parties. Also avoiding these limitations are PACs' "independent expenditures" that are spent on behalf of individual candidates without the knowledge or assistance of the candidate's campaign. Furthermore, there are ways groups can spend operating funds or dues on elections without using voluntary contributions made to their PAC. Soft money contributions are one way to do this. Others include "issue advocacy" ads and direct communication with members of the organization. Groups can directly endorse candidates in communications with their own members, for example, in a group newsletter, and can spend as much as they want on such promotions. Issue ads are aimed at the general public rather than members of the organization. They are protected as free speech by the courts (*Buckley v. Valeo*, 1976; *Federal Election Commission [FEC] v. Massachusetts Citizens for Life, Inc.*, 1986) as long as they do not directly advocate the election or defeat of a particular candidate. Thus, groups can spend money on ads positively associating a candidate with popular issues and associating his or her opponent with unpopular positions. These ads clearly imply which candidate the voter should support, but are acceptable as long as no direct endorsement is made.

5. *Targeting*. Group resources are finite, so groups must prioritize how they will spend limited money and time. Thus, they need to be concerned with helping supporters who are competitive yet need assistance to win. Some candidates are likely to win without vigorous assistance from the group; others are destined to lose regardless of the group's efforts. In either case where the results seem preordained, any man hours or funding by the group is wasted since these misallocated resources could instead be devoted to candidates for whom assistance would have a higher probability of payoff. In the past, labor has been more successful targeting financial contributions than manpower to competitive congressional races (Burns, Francia, and Hernnson 2000).

6. *Coalitional activities*. The resources of an individual organization may be limited, but their effectiveness can be multiplied by coordination with other like-minded organizations (see Hojnacki 1997; Hula 1995). The AFL-CIO itself is a coalition of labor unions. Politically, unions with membership strength in certain regions can focus their efforts on local campaigns, while relying on unions with membership strength in other regions for mobilization in those campaigns. Likewise, coalitions are frequently built with other like-minded organizations. Unions have long worked with other liberal groups to turn out voters for Democratic candidates. These include organizations of racial minorities, women, environmentalists, college students, and the elderly. Unions themselves sponsor organizations devoted to these purposes: A. Philip Randolph Institute (African Americans), Coalition of Labor Union Women, Working Women's Vote, Council of Senior Citizens, League for Latin American Advancement, and Frontlash (college students).

ORGANIZING STRATEGY

Much of the AFL-CIO's new strategy is based on a reinvigorated emphasis on its membership. That includes both increasing, or at least stabilizing, the size of its membership after years of decline as well as educating and mobilizing existing members.

A group's membership are the constituents of elected officeholders—the citizens they represent in government and the voters who decide to continue or end their service. Many believe that labor unions need to reverse the decline in membership, not just as a matter of preserving unions as workplace organizations, but as a means of strengthening unions' political voice. One national AFL-CIO officer explains: "We must be bigger and have members who believe in the movement as a precursor to policy influence. We need a stronger movement before politicians will be reliable." By broadening its appeal to low-wage workers and forming alliances with local religious leaders, immigrant groups, environmentalists, and college activists, it also helps labor present a "social movement" public image articulated by Sweeney rather than being dismissed politically as an ossified and out-of-touch special interest.

We have already documented the long-term decline in union membership in the United States. This decline has been accompanied by a decline in the proportion of union funds spent on organizing new members. Unions spent 39 percent of their funds on organizing in the 1950s; this had fallen to about 3 percent by the mid-1990s (P. Johnson 1991; Kosterlitz 1999).

To increase organizing by locals, the new AFL-CIO strategy is to provide them with more money and manpower assistance. One AFL-CIO officer comments: "We want to shift priorities to organizing, not just to exclusively service members as in the past. This means shifting money, staff, and members into organizing." Sweeney wants locals to devote 30 percent of their budgets to organizing. The AFL-CIO will provide $20 million in matching grants for organizing drives and another $60 million for a public relations campaign to improve labor's public image to create a more favorable climate for organizing (Greenhouse 1997).

The AFL-CIO will also target its organizing resources more carefully toward certain localities and industries. A national AFL-CIO officer explains:

> Our new strategy is organizing in more places, being more experimental, having more cooperation between unions, and pooling our resources. We will target certain industries and certain locations and will organize the whole market. That's the only way to have any leverage over employers. For example, [the Teamsters] won the UPS [United Parcel Service] strike because 80% of UPS is organized. We need to do the same with others.

Having learned the lessons of many manufacturing jobs moving to foreign countries, many of the industries targeted for organizing are those that cannot move—health care, tourism, building services, and food processing (Meyerson 2000). This targeted strategy has been implemented most prominently in Las Vegas, where the AFL-CIO has engaged in a drive to organize hotel and casino workers, and in Los Angeles, where seventy-four thousand health service workers have organized.

The Las Vegas and Los Angeles examples showed the type of workers organizing drives are targeting. They were low-paid workers, often female, minorities, and immigrants, who had not been the focus of union organizing in the past. Service sector unions have increasingly seen these workers as major opportunities, in contrast to industrial unions who often saw immigration as a threat to the jobs and wages of American workers. The AFL-CIO's new emphasis was shown clearly at its executive council meeting in February 2000 when it called for an amnesty on illegal immigrants and the repeal of a law imposing sanctions on employers who hire them—a law labor lobbied to pass in 1986 (Swoboda 2000c).

Another targeted region is the traditionally union-hostile South (Sweeney 1996, 131). To organize effectively in the South, labor will emphasize greater coalition-building with civil rights groups and churches. The AFL-CIO's former director of organizing explains: "We want to make the right to organize a civil rights issue by focusing on poor, minority industries. . . . Denny's doesn't care if they're called union busters. They do care if they're called racist." The aim of this southern organizing strategy and coalitional activity is to create access to and to mesh with the existing concerns of southern Democrats who are not necessarily prounion. Success means creating a constituency base for labor outside of its traditional strength in the Northeast and Midwest.

These examples are part of a broader strategy to change the way in which the AFL-CIO organizes new unions. The new emphasis began in 1991 with the formation of the Organizing Institute. The aim of the institute has been to train organizers of affiliates to use the community organizing tactics of Saul Alinsky. These tactics are more aggressive than quietly persuading workers in an individual firm; instead, protests and boycotts are used to grab media and public attention and to help build coalitions with other community organizations. Richard Bensinger, a former AFL-CIO vice president for Organizing, explains: "We need to change the climate in which organizing is done. We won't have legal change in a short period of time to assist us. Instead, we must look more like a social movement. We must mobilize our base. We need to put emphasis on local members as organizers, get support from local politicians, ethnic community leaders, and the health and safety community." Indeed, Peggy Taylor, the AFL-CIO legislative director, explains how the AFL-CIO has incorporated the organizing emphasis into its lobbying:

> Organizing now is our highest priority. Increasingly, we talk to members of Congress about supporting organizing drives in their districts, not about legislation on reforming labor law per se. We want to get members of Congress to understand the workplace, employer-employee relationships, and the way we conduct organizing drives. Most members of Congress have never been

in an employee-employer relationship. They're lawyers or owned their own business. We try to show good and bad organizing drives. At the [congressional] Democratic retreat recently, we brought in workers to explain the difficulty of organizing drives.

The AFL-CIO's pitch to Democratic members of Congress is that it is in their electoral self-interest to help labor's organizing drives. Increasing the number of union members in their districts increases the number of union households likely to vote Democratic and the number of union activists available to volunteer for their reelection campaigns.

The importance of gaining the support of local politicians can be seen in the Service Employees International Union's organization of health care workers in Los Angeles. To overcome a court ruling that found that these workers did not have the right to organize, SEIU had to persuade the state legislature and the governor to change state law, and Los Angeles County officials to establish a board with which the workers could bargain (Greenhouse 1999c). Without action by government officials and the electoral support unions had given these officials over the years, labor's largest organizing drive since the 1930s could not have occurred.

A final innovation in organizing strategy is "bargaining to organize." In contract negotiations with companies who are already unionized, unions have received assurances that these employers will prod their nonunion suppliers and subsidiaries to ease their obstruction of organizing. Ideally, unions attempt to convince employers to recognize the union once a majority of members have signed "check cards" that affiliate themselves with the union. Alternatively, unions have asked for expedited union certification elections. These methods seek to avoid the long process of a National Labor Relations Board election during which employers often mount extensive antiunion campaigns. At the least, unions seek to get assurances that their organizers will be able to meet with workers inside the organizing site and that the employer will not threaten to cut jobs during the organizing drive. In the Las Vegas organizing drive, the Hotel Employees and Restaurant Employees union agreed to changes in work rules at hotels with which it had contracts in exchange for check card recognition at a new hotel run by the same management (Meyerson 2000).

The new aggressive tactics and strategic emphasis on low-wage workers does not mean that unions are ignoring opportunities to organize white-collar workers when they arise. Doctors and other medical professionals are showing increasing interest in union protections due to threats on their incomes and autonomy from managed care organizations. Unions are making increased efforts to organize graduate assistants on university campuses—particularly in the California state system. A successful strike by engineers at Boeing was trumpeted as evidence that would show other white-collar workers the benefits of unionization (Greenhouse 2000e; Cole 2000).

Some success in the new emphasis on organizing is apparent. The average share of union budgets devoted to organizing has risen from 3 percent to 10 percent (Kosterlitz 1999, 2474). Behind this overall increase is considerable variation: the SEIU spends 45 percent of its budget on organizing, ten times the percentage of most unions (Greenhouse 2000c). The aggregate number of union members has increased two years straight by 100,000 in 1998 (Swoboda 1999b) and by 265,000 in 1999 (Greenhouse 2000d). Even the number of members in the private sector increased in 1999.

Furthermore, the new emphasis on organizing has direct political implications beyond that of increasing membership strength. The skills and tactics useful for coordinating campaigns to organize unions are quite similar to those skills and tactics useful for coordinating political campaigns. College students who were trained by the AFL-CIO and spent their summers as organizers and community activists in union summer programs have returned to their campuses to organize teaching assistants and to mobilize against the manufacture of college merchandise by sweat shops (Greenhouse 1999a). Likewise, experienced union organizers, though their primary responsibilities are not political, can quickly become election volunteer recruiters and trainers. One AFL-CIO officer comments: "Up 'til now, there hasn't been much synergy between political organizing and union organizing. Our latest organizing drive in Las Vegas is a good example of how we can move union organizers into political organizing. When we did that, the incumbent [Republican candidate] went from thirty [points] up to ten points down [in a public opinion poll]." Union political organizers at the grassroots level are a core part of the AFL-CIO's new political strategy. The new strategy consists of more than just greater aggressiveness in recruiting new members. It also involves greater aggressiveness in mobilizing current members and influencing the political beliefs of the general public.

POLITICAL STRATEGY

After Sweeney's election to the AFL-CIO presidency, the planning of the new political strategy began. Gerald W. McEntee, the AFSCME president, which is a major federation of public employee unions, was appointed as the chair of the AFL-CIO's political affairs task force. Steve Rosenthal was appointed as the new COPE director.

Labor sought to learn from the tactics used by the small business and insurance industries to defeat Clinton's national health care proposals (see Johnson and Broder 1996, Skocpol 1997). The keys to their success were coalition building, grassroots mobilization, and media savvy. One union's national political director quipped: "We owe it all to Harry and Louise" [the fictional couple who starred in the anti-Clinton plan ads].

McEntee needed to demonstrate to the AFL-CIO that the new strategy would be successful. To do so, AFSCME joined forces with a dozen other liberal groups, including Citizens Action, the National Council of Senior Citizens, and several environmental groups to form Project '95. The coalition developed a grassroots lobbying campaign to oppose Republican proposals on health, welfare, education, and the environment. A $1 million budget sent organizers into fourteen Republican congressional districts, particularly those represented by vulnerable freshmen (Kosterlitz 1996). The organizers worked with local groups to publicize votes that would be unpopular through protests, letters to the editor, and news conferences. As a second step, a coalition composed of many of the same organizations as Project '95, called Save America's Families, paid for television commercials that criticized Republican proposals on health and education.

Meanwhile, the AFL-CIO polled its members to find out what issues were important to them. They found that the economy, health security (Medicare), retirement security (Social Security), and their children's futures (education) were highly important. Originally, the purpose of the polls was to determine issues on which to mobilize grassroots lobbying campaigns. Later, they formed the basis for television ads during the 1996 election.

The AFL-CIO had a test run of its new political strategy during the January 1996 special Senate election in Oregon. The contest was between U.S. Representative Ron Wyden, a liberal Democrat, and Oregon Senate majority leader Gordon Smith, a conservative, to replace Bob Packwood, a moderate Republican who had recently resigned. The AFL-CIO sent thirty-seven full-time operatives to work for Wyden's campaign. They helped with voter registration, managed Get-Out-the-Vote drives, and signed up volunteers (who would spend thirty hours during the campaign telephoning and knocking on doors). Nearly five hundred thousand pieces of mail were sent to union members (Kosterlitz 1996). Campaign messages were tested comparing the candidates' positions on minimum wage, worker safety, education, and environmental protection. In the end, Wyden won.

THE 1996 CAMPAIGN

President Sweeney asked affiliates to contribute an extra $35 million dollars from their treasuries to be used in independent expenditures for the 1996 congressional races.[1] This money would go for two purposes. First, in conjunction with the other organizations of Project '96, it would pay for issue ads in targeted congressional districts. Internationals, rather than the AFL-CIO, contributed most of the union money to Project '96. In total, unions contributed approximately $100,000 (R. Gerber 1999, 85). Second, the money would pay for the Labor '96 campaign, whereby union volunteer coordinators were to recruit and train activists in targeted districts.

The AFL-CIO's $35 million independent expenditure campaign was not the only labor political spending. On top of it, unions gave $9.5 million in soft money contributions to the national parties and made additional independent expenditures of at least $6.7 million (Dark 1999, 185). Labor PACs increased their total contributions by 27 percent between 1992 and 1996, from $33.6 million to $46.3 million.[2] Corporate PACs increased their total contributions by 21 percent during the same period, from $54.6 million to $69.5 million. Labor PACs also improved the targeting of their contributions by giving 25 percent to competitive Democrats challenging incumbent Republicans in 1996, compared to only 8 percent in the 1992 elections.[3] House Democrats were increasingly reliant on union spending—45 percent of their total PAC receipts were from unions, up from 32 percent in 1992 (Stanley and Niemi 1998, 103). In the 1996 Senate campaigns, labor PACs focused on open-seat races by contributing 48 percent of their total PAC contributions. This is a substantial increase over the 25 percent given to open-seat Senate candidates in 1992.

The $25 million ad campaign was aimed at influencing the general public primarily in marginal Republican congressional districts.[4] In the last two months of the campaign, Anthony Corrado (1997, 163) estimates that unions' independent expenditures totaled about $10 million in twenty-one districts with Republican incumbents compared to $1.1 million in open-seat districts.

The objective of the issue ads was to set the agenda of the election and to control the debate early on so the contest would be fought on labor's terms (West and Loomis 1999). The theme was "America Needs a Raise." This focused the public's attention on popular economic issues, especially raising the minimum wage, which Democrats were pushing in Congress. The ads included an 800 number viewers could call to receive a voter's guide. As one union political director observed: "Every election before 1996, the focus of the campaigns was on guns and abortion rather than working family issues." So, explained another, labor sought to turn the tables on the Republican's aggressive attempts to pass their Contract with America: "This year we didn't wait for the election to go into districts to influence voters. The Republican leadership [in Congress] was introducing items that wouldn't be popular back home. So we went back home to make sure people knew about it." The AFL-CIO aired twenty-seven thousand ads in forty districts, distributed voter video guides in twenty-four districts, and ran radio ads in several others (Herrnson 1998a). [5]

The ads were also part of an intra-Democratic Party skirmish. Labor saw itself in a battle with Dick Morris, the presidential campaign consultant, and the moderate Democratic Leadership Council (DLC) over how Clinton and the Democrats should position themselves in the 1996 election. Morris and the DLC wanted Clinton to run as a moderate. Commented one labor campaign organizer: "They want to concentrate on yuppies and forget about workers. They think our voters are assured and they're not." The AFL-CIO saw the ads as an important means of forcing Clinton and the Democrats to defend traditional party themes and programs.

Where the ads were directed at the general public, Labor '96 was directed at union members. If the ads were the "air war," Labor '96 was the "ground war." First, during the early spring of 1996, COPE worked closely with state affiliates to develop campaign plans for congressional races. Originally, the plan was to send 175 volunteer coordinators to 73 targeted districts. But as the campaign unfolded, more state affiliates requested that local congressional districts be targeted. As more locals, state affiliates, and internationals committed staff to COPE, the AFL-CIO increased its involvement to 105 congressional districts, 14 Senate races, and 2 gubernatorial races.

One part of the volunteer coordinator's job was to meet with local union officers to develop and coordinate the campaign plan for that congressional district. A union political director explains the costs and benefits of assigning national staff as volunteer coordinators in congressional races:

> When a Washington staffer is assigned to Alabama, the person loses time becoming familiar with the area. This is why institutionalized training of activists at the local level is important. The national representative should be the servant of those at the local level. They're easier to shift around wherever needed and help the locals become more organized. But we must have a base of local activists to make it work, to hold candidates accountable for how our [PAC] money is spent. . . . Most of the focus of state federations is on the state capitol and the Central Labor Councils on their cities. The national rep assures the federal level isn't being ignored.

The other part of the volunteer coordinators' job was to train twenty-five hundred local activists who would recruit campaign volunteers for the final month of the campaign. Each local union coordinator would recruit one activist for every ten to twenty members of the local (R. Gerber 1999). The activists would talk to members on a one-on-one basis, distribute campaign literature, and mobilize turnout and volunteer participation.

As part of Labor '96, activists distributed 9 million comparative voter guides and made 5.5 million phone calls to other union members. They coordinated local mobilization activities with the A. Philip Randolph

Institute, Citizen Action, Interfaith Alliance, National Baptist Convention, National Rainbow Coalition, Rock the Vote, Women's Vote Project, and dozens of others (AFL-CIO 1996; R. Gerber 1999).

The AFL-CIO has also begun to institutionalize its development of political operatives through its Labor Political Training Center. The center schools labor political activists, campaign managers of friendly candidates, and union members interested in running for public office. In 1996, the center held an issues seminar for fifty House and Senate challengers and twenty-five of their campaign managers to familiarize them with labor's priorities (AFL-CIO 1996). The AFL-CIO planned a "Goals 2000" campaign to recruit 2000 members to run for local and state offices. In the end, 901 union members ran (AFL-CIO 2000). Electing union members would create sympathetic public officials at the state and local levels and also provide a source of quality candidates for higher office in the future.

Labor '96 was different from past campaigns in a number of ways. First, there was a greater emphasis on coalition-building than in the past. This was true of AFL-CIO affiliates cooperating through the federation as well as the AFL-CIO coordination with other interest groups through Project '96. While coalitional activities occurred in previous elections, there were higher levels of coordination with a larger number of organizations in 1996. An officer of the Ohio Building Trades Council explained the improvement in coordination within the AFL-CIO: "The national, state, and local networks meshed more closely [in targeted races]—better coordination. [The Building Trades Council] also worked entirely through the AFL-CIO and central bodies [CLCs] this time. Before, individual internationals and locals would want to work independently so they could take credit with the candidate." In total, a record thirty AFL-CIO affiliates contributed staff to the Labor '96 campaign (AFL-CIO 1996).

Second, national and state federations coordinated closely to develop campaign plans. Previously, state federations and CLCs largely developed their own plans and the national federation supplied the money. Those funds were the national federations' primary involvement. Only in the last month before the election would national staff be assigned to the states to help to recruit volunteers, primarily for Get-Out-the-Vote drives. States whose political operations were ineffective were left on their own; there was little attempt to improve them.

Third, there was greater coordination between COPE and the AFL-CIO legislative department. Again, the difference is a matter of degree. The original membership polls and district-level ads were used to generate members' participation in grassroots lobbying campaigns against Republican legislation. But messages that are effective in mobilizing members in between elections can also be effective for mobilizing during elections. The grassroots lobbying campaign fed into the advertising blitz and the

Labor '96 election campaign. And the America Needs a Raise theme of the advertising fed into the AFL-CIO's successful legislative efforts to increase the minimum wage.

Finally, the ads provided an important complementary strategy to the membership mobilization of Labor '96. Since the issues were based on a poll of the membership, they resonated. Since the issues were broadly framed, they were effective in any international. In previous elections, affiliates tended to focus on the issues that were of greatest importance to their own members. This made it more difficult for unions to coordinate campaign messages. The ads provided a framework for union members to understand their own workplace concerns, and at the same time to see the wider implications. The broader message focused on strengthening the economic position of workers—the purpose of both unions and union political involvement. As one AFSCME political operative described the new messages frames: "The lesson is to connect with them as workers, not as AFSCME members. They need to see that the union sees them as more than a member. So we must speak to them as working families and can't put our institutional blinders on anymore. We must define our own mission as helping working families." The message's consistency across unions also provided the reinforcement necessary for it to be absorbed. The ads provided the message for the volunteer coordinators to use in mobilizing grassroots activists.

Furthermore, the content of the ads was different from ads traditionally run by labor. The poll of members found that they did not like their unions making partisan appeals or being told for whom to vote; however, they did like information from their union on the candidates and their issue positions. (The National Education Association [NEA] did a similar poll of its members and reached the same conclusion.) One national leader characterized the poll results: "They don't like being told who to vote for. They find that insulting. [Union] leaders don't have the credibility. They like receiving information on issues they care about." Thus, unions shifted to literature "comparing" the candidates on major issues. One union political director describes the change: "We stopped telling members who to vote for. We told them what to consider. We stopped what I call our Russian ads: pictures of healthy workers with lunch pails that just told our endorsement. [This year] we used candidate issue stand ads instead." Another comments: "We used [candidate] comparisons on leaflets and voter guides, the Christian Coalition was our model, and did massive distributions at work sites. We didn't tell them who to vote for, they weren't prounion or antibusiness as in the past. There was a new working family focus. Members could figure it out for themselves." Not coincidentally, by focusing on "issues" and not explicitly endorsing a candidate, unions could claim the ads and the literature were "issue advocacy," and thus could be paid for with operating funds rather than PAC funds.

There was a major downside to the ad strategy, however, by becoming visibly involved very early in the election, Republican candidates had time to respond. Business groups, led by the National Federation of Independent Business and the U.S. Chamber of Commerce, formed the "Coalition" to spend $5 million on issue ads and voter guides in thirty-seven districts (Herrnson 1998a, 125). Some ads decried the "outside interference" of the "big labor bosses" to make the unions themselves the issue.

The AFL-CIO believes the new Labor '96 strategy was effective in influencing members during the election. Polls document the difference in voting and turnout between union members and nonmembers (AFL-CIO 1996). Male union members supported President Clinton at much higher rates than male nonmembers, 61 percent to 38 percent, respectively. The gap between union and nonunion members in congressional elections is just as dramatic: 61 percent of white male union members supported Democratic congressional candidates, while 63 percent of white male nonmembers supported Republicans. Female union members were also more supportive of Clinton than nonunion women, 72 percent to 52 percent, respectively. The turnout of voters from union households increased by 2.3 million from 1992 to 1996, despite the fact that both overall turnout and union membership declined.

Of 105 targeted congressional districts, the labor-endorsed candidate won 47. Seventeen of the victors were incumbent Democrats that labor was trying to protect, twelve involved open seats won by Democrats, eighteen were incumbent Republicans who lost, and another twenty-five targeted Republicans won with less than 52 percent of the vote (AFL-CIO 1996). Labor-endorsed challengers won in nearly one-third of their campaigns, a considerable achievement since congressional reelection rates typically top 90 percent. Gary C. Jacobson (1999) provides evidence that the success of Labor '96 would have been even greater had the Democrats been able to recruit more experienced, well-financed challengers to Republican incumbents. The AFL-CIO's efforts were also undermined by revelations of questionable fund-raising by Clinton and the Democratic National Committee during the last weeks of the campaign. Voters who decided in the last week of the campaign favored Republicans, 55 percent to 41 percent, compared to voters who, deciding a month or more before the election, favored Democrats, 51 percent to 47 percent (AFL-CIO 1996).

THE AFTERMATH

In the 1998 midterm elections, the AFL-CIO continued to emphasize grassroots mobilization but shifted away from the issue ads. Attempting to mobilize broad sections of the public through television ads is an extremely expensive and inefficient strategy relative to targeting and activating one's own membership (Schier 2000). One AFL-CIO political officer explained the change in emphasis: "In 1996, our media campaign made us the target. And the ads were not targeted to our members, so they were not effective in getting them out to vote. In 1998, we couldn't spend as much. It is more effective in the short and long term to focus on our members. The best predictor of whether a member turns out to vote is whether [he or she] had a direct contact in the workplace." With little legislative activity occurring in the 105th Congress, there were few highly salient issues that could effectively stir the public. And by maintaining a lower profile, business organizations were less likely to countermobilize and demonize the labor bosses. The AFL-CIO decreased its independent expenditures to $28 million and targeted its ads more narrowly on thirty House districts (Cassata 1998, 1113). Turnout was expected to be low, and the outcome was expected to hinge on which party got its supporters to the polls, so labor focused on Get-Out-the-Vote drives. The AFL-CIO invested in 392 field organizers, and in 9.5 million pieces of mail and 5.5 million phone calls to union households (Balz and Broder 1998). Success was indicated by the increase in labor households' share of the electorate from 14 percent in 1994 to 22 percent in 1998 and the unusual gain of five seats by the president's party in the House in a midterm election, especially in a second term. Seventy percent of those union voters claimed to have voted for Democratic congressional candidates—an increase of 7 percent over 1996 (Foerstel 1998, 3298).[6]

The emphasis on grassroots mobilization continued in the 2000 presidential and congressional campaigns. Each international within the AFL-CIO appointed a volunteer coordinator in each state (Eilperin 2000). The statewide coordinator recruited representatives in each union, who, in turn, would recruit a point person on each shift. The AFL-CIO trained 1,000 coordinators at local worksites with the goal of recruiting 100,000 rank-and-file volunteers (AFL-CIO 2000). It sent 12 million pieces of mail, 60,000 e-mails urging people to vote, registered 2.3 million union household voters, and made 8 million phone calls to union households. Labors' Get-Out-the-Vote efforts were apparent as union households' share of the electorate rose to 26 percent, up from 23 percent in the last presidential election in 1996 (Broder 2000). Sixty percent of voters from union households supported Al Gore. Union turnout was particularly important in swing states such as Michigan, Pennsylvania, and Wisconsin. In Michigan, the United Auto Workers negotiated election day as a paid day off. Forty percent of voters in Michigan were from union households, helping Al Gore win the state and helping Democratic Representative Debbie Stabenow upset Republican Senator Spencer Abraham.

Labor's strategy is to continue to build its grassroots membership and political strength. It will continue to use membership polls to decide issues to emphasize and to use the media and issue mobilizations well before the election not only to influence legislation in Congress, but also to set the issue agenda for the next campaign. By focusing electoral debate on issues that are already popular with members, it is easier to mobilize members and to get them to see the relevance of politics. By allowing them to see how legislators respond to their issue mobilization, members can test for themselves the quality of representation they are receiving from their legislators and can understand why they should support candidates who share their issue positions rather than relying on union endorsements alone.

CONCLUSION

Unions have a membership that has diverse political beliefs—on political party affiliation, ideology, issue opinions, and the appropriateness of union political involvement—and is increasingly diverse sociodemographically as well. Although union leaders can appeal to members who share union political goals for political mobilization, the difficulty is mobilizing sufficient members to have an effect on political outcomes. Mobilizing members who are indifferent to politics or those who disagree with unions' political positions to some degree would help to make labor politically effective, but persuading these members to participate is difficult. Rather than spend the effort educating and persuading members, especially across the interests of a variety of internationals that organize different economic sectors, labor found it was easier to rely on organizational resources that leaders controlled: lobbyists, staff and officer contacts, and campaign contributions. This strategy worked politically as long as labor had inside access through a sympathetic Democratic Party leadership.

Since the 1994 Republican victories, labor has had to develop political strategies to unite the diversity of its membership and internationals. A combination of the external threat of Newt Gingrich's Republican Congress and Sweeney's coming to power within the AFL-CIO has led to a more aggressive, grassroots-oriented political strategy. Labor has had to invest in the costly and difficult efforts of organizing new members and educating and mobilizing existing members. It has coordinated its lobbying strategies more closely with its electoral strategies (Heberlig 2000). It has had to reach beyond its members to the general public through media campaigns and to other like-minded interest groups and their members through coalition-building. The 1996, 1998, and 2000 congressional elections saw labor implement and hone its new political strategy. Above all, labor learned how to educate and mobilize its members most effectively without also countermobilizing the opposition.

Labor will face a number of difficulties in sustaining this new political strategy. To what extent can it continue to invest heavily in organizing and political mobilization, and at the same time, continue to emphasize collective bargaining, grievance adjudication, and other economic activities that members expect first and foremost? To what extent can it keep activists continually "fired-up" without leading to burnout? To what extent can it stay one step ahead of its political opponents as they adapt their political strategies to labor's? As union membership continues to diversify, can unifying messages be found? These are some of the challenges that will face union leaders and political activists in the years ahead.

NOTES

1. A special convention in March 1996 approved a special monthly assessment on affiliates—15 cents per member—to cover most of the cost (Kilborn 1996). Larger affiliates and internal AFL-CIO funds covered the rest.

2. The source of all PAC contribution data is the Federal Election Commission (FEC) as reported by Paul Herrnson (1995, 117–9; 1998a 116–8).

3. In 1992, the Democrats held the majority in both chambers of Congress. Their strategy was to preserve this majority in a year of redistricting, mass retirements, and the House Bank scandal by protecting vulnerable incumbents. Thus, union PACs purposely gave more emphasis to helping incumbents than usual. With Republicans taking control of Congress in the 1994 election, Democrats needed to defeat incumbent Republicans in order to regain the majority. Thus, the strategy shifted to emphasizing competitive challengers.

4. The NEA also increased its efforts in 1996, but primarily focused on educating and mobilizing its own members, rather than attempting to influence the public. Unlike the AFL-CIO, its priority was reelecting President Clinton, rather than influencing congressional races.

5. Ads were not run in all the districts in which the AFL-CIO had volunteer coordinators, only those with the "most hostile and vulnerable" incumbents.

6. The party of the incumbent president usually loses seats in midterm elections. The 1998 election was expected to be no different, particularly with the fallout from President Clinton's relationship with Monica Lewinsky potentially tarnishing Democratic candidates. Labor PAC contributions to Democrats shifted slightly from the 1996 election cycle towards protecting incumbent Democrats: two-thirds of labor PAC contributions in both House and Senate races went to incumbents, 16 percent to challengers and 16 percent to open-seat candidates in both the House and Senate races (calculated from FEC reports).

6

Union Political Activists

AFL-CIO president John J. Sweeney's political strategy relies heavily on the activism of union members for labor to achieve its electoral and public policy objectives. Although the effort Sweeney and contemporary union officers are placing on mobilizing activists may be intensified, membership activism has long been a critical political resource for organized labor. Based on their study of union political action in the 1950s and 1960s, Derek C. Bok and John T. Dunlop (1970) argued unions' manpower, rather than their endorsements or campaign contributions, had the greatest effect on elections. More recent studies consistently confirm that unions are more active in attempting to mobilize their members for political activities than other economic and social organizations (Goldstein 1999, 114; Knoke 1990, chapter 10; Schlozman and Tierney 1986, 105; Verba, Schlozman, and Brady 1995, chapter 13). Thus, to understand the involvement and effect of labor unions in American elections, and the potential for Sweeney's strategy to succeed, it is critical to understand how unions mobilize their members politically. The major decisions regarding electoral strategy may be made at the national or state level, but ultimately these strategies are implemented at the local level. If labor is to have an impact on elections in ways other than as a financier of campaigns, local officers, activists, and rank-and-file members must respond.

In this chapter, we review the structures of unions and characteristics of their members that facilitate effective political mobilization. We use interviews with Ohio union officers and activists to describe union mobilization tactics. We use the Ohio union surveys to explain why members participate in response to union mobilization. We focus here on electoral activists—those who engage in activities that demand time, effort, and/or money and are designed to influence the participation and votes of others—rather than those who merely turn out to vote. We find that

members' commitment to the union and agreement with political positions of union leaders are important explanations. Finally, we compare the
political participation of labor union members to that of nonmembers in
U.S. elections and find that union members participate at slightly higher
rates.

LABOR UNIONS AND GRASSROOTS MOBILIZATION

Unions have organizational characteristics that facilitate the mobilization
of their members for political action. First, they have a large membership
spread over substantial portions of the country. Most interest groups are
precluded from using such a strategy based on the simple fact that they
do not have large membership bases (Salisbury 1984; Schlozman and Tierney 1986; Walker 1991).

Yet labor union members do not join their union in order to support its
political agenda. They join for the work-related benefits and protections
or because they were forced to join by a union-shop agreement. This limits the willingness of some members to participate in union political mobilization. Moreover, unions organize diverse sectors of the economy and
increasingly organize white-collar workers and the public sector. The diversity of interests of union members makes it difficult for the movement
to represent its membership politically or to mobilize members with a single appeal. Union membership is also unevenly distributed across the
country. Labor has high levels of organization in the industrial states of
the Northeast and the Midwest (20 percent of workforce) and low levels
in right-to-work states in the Rocky Mountains and the South (9.5 percent
and 7 percent of the workforce, respectively) (Hirsch and Macpherson
1997).

The second attribute of unions that facilitates political mobilization is
their history of collective action. In the workplace, members are urged to
band together to leverage better working conditions, benefits, and job security from their employers. Solidarity with one's fellow members is a
central element of the union movement. Since the 1930s, and particularly
since the passage of the Taft-Hartley Act (Bok and Dunlop 1970; Greenstone 1977), unions have expanded their collective action from the workplace to the political arena. This stands in contrast to groups like consumers or the working poor, who are largely unorganized by interest
groups, and do not share a group identity that would facilitate collective
action.

Finally, unions' organizational structures facilitate grassroots mobilization. Union political organization is both fragmented and decentralized. The
fragmented structure allows each international to emphasize issues that are

the greatest concerns of its own members and are most likely to be effective in mobilizing them. An officer of the United Auto Workers (UAW) explains: "We concentrate on our own members as do the other internationals of the federation. We focus on issues specific to the UAW. We use more specific messages for different groups when we can: retirees, unemployed members, active members, issues important in specific communities."

Decentralization is important because local officers are available to ask members to participate. The presence of local chapters is a consistent predictor of the use of membership mobilization strategies by interest groups (Gais and Walker 1991; Hojnacki and Kimball 1999; Kollman 1998). Individuals are most likely to respond positively to mobilization requests when the request comes from a personal acquaintance (Verba, Schlozman, and Brady 1995, 142).

Union organizational structures also put staff in place at the national, state, and local levels to help local unions with political mobilization. Staff can be moved to help in regions where unions are targeting particular campaigns for special assistance or regions where local officers are inactive or need assistance. Staff help to promote local political involvement and coordinate joint activities of locals. They coordinate between unions and candidates' campaign organizations. They provide training, communications assistance, and logistical assistance that make it easy for members to complete preplanned activities. Without structures and personnel to facilitate political action, unions would have to rely on members to volunteer on their own, decreasing the likelihood that unions would generate sufficient activity to have a significant impact on elections.

THE ROLE OF LEADERSHIP IN POLITICAL MOBILIZATION

Group members will not automatically participate in activities that will help the group produce benefits for themselves and their compatriots. As demonstrated by economist Mancur Olson (1965), individuals will not contribute to the production of collective goods—goods that, once produced, are available to everyone—unless the benefits of participation outweigh the costs and the individual's contribution makes the difference in allowing the good to be produced. Individuals would prefer to be "free riders"—that is, acquire the benefits of group membership and allow others to bear the costs. Groups may solve this problem in organizing by providing "selective" benefits to members only or by coercing members to join (such as unions' closed-shop agreements), but groups face the free rider problem again if they need existing members to participate in group-sponsored political action. The challenge for group leaders is to persuade members to engage in activities for the collective benefit of the

organization when such activities are beyond the conditions of employment or group membership.

There are also informational barriers to members' participation in organizational political activities. There are a variety of details members
must know in order to engage in group political action: what is happening in the political arena, how these events affect their personal interests
and the organization's interests, what they can do about it, and when,
where, and how to get involved effectively. In the words of one National
Education Association (NEA) activist: "Mobilizing works best when you
bring the 'road show' to the people: bring [NEA] officers to local meetings, provide legislative updates. If members know what is happening
and the implications of it, members will have the motivation. If you give
them the means, they will do it. Let them know what they can do."

Union leadership plays an important role in getting members involved
in political action. Members have other interests and demands on their
time other than union events and political action. Without clear reasons
for participation and opportunities to do so, the other responsibilities of
life are likely to take precedent over group participation. Thus, the critical
task of group leaders is to find ways of making it easier for members to
participate.

OPPORTUNITIES

First, the group makes it easier for members to become involved by providing opportunities through sponsorship of political activities. Interested members do not have to seek out political parties or candidates'
campaigns on their own. They can participate with their coworkers in activities provided by the union. In the Ohio union surveys, we asked members if their union engaged in the following activities: operating phone
banks, distributing campaign literature, placing yard signs, registering
voters, providing opportunities to meet with candidates (such as candidates' nights or gate visits), raising money to contribute to candidates or
issues, or working at party headquarters. In 1996, we also asked about
Get-Out-the-Vote drives. Table 6.1 presents the percentage of members
who perceived that their union offered each activity across the four election cycles.

Union distribution of campaign literature is the activity that is most
often noticed by members. More members may be aware of this activity
because they are handed the literature with the union endorsement. They
do not have to take any action or even pay close attention to union activities to be made aware of literature distribution. Most of the other activities attain relatively equal status, 20 percent to 30 percent, in members'

TABLE 6.1
Union Campaign Participation (% of members who perceived that their unions participated in each activity)

	1990	1992	1994	1996
Distribute Literature	61	66	71	69
Campaign Contributions	28	35	39	40
Phone Banks	24	30	26	25
Voter Registration	24	32	31	26
Candidate Meetings	24	22	32	28
Yard Signs	14	21	25	23
Work at Party Headquarters	10	14	13	12
Get-Out-the-Vote Drives	NA	NA	NA	57

Source: Ohio union surveys.

awareness. These tend to be time-intensive activities. Members perceive the least participation in working at party headquarters, the most time-intensive and partisan of the activities. There is considerable stability in members' perceptions across the four election cycles. Few activities have ranges greater than ten percentage points and no activities show clear trends in perceptions of greater or lesser activity.

Another way to examine the provision of opportunities by unions is to count the number of activities the member perceived his or her union to have sponsored. Table 6.2 shows the results. Most members perceived some level of political activity by their union. Over 80 percent of members thought their union engaged in at least one electoral activity, with the exception of 1990. At the same time, the majority of members in each year noticed two or fewer union political activities. Few members (around 10

TABLE 6.2
Number of Opportunities to Participate in Union Political Activities as Perceived by Ohio Union Members

Number of Activities	Number (and Percentage) of Members			
	1990	1992	1994	1996
0	375 (47%)	110 (18%)	77 (12%)	99 (16%)
1	161 (20%)	143 (23%)	141 (22%)	140 (23%)
2	106 (13%)	118 (19%)	140 (22%)	142 (23%)
3	67 (8%)	96 (16%)	100 (16%)	106 (17%)
4	40 (5%)	75 (12%)	75 (12%)	67 (11%)
5	27 (3%)	47 (8%)	50 (8%)	36 (6%)
6	17 (2%)	17 (3%)	24 (4%)	20 (3%)
7	5 (.6%)	7 (1%)	18 (3%)	8 (1%)

Source: Ohio union surveys.

percent) thought their union engaged in five or more activities. There is a substantial increase in the number of sponsored activities between 1990 and 1992, but thereafter no trend is apparent.

INFORMATION AND PERSUASION

Just as they provide opportunities to participate politically, staff and officers provide the information and training necessary for the members to be effective political activists. The district political coordinator for the Communication Workers of America explains: "Ignorance, not knowing what to do or what they can do, is the main excuse for not participating. So the key in getting members to participate is to show people what to do." Staff put together manuals on many political topics including how to run a phone bank or Get-Out-the-Vote drive, how to solicit political action committee (PAC) contributions, and how to contact a member of Congress. Political topics are staples of union leadership training sessions. Federal employee unions put special emphasis on training members about the ways in which they can participate in politics without violating the provisions of the Hatch Act, which bans partisan political activity by civil servants.

Many interviewees believe that a group's ability to mobilize its members effectively depends on constant and long-term education. One NEA activist argues: "The key [to NEA's success] is that it is a constant mobilization process. When NEA trains EPAC [Educator's Political Action Committee] representatives, they stress the key to the job is keeping members informed: keep in contact, answer their questions, give them information." Union leaders admit that in most issue and electoral mobilizations, member education occurs more through contacts at the time of mobilization than through long-term educational efforts.

Providing information is closely linked to persuasion, which entails actively convincing the member that he or she should become involved. Leaders can connect the mobilization appeals and activity being undertaken by the group to the specific interests and values of the member. Leaders can clarify the benefits of action and risks of inaction for the member. The district political director of the United Steelworkers of America (USWA) explains:

> This is the key educational task that the union must do: show members how politics and policies affect them individually. If members focus on gun control, the union needs to show them how the bills and budget cuts pushed by the Republicans will make a difference to them personally. For example, cutting student aid means working longer hours to put your kid through school at a cost of spending less time with family or fishing.

Similarly, another NEA activist explains the importance of persuading members to become politically active: "Some teachers have the long-standing mind set that 'Educators should be educators' and should not be involved in politics. But everything in education is political: the existence of schools, how, what, and who we teach is determined by politics, salaries, retirement; and politics occurs at both the state and local levels. My job is to convince them that they must be involved."

Personal contacts by leaders not only provide the relevant information regarding what to do and why, but also place social pressure on the member to accede to requests to join in the group effort. The Ohio AFL-CIO Phone Bank Manual, in bold and capital letters, states quite clearly: TO THE [GREATEST] EXTENT POSSIBLE, PROSPECTS SHOULD BE ASKED TO VOLUNTEER BY PEOPLE THEY KNOW. IT MAKES IT MUCH HARDER FOR THEM TO SAY "NO" (Ohio AFL-CIO COPE 1994b, PM-8).

Union leaders understand the necessity of making personal contacts with members during the mobilization process. One put it concisely: "If you don't ask, nobody will do it." Another argued: "It takes a local leader recruiting and saying 'We're going to do it.' You don't get participation from putting a flyer on the bulletin board. You get it from going face-to-face, nose-to-nose, toe-to-toe, asking people. That's what works." Similarly, the AFL-CIO Committee On Political Education's (COPE) Checkoff Yes Pamphlet on how to raise COPE contributions argues emphatically: "Members *will* respond . . . there's proof of that. An AFL-CIO national poll of union members showed 64 percent of members willing to contribute to their union PAC *if they're approached*" (n.d., 13, emphasis in the original). Thus, to explain members' participation in union political action, it is important to understand whom the union contacts.

LIMITS TO MOBILIZATION

The same decentralized union structures that facilitate political mobilization through personal contacts have a liability as well. Local leaders must be convinced to recruit their members. There are no assurances that they will do so. A 1982 survey of Ohio union officers found that less than 20 percent of Ohio locals were "very active" in state or local campaigns. About one-quarter of the locals were "somewhat active" and a clear majority, 60 percent, were classified as "not very active" by their officer (Clark 1982). Tables 6.1 and 6.2 show that most members perceive some level of activity by their union in the 1990s, but that few unions sponsor a wide variety of electoral activities. Whatever benefits there may be to local organizations and the personal touch, such benefits cannot be realized if local officers do not mobilize.

There are several important obstacles that impede local officers' contacting their members. First, both local officers and rank-and-file members have competitive demands on their time. Some large locals have enough officers and staff so that one person can be assigned to organize the local's political activities, but many locals do not have the resources to afford this luxury. For most, union political action is one activity the officer *should* do along with many activities he or she *must* do to manage the internal affairs of the local; this may include involvement in collective bargaining, grievance procedures, internal finances, union committees, internal communications, and external reports. Political action can get lost in the shuffle.

Furthermore, officers at times request participation from members in nonpolitical union activities. Like their officers, members' time is limited. They face multiple demands of family, work, recreation, and other voluntary activities. Thus, local officers must decide when to ask members for additional contributions and for what purposes. An officer of the International Association of Machinists and Aerospace Workers argues: "You pick and choose where you ask members to get involved. You don't want to ask them to do too much too often. We are also asking them to volunteer for nonpolitical union activities, such as organizing, so we don't want to over-ask." An NEA activist concurs: "People can't be bothered every week. You must mobilize them judiciously." The risk of trying to limit the number of times members are asked is that they are not asked at all. This is exemplified by the first and last sentences of an international officer's explanation of the difficulties of mobilizing members: "Our members have too many other activities competing for their time. . . . Maybe we need to ask more."

The second obstacle to local officers' political mobilization is that union members elect their officers. Local union officers, like others who run for office, can be reticent about discussing subjects or making requests that might risk losing the votes of their constituents. An Ohio Building Trades Council officer asserts: "We have a problem in getting [political] activists. Local leaders are afraid to ask their members to get politically involved, so political activities are done mainly by officers. Talking about politics risks offending the members. Local leaders must stand for election and don't want to alienate their members." The problem some local officers have with talking politics with members reinforces the point that union members are not members of the organization because of their political agreement with the organization and thus are not necessarily likely to be mobilized or to participate based merely on their preexisting agreement with the positions of the group.

Third, even if local leaders are interested in political action, recruitment of members for voluntary political action is not the highest priority in

COPE electoral mobilizations. The fundamental activities of COPE include: endorsements of candidates, voter registration, political education, Get-Out-the-Vote drives, and coordination with other community groups. Much of this activity is technically "nonpartisan" so that unions can reach out beyond their own memberships.[1] Recruiting activists thus may not be the focus of a local officer's political activities. A comment from the coordinator of the UAW's Ohio Community Action Program is revealing, given that the UAW has the reputation of being one of the most politically active unions in Ohio: "The primary activity we try to get rank-and-file members to do is to talk to relatives about voting for endorsed candidates. Members are scared off if you ask them to do too much." Similarly, one AFL-CIO Central Labor Council (CLC) officer asserted that he seeks quality participation over mass mobilization: "You can have too many people. The key is not the number of people, but getting people who can do the job." Union staff does most of the "activist" work.

Despite these problems, unions still are more active in political mobilization and are more successful at producing campaign volunteers than other organizations (Knoke 1990, 199; Herrnson 1995, 70, 197).[2] Officers alone cannot undertake labor-intensive electoral activities such as leafletting, voter registrations, Get-Out-the-Vote drives, and filling PAC coffers. Indeed, the Ohio AFL-CIO COPE 1994 Phone Bank Manual clearly, and in bold in the original, urges officers to seek out volunteers: "*all* key campaign officials should make every effort—at every opportunity they have—to increase the volunteer force, whether for their own specific area of responsibility or for other activities. Volunteer recruitment is *everyone's* job" (1994b, 7, emphasis in the original). Even if informing members about endorsed candidates and getting them to the polls are higher priorities, promoting volunteerism is still a core union political activity.

In sum, there are costs of political mobilization to local officers in terms of time, energy, and members' support, which may create uneven mobilization effort across local unions. Yet, if members are likely to respond positively when asked, as asserted by AFL-CIO manuals, explaining which members are asked to participate by local officers may be a key to explaining which members actually participate.

WHO IS ASKED TO PARTICIPATE?

Since union officers have competitive demands on their time and energy, they are likely to mobilize those members who are most likely to respond as desired (Brady, Schlozman, and Verba 1999; Rosenstone and Hansen 1993; Schier 2000). To examine which members are mobilized, we first asked members whether their union had sponsored a particular activity (see the list of opportunities mentioned in the previous section). If members claimed their union had sponsored the activity, we then inquired whether anyone in their union asked them to participate in that activity.[3] We asked members whether they were mobilized in only the 1994 and 1996 Ohio union surveys. In 1994, nearly one-half of Ohio union members, 46.2 percent (283), were asked to participate in at least one union electoral activity. There are important differences in levels of mobilization among the three union samples. The Ohio Education Association (OEA) mobilized the highest proportion of its members (65 percent), followed by the AFL-CIO (42 percent) and the Ohio Civil Servant Employee Association (OCSEA) (33 percent). In 1996, 42 percent of members were asked, with 61 percent of NEA members and 34 percent of AFL-CIO members receiving requests.[4]

Which characteristics of members lead to an invitation to participate? First, a member is more likely to be contacted if he or she is accessible to union officers. Members who are frequently in contact with officers can be asked to participate politically with little extra effort. (The measurement of each of independent variable is presented in appendix C.) Table 6.3 re-

TABLE 6.3
Probit Estimates of Receiving a Request to Participate
in a Union Electoral Event, 1994 and 1996

Variables	1994 Coefficient	1996 Coefficient
Accessibility		
Participation in the Union	.42*	
Ability to Participate Effectively		
Education	.20**	.25**
Political Agreement		
Local Union Context		
Active Union	.04*	
Geographically Active	.38*	
Targeted		
Awareness of Political Appeals		
Political Interest	.20*	.21*
Informational Dependence		.35**
Tenure		
Voluntary Membership		.27*
Constant	−2.80**	−3.08**
Number of Cases =	416	478
Pseudo R^2 =	.11	.10
% Predicted Correctly =	67.3%	65.7%
Log Likelihood =	−255.45	−295.98

Note: Only variables significant at $p < .10$ are displayed; *$p < .05$; **$p < .01$ two-tailed test.

ports the probit analysis results of the relationship between independent variables and receiving a request to participate. Accessible members were significantly more likely to be asked to participate in the 1994 election, but not in the 1996 election.

Second, union officers are likely to ask the members who are most likely to respond effectively and appropriately (in the officers' view) to their appeals. Officers seek out members who support the political position of the organization and who have the political skills to deliver the message. Based on the perceived differences between members' and officers' perceived party identifications and ideologies, a "political agreement" scale measures the similarity of political beliefs between members and officers (see appendix C). The member's level of education is critical to effective participation. Education is highly related to many "civic skills" necessary to participate effectively in politics: planning, organizing, making decisions in group settings, and making speeches and presentations (Verba, Schlozman, and Brady 1995). Thus, education acts as a proxy for political skills.[5]

The member's level of education is significantly related to receiving a request to participate. In fact, the chances of a member receiving a request because of his or her level of education are greater than those for any other characteristic in both years (not shown). By contrast, the member's proximity to the political positions of union leaders is not related to whether or not he or she is asked to participate in either year. Put differently, union leaders are not more likely to mobilize Democrats or liberals than Republicans and conservatives. (In both years, the correlation between requests and party identification is −.05 and between requests and ideology is −.04.) Union leaders are more concerned with recruiting those members who have the knowledge and skills to participate effectively than those who agree with union political positions.

Mobilization also depends on the local union context—that is, whether officers are actively recruiting their members. As one union officer stated: "It is clear that local union leadership is absolutely the key [to members' mobilization and participation]." We analyze three measures of local officers' activity: the traditional level of political mobilization of the member's international, the traditional levels of union political mobilization where the member lives, and whether the member lives in a legislative district targeted by his or her union for extra campaign assistance.

Members who live in regions that are traditional hotbeds of union political activity and those who are members of internationals that have reputations for political activism were more likely to be asked in 1994, but not in 1996. Residence in a targeted district is unrelated to receiving a request to participate in either year. This shows mobilization is more a matter of long-term efforts by local union leaders than an effort to give special emphasis to a competitive race in a single year.

Finally, some members are more likely than others to be aware of political mobilization appeals. Union leaders can send out general invitations to participate at a meeting or in a newsletter, but members vary in the extent to which they notice political appeals. Members who are interested in politics or who look to their union for political information are more likely to be aware of the mobilization activities of their union. Those who have longer tenures in the organization and who have voluntarily joined the union are also more likely to be aware of union mobilization. These hypotheses are largely supported in table 6.3. Members who are more interested in politics were more likely to be asked in both elections. Members who rely on the union for political information, and who voluntarily joined the union were more likely to receive requests for political participation in 1996 only.

These findings support our hypotheses that leaders are likely to recruit some members more than others. It is particularly noteworthy that in both years the members' level of education is clearly the most important factor in explaining which union members are contacted for political participation. Leaders ask those members who they think have the skills and abilities to get the job done. Education is the basis of civic skills (Verba, Schlozman, and Brady 1995). The evidence also indicates that union officers do not recruit the members most likely to deliver the political message desired by the organization—that is, those members who perceive themselves to be in political agreement with their officers. In contrast to skills, which officers may see demonstrated in the workplace, officers may be uninformed of the political preferences of individual members when recruiting political activists—or the need to produce anyone who can show up and get the job done may overwhelm the need to seek out partisan and ideological soul-mates.[6]

SEEKING COMPLIANCE WITH REQUESTS FOR ACTIVISM

Asking members to participate is only the first step in mobilization (Brady, Schlozman, and Verba 1999). Members can turn down the request. Family, recreation, or other personal interests may take precedence over political action. The difficulty of getting members to accede to requests for political action is noted by James N. Rosenau: "If getting family and friends to make simple and clear responses is often a vexing and delicate task, getting unknown persons to give time, energy or money on behalf of distant goals that may or may not be realized seems awesome" (1974, 408). Thus, we now seek to explain why members comply with requests for political participation and what leaders can do to encourage members to comply. These tactics show the ways in which unions attempt to make it easier for rank-and-file members to participate.

There are three basic reasons an individual would comply with a request to do something (Brehm and Gates 1996; Levi 1988). The first reason is coercion—the individual is forced to comply under the threat of punishment. For example, workers can be fired for not doing their jobs properly. But in the political context, members are being asked to make contributions above and beyond the duties of their jobs or responsibilities to the union. Unions cannot force members to become politically involved.[7] Indeed, when asked how they get members to participate, union leaders responded by shaking their heads and quipping "We beg," or "I hope your study will tell me." This hardly indicates coercive powers.

The second basis for compliance is an instrumental or selective benefit. That is, the member complies in order to receive some reward promised to him or her personally in exchange for cooperation. The most well-known list of organizational incentives is offered by Peter B. Clark and James Q. Wilson (1961). They argue that people will respond to material incentives (such as money or goods), social or solidarity benefits (such as the enjoyment of spending time with other compatible individuals), or "purposive" or "expressive" incentives (such as the desire to feel good about contributing to a favored cause) (Salisbury 1969).[8] Few organizations have substantial incentives that they can offer only to political activists. As will be discussed, unions have some instrumental incentives that can be used to entice members to participate, but these incentives are weak.

Margaret Levi (1988) and John Brehm and Scott Gates (1996) label the third basis for compliance "ideological." Members participate because they think it is the right thing to do. The ideological incentive is close to Clark and Wilson's "purposive incentive." The critical reason for the distinction is that the feeling of "doing the right thing" cannot be provided as an incentive by group leaders, though they can supply rhetoric to assure the member that it is the right thing to do. When members comply for ideological reasons, they are not doing so because the group can provide them a specific reward. Even if members participate largely for ideological reasons, mobilization by the leadership is still important because it provides members with the opportunities and information necessary to participate. By making participation easier, it is more likely that members will express their ideologies through the group rather than spending their time doing other things.

In the union context, ideological compliance can be based on the member's commitment to the union or his or her agreement with the union's political positions. Both of these topics were explored in chapter 3.

Committed members are more likely to participate because those who are loyal to the group are more likely to comply with requests for activities based on their willingness to respond to group norms, to do what "good" group members are doing in a given situation.

We argue that union members comply with requests for political participation mainly for ideological reasons. But first we will review how union leaders use instrumental incentives and attempt to make participation easier in order to entice more members to contribute money to union political action committees (PACs) and to volunteer their time for political activities.

RECRUITMENT TECHNIQUES AND INCENTIVES

PAC contributions are raised from rank-and-file members by local officers and activists, so that there is some social pressure to accede to the request, pressure that would not be present in a request from an unknown staffer from central office. In the words of one NEA activist: "The number one reason for giving is to please the person who asked. The keys to getting a contribution are friendship, credibility, and personal contact." Social events such as dinners and picnics are frequently used for fund-raising.

Unions try to make it easy to contribute by using payroll deductions, where the member agrees to have a certain amount deducted from each paycheck for the PAC. In the opinion of one NEA activist, "The key to fund-raising is simplification. By making the contribution automatic, you make the member's job easier." Payroll deductions also make it easier on the fund-raiser—once the member is signed up, one does not have to ask for a contribution every year. This creates a potential liability, however. If fund-raisers no longer need to engage in personal contacts in order to get a contribution, there is no longer the opportunity for these contacts to be used for political discussion and persuasion or to strengthen the relationships between leaders and the rank and file (Mundo 1992, 125). This may weaken the ability of unions to mobilize members for other purposes or to convince members to follow endorsements.

Payroll deductions must be negotiated as part of a collective bargaining agreement, so not all locals have them. For unions without the payroll deduction option in their contracts, other methods can be used to make contributions easier. These include credit card contributions, automatic transfers from the member's bank account, or payroll deductions from his or her local credit union.

Unions also use instrumental rewards to promote PAC contributions. The NEA gives prizes (e.g., a recognition dinner) and commendations to the school buildings, locals, and NEA districts that raise the most PAC money. An International Union of Electrical, Radio, and Machine Workers (IUE) officer describes their method: "We have developed a reward system to encourage members to solicit contributions. For example, we give away appliances our members make so it doesn't cost us anything [he points out the TV, VCR, and TV cabinet in the room]. Sign up twenty-five members on the COPE checkoff, get a watch; sign up ten, get a tote bag or jacket with the IUE COPE symbol." The prizes give members an incentive to participate, the recognition is a social reward for those who follow group norms.

Similarly, activists are recruited with the personal touch and by making participation easier. Many agreed with the comments of one NEA activist: "A letter won't do. It's hard to say 'No' in person." Many unions keep lists of people who have participated in political activities in the past and rely on members who are active in all elements of union activity, particularly officers.

Inevitably, new activists are needed. One NEA activist joked that he starts by asking "friends and people who owe you." Others were more serious about asking people who owe them. An officer of the Plumbers and Pipefitters explains: "Once the union helps an individual, we use that as leverage to get them involved. Our message is: 'We helped you out when you needed it, you've seen how union political action is important, why don't you return the favor to benefit someone else?' "

Building Trades Council apprenticeship programs provide an example of how participation can be made easier for new members. New members must go through the training programs to be certified and receive full benefits. Although the benefits of unionism and political action are part of the curriculum, the Plumbers and Pipefitters also allow apprentices one night of schooling off to go out and work with a veteran activist on political activities. In addition, explains an officer, "the social aspect helps and makes them want to come back."

Another successful tactic in recruiting new volunteers is to find people who are interested in politics and give them something "doable" as a starter. Members, particularly ones who have not been politically active, can be "scared off" if they are asked to do a lot at once. One union officer explains in the context of recruiting for Get-Out-the-Vote drives:

> You have to give them [volunteers] a reasonable workload. A reasonable workload is one run on Sunday when people are more likely to be at home. The member is less likely to get frustrated at not being able reach people and slack off and end up in a bar before their second or third runs [if Get-Out-the-Vote drives were on election day rather than Sunday]. I did this myself once upon a time. . . . If a member is frustrated by too many runs or too many people not at home, they won't enjoy it and won't come back. If it is a reasonable amount of work, they will enjoy it and will come back.

Others agreed that once a member initially becomes involved, he or she will be willing to undertake more.

Instrumental incentives also matter in generating voluntary activities. Taking time off work, especially if unpaid, makes it more difficult to participate in union activities, so unions try to remove this barrier. Some unions provide members with "lost time," or paid time off work for union activities. The equivalent in the NEA is "Association Days" that members can take to participate in Lobby Day visitations to legislators. However, Association Days (and lost time) must be negotiated in the contract, and it is up to the district superintendent to decide whether Lobby Day activities count as an Association Day or a personal day.

We find that the effectiveness of lost time is very limited as a political incentive due to its lack of availability or members' lack of awareness of its availability. In the Ohio union surveys, we asked members: "Does your union pay its members for participation in any campaign activities?" In 1994, only twenty (3.3 percent) said their union did; in 1996, sixteen (2.6 percent) respondents said so. These few members who were aware of lost time provisions may have other reasons for participation. Clearly an incentive that is available to such a small proportion of members cannot generate much political participation.

WHY MEMBERS PARTICIPATE

In studying union political mobilization, we need to be ensured that members are participating in union political events rather than in the activities of candidates, political parties, or other interest groups. To limit members to the union context, we first asked members whether their union had sponsored a specific political activity (see the list of activities in table 6.4). If the member responded positively, we then asked whether or not they participated in that activity. We asked about electoral participation in the 1992, 1994, and 1996 Ohio union surveys.

The proportion of members participating in at least one campaign activity remains rather stable, around 25 percent, over three election cycles. Specifically, 23.5 percent of members participated in 1992, 28.2 percent in 1994, and 26.1 percent in 1996. Members could participate in multiple events. When totaled, there was greater participation in 1994 (307) and 1996 (276) than in 1992 (225).

Activities vary in popularity, as shown in table 6.4. Slightly more members claimed to have donated money and attended meetings with candidates. These activities probably were the most popular because they are the easiest to do: members can donate money by payroll deductions or by quickly writing a check when asked; they can meet candidates at the gate

TABLE 6.4
Union Members' Participation in Electoral Activities

Activities	*Number (and Percentage) of Members*		
	1992	*1994*	*1996*
Donating Money	76 (12.4%)	85 (13.9%)	80 (12.9%)
Candidate Meetings	34 (5.5%)	62 (10.1%)	56 (9.1%)
Literature Distribution	34 (5.5%)	54 (8.8%)	57 (9.2%)
Registering Voters	35 (5.7%)	30 (5.4%)	23 (3.7%)
Phone Banks	23 (3.8%)	36 (5.9%)	23 (3.7%)
Placing Signs	19 (3.1%)	33 (5.4%)	29 (4.7%)
Party Headquarters	4 (0.7%)	7 (1.1%)	8 (1.3%)
Total Participation	225	307	276

Source: Ohio union surveys.

when leaving work or at a union meeting they are attending anyway. Little additional time or effort is necessary to undertake these two activities. The fewest members worked at party headquarters. Working at campaign headquarters is likely to be the most time intensive of the activities and to be of interest to only the most partisan members.

Members can participate in union activities through mobilization—being recruited by someone in their union—or through volunteering without receiving a request. Members were counted as volunteering spontaneously if their union had sponsored a given electoral activity and they participated in it, yet someone in their union did not recruit them. In 1994, forty-four members engaged in a total of seventy-one spontaneous acts (23 percent of total participation). In 1996, forty-six members spontaneously participated in a total of fifty-seven activities (21 percent of total participation). A number of members, twenty-nine in 1994 and twenty-seven in 1996, spontaneously participated in some events but were mobilized for other events. Clearly, most union political activity is mobilized.

Which members participate? Which members respond to union political mobilization efforts? We believe that the member's level of commitment to the union will be critical in explaining whether or not members participate in union-sponsored political activities. But other factors may be related to participation as well. For example, there are other facets of members' relationship with their unions such as their view of the appropriateness of union political activities, their length of tenure in the union,[9] and whether union membership is voluntary. Members who believe union political activism is appropriate, those with longer tenures, and those who have joined voluntarily are more likely to participate (see appendix C for measurements).

The bivariate correlations presented in table 6.5 offer considerable support for these generalizations. In all three elections, the higher the

124   *Chapter 6*

TABLE 6.5
Correlates of Electoral Participation

Independent Variables	Number of Events in Which Member Participated		
	1992	1994	1996
"Ideological" Compliance			
Commitment	.21**	.14**	.18**
Political Agreement	.18**	.14**	.17**
Appropriateness	.21**	.13**	.26**
Tenure (Linear)	.06	.11**	.07
Tenure (Log)	.10*	.12**	.08
Voluntary Membership	.10*	.12**	.08
Participatory Attitudes and Resources			
Efficacy	NA	.13**	.04
Political Interest	.20**	.08*	.15**
Education	.09*	.16**	.19**
Local Context			
Active Union	.01	.13**	.06
Geographically Active	.08*	.15**	.06
Targeted	.01	.02	−.02

Note: *p < .05; **p < .01.

member's level of commitment, political agreement, and belief in the appropriateness of union political activity, the more often he or she participated. Tenure and voluntary membership are related to more frequent participation in 1992 and 1994.

Second, members who participate in union political mobilizations may be those who generally participate in politics, so we need to account for their political attitudes and resources. Those who are interested in politics and who have high levels of political efficacy (those who think they can make a difference in the political arena) are more likely to participate in organizationally sponsored political activities. Education plays a central role in individuals' ability to participate in politics (Verba, Schlozman, and Brady 1995, 433–6; Nie, Junn, and Stehlik-Barry 1996). Education develops one's civic skills and cognitive skills for understanding the political world, both of which are necessary to engage in many political activities.[10] Indeed, higher levels of both political interest and education increase levels of participation in all three elections. Efficacy is significantly correlated with participation in 1994.[11]

Finally, local union context may influence whether members participate (Leighley 1995; Huckfeldt and Sprague 1993). We use the ratings of an international's traditional level of political activity, the traditional level of union political activity in the member's geographic region, and residence in legislative districts targeted by the member's union to account for context. Table 6.6 shows that the relationship between context and participation is inconsistent across the three elections. Residence in a region of traditional union activism is related to participation in 1992 and 1994. Membership in a traditionally active international is related to participation in 1994. Residence in targeted districts is not related in any election. No contextual variables are related to participation in 1996.

Receiving a mobilization request largely explains participation in union electoral activities. The correlation between the number of requests received and the number of events in which the member participated is very high (.76 in 1994). Indeed, multivariate models of member's participation in union-sponsored electoral activities find that few other factors predict member's participation once we take into account the number of times they were asked to participate. Similarly, statistical models demonstrate that it is difficult to predict which types of members are more likely to volunteer spontaneously (Heberlig 1997).

TABLE 6.6
Union Member Response to Electoral Mobilization Appeals,
1994 and 1996 (Poisson regression estimates)

Variables	*1994 Coefficient*	*1996 Coefficient*
"Ideological" Compliance		
Commitment	.11	.11**
Political Agreement	.06*	.11**
Appropriateness		.23**
Voluntary Membership	.48**	
Tenure (Linear)	−.03*	
Tenure (Log)	.61*	
Participatory Attitudes and Resources		
Efficacy		
Political Interest		
Education	.12	.40**
Local Context		
Active union	.05**	
Geographically Active	.29*	
Targeted		
Constant	−5.77**	−5.81**
Number of Cases =	437	414
Pseudo R^2 =	.10	.13
Log Likelihood =	−337.08	−285.04

Note: Only variables significant at $p < .10$ are displayed; *$p < .05$; **$p < .01$ two-tailed test.

Even if mobilization is critical to explaining participation, some members respond positively to mobilization appeals and others reject the appeals. In 1994, 43 percent of those asked responded positively; in 1996, 47 percent of those asked participated. Who responds and why? To find out who responds to mobilization appeals, we eliminated spontaneous acts to count only those acts that were mobilized. Since the mobilization question was asked only in 1994 and 1996, our analysis is limited to those two years.[12] We use Poisson regression as the multivariate estimation technique.[13] Table 6.6 presents the results.

After the introduction of controls, only three variables are significantly related to the probability of individuals' responding to larger numbers of mobilization appeals in both the 1994 and 1996 elections: higher levels of commitment, political agreement, and education. Committed members have a greater probability of overcoming the incentive to free ride. The success of the organization is important to them personally. So they are willing to contribute to collective efforts out of their loyalty to the group—that is, to do what they think "good" group members should do. A member's level of agreement with the political positions of the organization is also critical to explaining whether or not the member responds to mobilization appeals. And, as expected based on the traditional explanations of political participation, members with higher levels of education are likely to participate when asked.

COMPARING UNION MEMBERS' ACTIVISM
TO THE GENERAL PUBLIC'S

In order to judge the effect of labor's mobilization of activists, it is useful to compare the political participation of labor union members to that of nonunion members. Our first comparison uses our Ohio surveys. In 1996, we asked the same activism questions to our random sample of Ohioans as we did to our union sample. We found that the level of activism among union members was actually slightly lower than the general public's. Twenty-six percent of the union sample participated in at least one event, while 29 percent of the random sample participated. A couple of caveats are necessary, however. First, if we also count participation in Get-Out-the-Vote drives, a common union activity, the levels of participation were even, 30 percent, between union members and nonmembers. Second, union members were only asked about participation in union-sponsored activities. To the degree that some members are politically active outside the union context, union members' levels of participation would likely be higher.

We also can go beyond our data on Ohio to compare union members and nonmembers nationwide by using the American National Election

Studies (ANES). Respondents are asked about their participation in five different electoral activities: talking to others about the election, placing yard signs, attending campaign meetings, working for a political party, and giving money to a party or candidates. Although there is some overlap with the activities asked about in our Ohio surveys, our surveys did not ask about talking to others about the election. This activity is easy to do and is the most popular. For this reason, the participation rates in the ANES are higher than in the Ohio surveys.

First, we examine activism in at least one campaign activity. Table 6.7 shows that union members participate at slightly higher rates on average (41 percent) than nonmembers (35 percent) in presidential election years. This table also compares the extent to which union members and nonmembers participated in multiple campaign activities. Here, the union advantage disappears; members and nonmembers participate at basically the same rate (14 percent and 12.5 percent, respectively). Unions are more successful in getting their members to do something than in getting them to do a lot. This is consistent with officers' descriptions of their mobilization efforts—they try to get their members out to vote, but do not ask for much more.

It is also interesting to note that activism declined for all union members, union households, and nonmembers between the 1992 and 1996

TABLE 6.7
Nationwide Campaign Participation in Presidential Years, 1952–1996
(% participating in election campaigns)

Year	One or More Act			Two or More Acts		
	Union Member	Union Household	Nonunion	Union Member	Union Household	Nonunion
1952*	32	27	27	6	6	7
1956	50	37	37	22	14	15
1960	44	42	42	20	20	20
1964	41	42	39	14	16	16
1968	42	34	35	12	13	14
1972	37	28	33	15	11	14
1976	40	32	36	12	10	10
1980*	41	31	35	10	5	8
1984	41	37	36	18	10	12
1988	38	38	32	17	8	11
1992	51	40	40	16	10	14
1996	38	30	31	9	10	9
Average	41	35	35	14	10	12.5

Source: American National Election Studies 1952–1998.
*Four campaign-related questions were asked in these two years; five questions were asked in all other years.

elections. This is somewhat surprising given the substantial efforts at membership mobilization as part of Labor '96 that did not have a parallel in 1992. However, at the presidential level, 1992 was a much more competitive election than 1996. In 1992, Bill Clinton was aiming to unseat incumbent George Bush to become the first Democrat to occupy the presidency in twelve years. In 1996, Clinton was the incumbent with a record of peace and prosperity. He maintained a large lead in the polls throughout the election, so the race was never very competitive (Goldstein 1997). Participation is generally higher in competitive elections than in those that are not (Rosenstone and Hansen 1993). The OEA governmental affairs director explains the OEA's difficulties in mobilizing activists in the 1996 election: "Part of the problem was that the Clinton race overshadowed all the others and he had a large lead. There was a lack of excitement about local races. It also hurt that the Democrats recruited some poor quality candidates. The candidate would come into a meeting and our members would say, 'Where'd they get this guy?' You need attractive candidates to get the members to want to work for them."

Some evidence for the effectiveness of the AFL-CIO's new mobilization strategy might be seen in activism rates nationally in the 1998 midterm elections. ANES data show that 40 percent of union members participated in at least one activity. This is notable for several reasons. The rate of participation in 1998 is substantially higher than in the preceding midterm elections. In 1990, 26 percent of union members engaged in at least one activity; in 1994, 22 percent did. It is also slightly higher than union members' activism during the 1996 presidential election. Typically, participation is much higher in presidential election years (Rosenstone and Hansen 1993). Also, nonunion member participation declined in 1998 to 27 percent, creating a substantial thirteen-point gap between union members and nonmembers. Similarly, 14 percent of union members engaged in two or more activities in 1998. This is five points higher than members' participation in the 1996 presidential race, six and seven points higher than in the midterm elections of 1990 and 1994, respectively, and five points higher than the percentage of nonunion respondents who engaged in two or more acts in 1998. Union election activists were easier to find nationally in the 1998 campaign.

We should not declare a new era of labor political activism yet. One election is not sufficient to indicate a trend and the rate of participation in the 1998 midterm election, while substantially above the previous midterms, is about at the average of rates of participation in presidential elections between 1952–96. Nevertheless, the fact that the change in participation corresponds to labor's strategy shift is noteworthy. It provides evidence that unions have some capacity to reenergize their members.

CONCLUSION

The mobilization of grassroots participation of rank-and-file members is an important component of the electoral strategy of labor unions in the United States. Although much scholarly and media attention is focused on the role and impact of PACs' campaign contributions, less attention has been given to the role and impact of "sweat equity" provided by the members of interest groups and volunteer fieldwork more generally. Both money and volunteers are critical campaign resources, and volunteers are especially important in local elections in which television commercials do not dominate. This gives unions the potential to exchange their manpower resources for policy pledges from candidates (Uhlaner 1989).

Labor's membership strength, history of collective action, and decentralized organizational structure provide advantages in grassroots political mobilization that many other interest groups do not have. The major asset of labor's political structure is the potential for personal contacts. Such contacts make it easier for members to participate by providing the opportunities and information, supplying social pressure, and invoking group norms. In order to mobilize effectively, however, local officers must be convinced to recruit their members. As the evidence in this chapter demonstrates, it is not automatic that local officers will do so. When they do mobilize, members are very likely to respond. To the extent that labor unions can ask more often than other interest groups, they have a substantial ability to generate participation from their members. Some support for this is found in the consistently higher rates of campaign participation of union members than nonunion members in the ANES.

Since the election of John J. Sweeney to the AFL-CIO presidency, the AFL-CIO has become more directly involved in grassroots mobilization by sending national staff into targeted congressional districts as volunteer trainers and coordinators. If receiving a request for participation is necessary for most members to act, making political mobilization the responsibility of union staff and officers is a potentially effective method for increasing labor's grassroots participation in the future. Likewise, to the degree that the national staff can train and create local cadres of activists who will mobilize members from their own locals, the effectiveness of mobilization will only increase as members are recruited by people they know. However, it takes substantial resources to undertake this level of mobilization effort nationally. The critical question is whether this effort can be sustained given other competing demands on unions' treasuries and officers.

When mobilization is attempted, union officers tend to contact their most highly educated members. It has long been known that the highly educated are more likely to vote and engage in other participatory acts (e.g., Verba and Nie 1972). Education gives people the cognitive ability to understand complex and conflicting political information and sorts people into social networks in which participation is encouraged (Nie, Junn, and Stehlik-Berry 1996). The highly educated are especially sought after to engage in intensive electoral activities beyond voting because they have the "civic skills"—particularly the organizational and communication skills—necessary to complete these activities successfully. Though union members have fewer civic skills than members of many other types of organizations (Verba, Schlozman, and Brady 1995, 378), our evidence demonstrates that officers seek out the members who have them.

Although the bias towards those of higher social status in interest group activities is well known (Schattschneider 1960; Schlozman and Tierney 1986), the fact that unions mobilize their high status members as well is quite interesting. In fact, it points out a persistent problem in political mobilization in the United States—that individuals of lower social status, particularly those with few skills, are extremely hard to mobilize (Piven and Cloward 1978). Despite their professed desires to "act as a social movement" (Sweeney 1996, 106), this evidence indicates that union leaders do not target the quiescent. Like leaders of other interest groups, union leaders rationally target those who are most likely to participate, rather than attempting to assure equal representation of all voices within the organization.

However, even if unions do not mobilize their members with the least social status, other union political activities are directed at mobilizing a broader cross-section of the working class. Unions target their nonpartisan voter registration and Get-Out-the-Vote drives to mobilize nonmembers in precincts with high levels of working-class, low-income, and/or minority voters with the intention of increasing the turnout rates of those voters most likely to support union-endorsed candidates (Democrats). Unions engage in substantial coalitional activities during elections with other interest groups whose memberships are dominated by the nonelite. And in lobbying, unions often take positions and join in coalitions with other liberal groups to support the perceived interest of the working and lower classes. This suggests that unions attempt to decrease the organizational bias of the interest group system by speaking on behalf of those without high social status, but do not decrease the bias in individual participation.

The fact that commitment is important to explaining why members respond to mobilization appeals emphasizes the importance of group identity and solidarity that unions foster. To the extent that other interest groups are less able to generate commitment, they may be less effective in mobilizing their members. Labor's efforts at political education can help to convince members that they are in political agreement with union leaders—another critical "ideological" explanation of participation.

Finally, it is labor's membership that makes grassroots mobilization possible. To the extent that labor continues to lose membership, it also loses activists who can participate in elections. With a smaller membership base, additional mobilization of members is necessary just to maintain a relatively constant number of activists. Thus, labor's success in political mobilization is dependent on its economic success. Union organization is necessary to maintain a membership base and success in providing the benefits desired by members keeps them committed to the union and willing to respond to its political appeals. This evidence supports Sweeney's argument that a "seamless garment of activism" (1996, 99), which includes organizing, bargaining for contracts, and political mobilization, is necessary for labor to succeed politically.

NOTES

1. Federal election laws restrict union staff contacts regarding political action to union members only. Likewise, union dues cannot fund political communications to nonmembers that expressly endorse certain candidates or parties (though PAC money can) in federal elections.

2. Sidney Verba, Kay Lehman Schlozman, and Henry E. Brady (1995, 384–8) estimate that churches produce a higher aggregate number of political volunteers than unions. This is mainly due to the fact that many more people are members of churches than are members of unions. They find that unions have higher efforts at political mobilization than churches, but higher rates of recruitment are unable to overcome membership differences.

3. Our definition of "mobilization" follows James N. Rosenau's: "The mobilized act occurs only in response to requests for support" (1974, 99).

4. In 1996, the OCSEA chose not to participate the in the survey.

5. Officers ask capable individuals to participate because they have observed their skills in the workplace; officers are not likely to be aware of the actual level of educational attainment of potential activists.

6. Controlling for NEA membership does not remove the relationship between education and mobilization in either year.

7. Drawing the line between coercion and social pressure is difficult in an organizational context. As noted by campaign finance scholar Frank J. Sorauf: "Evaluating the charges, though, founders on the difficulty of agreeing on an operational definition for 'coercion.' Is it persistent solicitation, in the bringing of peer pressure? If these conditions are coercive, one must conclude that coercion is an integral part of American voluntarism. Better instead is a standard of coercion that hinges on substantial personal costs (for example, denial of material incentives, status, or social acceptability) to the reluctant donor" (1984–1985, 601).

8. Our purpose here is to list the type of incentives to which members are likely to respond. The fact that we emphasize the selective benefit of each incentive does not preclude the fact that these incentives may have collective

components as well. For example, a union contract is a material incentive that benefits all members.

9. Both the linear and logarithmic terms for tenure are used to capture diminishing marginal returns (Rothenberg 1992). In his experiential model of activism, Lawrence S. Rothenberg argues that members learn about the costs and benefits of participation over time, but that if the member is not attracted to the benefits of activism within a few years of joining, he or she will not participate regardless of the length of time he or she belongs to the organization.

10. Income is also a common predictor of political participation (Verba, Schlozman, and Brady 1995; Verba and Nie 1972). However, once education is controlled, income is not a statistically significant predictor of participation, it adds no explanatory value, and it does not substantially effect the estimation of other variables in the model. Thus, income is not included in the reported results.

11. We did not ask the questions used to measure efficacy in the 1992 survey.

12. In 1992, we can use the number of times the member participated as the dependent variable rather than the number of times he or she responded to mobilization appeals. When a multivariate model is run using the same independent variables as in the 1994 and 1996 models (except efficacy), the following are statistically significant: commitment, political agreement, voluntary membership, tenure (logarithmic value), political interest, and education.

13. Poisson regression is the appropriate estimate technique when the dependent variable is a count of discrete events (King 1989, 48–51, 122–4). Two elements are required to estimate a Poisson regression model properly. First is the incident rate: the rate at which the events occur. Here the incident rate is the number of activities in which the member engaged per election. The second element is the exposure rate. The exposure rate is the number of opportunities for political participation the member perceives his or her union to have sponsored. Controlling for exposure allows us to conclude that the characteristics of the member and behavior of officers led to higher levels of participation, rather than that some members merely had more opportunities to participate. Members who perceived that their union did not sponsor any activities are excluded from the Poisson estimation because they were not "exposed" to any opportunities to participate.

7

Election Day Outcomes

Thus far, we have discussed the preelection day activities of organized labor, including the endorsement of preferred candidates, the support of these endorsed nominees through financial contributions, and the efforts to mobilize union members to participate in a variety of political activities. But the ultimate test of organized labor's clout in the electoral arena is what happens on election day. Do rank-and-file union members actually vote and, if they do, do they support the union-endorsed candidates? Can the leadership of organized labor legitimately claim that it can deliver on election day? This chapter will examine both the turnout of union members and their loyalty to union-endorsed candidates.

TURNOUT

Turnout in elections raises some important challenges and opportunities for labor unions. To the extent that old labor was organizing unskilled and semiskilled workers at the bottom of the socioeconomic ladder, one might expect that turnout among such individuals, had they not been members of the union, would be low. But to the extent that such members were integrated into the union as an organization, participated in union activities, understood and supported the union's economic and political agenda, and were the target of Get-Out-the-Vote activities, their participation rates in elections would be higher than expected based solely on their social class and educational levels.

There is ample research in both the American and cross-national context to suggest that an effective labor movement and explicit labor-based political parties in other countries can sharply lessen the gap in participation rates between citizens characterized by high versus low socioeconomic status. For example, the cross-national research of G. Bingham Powell, Jr. (1980; 1986) shows that strong linkages between political parties and cleavage groups (defined by religion, social class, occupation, or other factors) enhance political participation and turnout. This occurs because the political parties better represent these cleavage groups, thereby providing an incentive for rank-and-file members to support their respective parties. In addition, mobilization is made easier by the commonalities between the party stances on issues with the political and economic interests of its members. In short, a labor-based political party can stimulate higher turnout than would be expected among the working class.

Benjamin Radcliff and Patricia Davis (2000) directly examine the impact of the strength of the labor movement on turnout rates in the fifty American states and nineteen other industrial democracies. Although they are not enamored of Powell's linkage variable, their conceptually similar measures show that the greater the share of workers that are represented by unions, the higher the electoral turnout. Part of the explanation of the higher turnout may be the direct mobilizing activities of the unions. But part of the explanation according to Radcliff and Davis is that the presence of strong unionism moves the ideological positions of political parties appealing to working- and middle-class citizens farther to the left. This then provides lower-status citizens with more meaningful and distinctive election choices and thus gives such citizens greater reason to cast a vote.

In the American case with our two major umbrella political parties, the linkages between cleavage groups and parties are not as strong even as the Democratic Party is seen as the party supporting organized labor and its aspirations. But even here the linkages are strained by the presence of international trade issues in which a Democratic president and some Democratic members of Congress fail to support organized labor's positions on these issues. However, even without the strong group-party linkages found in many western European countries and even with the tensions that periodically exist between organized labor and the Democratic Party, we find both in national survey data since 1952 and in our Ohio survey data in the 1990s some evidence that union members vote at higher rates in elections than their nonunion compatriots. However, we cannot automatically attribute the higher turnout of union members to union mobilization or the effects of union membership itself, a point we will return to shortly. Nevertheless, the fact that turnout among union members is somewhat higher enhances organized labor's reputation as a significant player in elections.

Tables 7.1 and 7.2 present the turnout rates for our Ohio samples between 1990 and 1996 and for national surveys of Americans between 1952 and 1998. Note that in our Ohio surveys, the turnout in the overall union

TABLE 7.1
**Self-reported Turnout Rates among Registered Voters
in Ohio, 1990–1996**

	1990	*1992*	*1994*	*1996*
Ohio Sample	75	85	80	82
Union Members	77	95	88	88
Union Households	80	88	86	80
Nonunion	74	83	79	82
Union Sample	86	93	91	96
Ohio AFL–CIO	83	91	88	96
OCSEA	89	94	92	NA
OEA	95	98	98	97

Source: Ohio union surveys.

sample is consistently and substantially higher than the turnout in the overall Ohio samples, averaging almost 11 percent higher in the union samples over the four elections between 1990 and 1996. Even within the overall Ohio samples, the union respondents consistently report a higher voting participation than do the nonunion respondents. The turnout rates presented in table 7.1 may seem excessively high. Certainly, one phenomenon in survey research is for respondents to overreport their voting participation, in part because they want to present themselves as conscientious, civic-minded citizens. But there is no reason to believe that union members are more prone to overreporting than their nonunion counterparts. The second reason why the Ohio turnout rates are high is that they are based on registered voters, not on the total adult population. Not only is turnout higher among our Ohio union sample than the overall Ohio sample, but so also is the registration rate in the union sample, which across the four elections averaged about 10 percent higher for the union sample. These higher registration and turnout rates for the Ohio union samples mean that the labor vote can have a disproportionate impact on the election outcome, especially if that vote is strongly loyal to the labor-endorsed candidates.

At the national level, the results are similar. Table 7.2 shows that union members—but not union households—consistently turned out at higher rates than nonunion members. Although the differences are not huge, there are some variations by time period. Prior to 1989, the average difference is 5 percent, but in elections in the 1990s, the gap doubles to an average of 11 percent.

Thus, the data are reasonably clear that union members do participate in elections at rates higher than their nonunion counterparts. But is this difference due to the effects of union membership including the

TABLE 7.2
Self-reported National Turnout in General Elections, 1952–1998

Year	Union Member	Union Household	Nonunion
1952	76	77	73
1956	80	71	72
1958	69	50	56
1960	84	73	83
1964	83	83	77
1966	65	59	62
1968	80	69	75
1970	61	54	57
1972	79	70	72
1974	61	56	59
1976	80	75	70
1978	61	50	54
1980	76	73	70
1982	66	64	59
1984	78	72	80
1986	56	53	52
1988	78	72	59
1990	54	49	45
1992	88	79	74
1994	68	64	57
1996	85	81	75
1998	69	63	51
Average Turnout	73	66	65
Average Turnout, Presidential Election Years	81	75	73
Average Turnout, Nonpresidential Election Years	63	56	55

Source: American National Election Studies, 1952–1998.

mobilizing activities of organized labor? Here the answer is mixed. One multivariate analysis of the 1978 congressional elections (Delaney et al. 1988) found that being a union member was statistically significant in predicting whether a citizen would vote; no such effects were found for members of union households. The authors suggest two mechanisms by which higher turnout among union members is generated—union political education programs that emphasize the importance of voting to the rank and file and the peer pressures that occur among union members encouraging voting participation. Another study (Sousa 1993) of the 1960 through 1988 presidential elections found that union membership had a statistically significant influence on turnout only in 1976, once other explanations of turnout such as income, age, strength of partisanship, and race were controlled. We replicated David J. Sousa's analysis for the 1990, 1992, 1994, and 1996 elections and found that once one controlled for the aforementioned factors, union membership did not have a statistically significant impact on turnout in any of these elections. But the replication of Sousa's voting model for the 1998 election showed that union members were significantly more likely to vote. Although this result is for only one election, it still is noteworthy given the shift in the political strategy of the AFL-CIO and its heavy emphasis on turnout in the 1998 midterm election. Indeed, the 1998 union turnout rate of 69 percent is the highest in any midterm election (tied with 1958). The 1998 turnout gap between union members and nonmembers (18 percent) is exceeded only in the 1988 presidential contest. Moreover, since the 1982 election, the average gap between union members' and nonmembers' turnout rates has doubled: it was six points between 1952 and 1982 and thirteen points between 1983 and 1998. Thus, in any era of declining participation rates, union participation rates have shown less slippage in comparison to the overall American population.

Because it is difficult to demonstrate in most election years a separate union impact on turnout, does that mean that unions are less significant players in elections? The answer is no, for a variety of reasons. First, union turnout rates are higher than nonunion rates. The fact that we cannot directly attribute that difference to union mobilizing activities and the effects of union membership itself does not wipe away the difference. The higher participation rates of union members are politically and electorally significant. Indeed, given some of the rates reported in this chapter, it may be very difficult for unions to raise those rates much higher. Nevertheless, as the unionized percentage of the workforce declines, one strategy for maintaining union influence is to stimulate higher participation in elections, particularly in those districts and states where the union vote can make a difference in the outcome. Finally, turnout is not the only factor that determines labor's clout in elections. One must also examine the loyalty of the union vote. Do union members support union endorsed candidates?

One last observation about turnout is appropriate. As the class and educational composition of union membership changes over time, the direct impact of union membership on turnout may shift. That is, to the extent that union membership becomes more white collar and increasingly recruits teachers and even doctors, then the independent effect of union membership on turnout may be less since such professionals would be expected to vote at a higher rate because of other resources that they already possess, including higher levels of political interest and education. But if the unions begin to recruit more workers, typically heavily minority, at the bottom of the economic rung, such as low-paid health care and food service workers, then the impact of union membership and mobilization activities on turnout may become more substantial. Indeed, the Sousa study cited earlier found that union membership narrowed the gap in black versus white turnout (1993, 751). In the eight elections he studied, white nonunion members' turnout exceeded black turnout by 15.5 percent, but the turnout among black union members trailed white turnout by only 5.8 percent. Union whites turned out at a rate only 2.5 percent higher than nonunion whites, but the comparable difference among blacks was almost 13 percent. Thus, as the unions move to target minority citizens working in low-wage industries, we may see more direct effects of union membership on electoral participation.

VOTE CHOICE

While turnout is certainly a key factor in organized labor's electoral clout, it does the union movement little good if union members vote, but not for the union-endorsed candidates. The union movement needs both high levels of participation and high levels of loyalty among participants in order to stake its claim as a key player in elections. Unions have traditionally had difficulty delivering their members as a cohesive block of votes. Many of the union officers we interviewed expressed frustration at rank-and-file members using social issues—especially gun control and abortion—as the basis for their voting decisions rather than job-related considerations. Many officers believe that members do not understand how the decisions of a legislature affect their ability to do their job. A lobbyist for the state employee union hammered the point home: "We have to get our members to see legislators as their bosses." She continued with an anecdote about a phone conversation with a member: "He was startled that the Republicans in the legislature were cutting funds for his program. He said he had voted for the Republicans, but didn't expect this. I asked him why he voted for the Republicans. He said, 'Because of "moral issues": guns, abortion, homosexuality.' He didn't consider their [Republicans'] positions on how they could affect him at work."

Union leaders know that few members will be swayed by endorsements, but think they need to make sure that work considerations are at least an element of members' voting calculations. One union officer explained: "Some members get quite upset and send me nasty letters when they oppose our endorsements. But the union isn't considering all issues, and can't. Likewise, if abortion or gun control is that important to members, they'll go ahead and vote on the basis of it. Our job is to make labor issues something to think about when voting—that members at least consider workplace issues in deciding how to vote."

Partisanship is a major roadblock to members supporting union-endorsed candidates. Many Republican members dismiss labor endorsements as knee-jerk backing of Democrats and thus ignore them. But if members can be convinced that endorsements are based on issues important to them, they are more likely to support endorsees from the opposite party. An Ohio Education Association (OEA) activist explained how she used the candidate responses to the endorsement screening questionnaire to persuade members to support endorsees:

> I review how candidates answer the most important questions. This helps show members why a certain candidate was endorsed. For incumbents, I show their OEA voting score. . . . In the 1992 presidential race, they [NEA] developed a fact sheet, creating a side-by-side comparison of Bush and Clinton on education issues to show why they had endorsed Clinton. . . . Doing the questionnaire comparisons is a big help in educating skeptical members, but some strong Democrats or Republicans won't be convinced no matter what.

The AFL-CIO's issue ads run in marginal Republican districts during the 1996 congressional elections were based on the centrality of issues to swing voters. As explained by Steve Rosenthal, the national Committee on Political Education (COPE) director: "We firmly believe we can't move our members around candidates. We can move our members around issues" (quoted in Grunwald and Wells 1996, 996). Rather than just speaking favorably of the endorsee and urging voters to support him or her, the ads compared the candidates on highly salient issues such as Medicare, education, and the environment. By emphasizing the endorsee's popular stance on the issue in contrast to the opponent's unpopular stance, voters were given the information to make up their own minds.

Thus, organized labor needs to craft messages and communicate them to targeted audiences to generate support for endorsed candidates. Organized labor also needs information about its members in order to craft these messages in the first place. The coordination of communications to the rank and file is a key responsibility of the national and state COPE staffs. Their goal is to create messages that will be effective in stimulating members across the labor movement to become active and to vote for endorsed candidates. National union political officers thought the America Needs a Raise theme of Labor '96 was much more effective in appealing across unions than appeals in previous elections. In addition to general communications in monthly magazines, election flyers, and the like, state and central labor council (CLC) staffs created targeted communications for specific locals and for specific races. Targeted messages were necessary because of the diversity of interests among the different affiliates of the AFL-CIO and the variety of local political contexts in which those unions operated. For example, the central office developed letters about candidates and their positions on issues important to the local union president. The COPE manual further recommended that the letters be copied onto local union letterhead and distributed with the signature of the local union president, because "union members are more likely to respond to information received directly from their local union" (Ohio AFL-CIO Committee on Political Education 1994a, CC-1).

Some union political mailings and phone calls were also targeted toward selected members. Traditionally, phone banks have been organized by CLCs and international unions. First, membership lists are obtained; the internationals use their own membership lists and also share their lists with the AFL-CIO federation office in Washington. CLCs get the membership lists from Washington. Then, the members are phoned and polled on their voting intentions in one or two races. Callers are trained to introduce themselves as representatives of the "Committee on Political Education" rather than "COPE." The rationale is that most members recognize COPE but do not identify the "Committee" as the union. With this ploy, COPE officials believe that members will provide more accurate responses rather than saying whatever the members think the union wants to hear. In these polls, usually around 40 percent are undecided. The member is also asked to give his or her opinion on four issues followed by the single issue that he or she thinks is most important in this election. If the members say they are voting for the union candidate, they get limited mailings to reinforce their preferences. If members say they are not voting for the union candidate, they are removed from the union list and ignored. The members who are undecided get a mailing from the union signed by union officers that explains the candidate's stances on issues the members care about most. Whenever possible, the local union sends the mailing to its own members on behalf of the CLC. CLC officers estimate that 80 percent of the locals will do this. The letters to undecided members are then followed up with phone calls and/or one-on-one communications with representatives of the local union such as the members' steward.

CLCs and locals are encouraged to cross-check their membership lists with lists of registered voters. Members who are not registered then become the target of union voter registration drives, and if they still fail to register, they are not contacted by COPE regarding the elections. A union political director explains the advantage of this strategy: "Because of the list, we know that each mailing would be a 'hit' [i.e., it would go to a voter in the district]. It's not a costly shotgun approach. Seventy-five percent of locals in [his congressional] district did the special mailings which contained a five-issue comparison piece and a cover letter from the local." Some CLCs also check the partisan registration of the members when checking voter registration lists. Subsequent mailings and telephone calls are then directed to registered Independents and Democrats and not to Republicans.

In 1996, COPE did the polling itself in targeted districts. It then provided union campaign volunteer coordinators in the district a list of members who were undecided or who could not be contacted in the three days that the poll was in the field. COPE also provided a cross-listing of registered members who lived in the district. Coordinators then gave the list to the locals and suggested the locals send mailings to their members on the list.

In summary, organized labor endorses candidates. It communicates those endorsements through carefully crafted messages to the rank and file, particularly targeting the likely supporters of the union's position as well as the undecideds. Now the questions become: What is the payoff on election day for the union movement? Do members follow the union endorsement?

THE ELECTION DAY RESULTS

The National Picture

At the national level, the consistent pattern between 1952 and 1998 is higher support for Democratic candidates for president, the U.S. House, and the U.S. Senate on the part of union members than from nonunion members, with union households in most cases falling somewhere in between (see table 7.3). On average, union members' support for Democratic presidential, U.S. Senate, and U.S. House candidates was about 17 percent higher than nonunion members' support. Even in an election year such as 1972 where less than a majority of union members voted for the Democratic presidential nominee, their support was still nine points higher than that given by nonunion voters. The explanation for this pattern is very straightforward; union members are Democratic in their party identification or partisan loyalties and therefore more likely to vote Democratic on election day. In their study of the 1992 election, Warren E. Miller and J. Merrill Shanks (1996) found that the effects of union membership (they examined union households) on vote choice largely vanished when controlling for party identification. They concluded that the union vote in 1992 seemed "to have been singularly based on union members' historical differences from non-union voters, and may have been based on party identification alone" (276). Sousa (1993) reached a similar conclusion is his study of the 1960–1988 presidential races. Once income, race, and party identification were controlled, union membership had no

TABLE 7.3
Percentage Support for Democratic Candidates
in National Elections, 1952–1998

	Presidential Vote				U.S. Senate Vote				Congressional Vote			
	UR	UH	NU	DIFF	UR	UH	NU	DIFF	UR	UH	NU	DIFF
1952	62	48	36	26	62	41	42	20	65	55	44	21
1956	57	47	36	21	64	58	50	14	65	59	49	16
1958					70	71	53	17	79	77	54	25
1960	65	62	44	21	74	64	50	24	67	71	51	16
1964	85	81	62	23	78	75	54	24	85	74	59	26
1966					67	55	46	21	73	59	53	20
1968	52	47	42	10	60	62	51	9	61	55	52	9
1970					71	72	60	11	70	63	53	17
1972	42	45	33	9	60	45	49	11	65	57	54	11
1974					70	68	54	16	74	69	58	16
1976	68	61	47	21	70	69	55	15	77	65	53	24
1978					71	48	47	24	72	67	54	18
1980	51	51	36	15	65	60	49	16	67	63	51	16
1982					60	54	54	6	70	71	54	16
1984	60	52	37	23	66	61	50	16	67	55	53	14
1986					68	55	52	16	68	56	59	9
1988	59	58	44	15	70	62	54	16	71	61	57	14
1990					87	69	55	32	74	69	62	12
1992	56	52	46	10	64	64	53	11	69	60	58	11
1994					61	49	39	22	64	55	43	21
1996	66	68	50	16	65	69	49	16	65	48	44	21
1998					67	64	50	17	53	57	43	10
Overall Average	60	56	43	17	68	61	51	17	69	62	53	16

Note: UR = Union Respondents; UH = Union Households; NU = Nonunion Households; DIFF = UR–NU.

significant effect on voting in any presidential contest in this time period. Our replication of the Sousa analysis for the 1992 and 1996 presidential races also produced the same result.

The notion that union members vote more Democratic because they are more Democratic in their psychological attachments to political parties than are nonunion members is certainly the case, but does not capture the full richness of potential union effects on vote choice. For example, to the extent that organized labor joins with the Democratic Party to support a broader political agenda beyond direct union issues, labor's efforts may stimulate nonunion citizens to support Democratic candidates. And more importantly, labor union membership may enhance loyalty to and identification with the Democratic Party among union members, thereby generating greater electoral support for Democratic candidates on election day. Jong Oh Ra posits that "union members' awareness of and identification with the union's political goals strengthen their Democratic partisanship" (1978, 55). He also argues that the longer members have been involved in the union, the greater the Democratic partisanship. Ra's point is that if one simply looks at the direct impact of union membership and Democratic partisanship on the vote, one might overlook the indirect effect of union membership on vote choice through its impact on party identification. Another way of stating this is that just because the relationship between union membership and vote choice may weaken or even vanish when the effects of party identification are controlled (as in the previously mentioned Miller and Shanks study), this does not mean that union membership is inconsequential for vote choice. Its effects may be more channeled through party identification.

The Ohio Picture

Introduction

Unlike the national surveys that we utilized in the previous section, our Ohio surveys were explicitly designed to study labor's impact on elections. This will enable us to construct multivariate models of the voting behavior of union members in Ohio to determine what factors promote voting loyalty to union-endorsed candidates. Some members are loyal and follow the endorsements; others do not. The question becomes why. Certainly one part of the answer focuses on the partisanship of union members discussed earlier and the partisanship of the candidates endorsed by unions. Obviously, when unions overwhelmingly endorse Democratic candidates, one would expect that Democratic union members would be more loyal to the endorsed candidates than would Independent and Republican union members. But not all Democratic union members support endorsed Democratic candidates, nor do all Republican unionists oppose endorsed Democrats. Motivational and psychological aspects of union membership also come into play.

One would intuitively expect that members who highly value their union membership and who believe in the appropriateness of union activity would be more likely to support union-endorsed candidates than members who do not share these beliefs. Likewise, one would expect that members who voluntarily join unions and who see the linkage between the economic and political objectives of the union would *ceteris paribus* be more likely to support endorsed candidates. But union members, like other voters, bring other attributes and attitudes to their voting decisions including partisanship, ideological orientation, issue preferences, and demographic characteristics. Thus, we need to construct a multivariate model to assess the relative importance of those factors that enhance and impede electoral support for union-endorsed candidates.

Other studies have investigated whether endorsements influence voting behavior (for a review of the literature, see Masters and Delaney 1987b). Previous research has shown that members of unions tend to vote differently than nonmembers (Sousa 1993; Delaney, Masters, and Schwochau 1990; Ra 1978), that union endorsements can have significant effects on members' vote choices (Rapoport, Stone, and Abramowitz 1991; Juravich and Shergold 1988; Converse and Campbell 1968; Kornhauser, Sheppard, and Mayer 1956), and that unions may also influence voting indirectly by strengthening rank-and-file members' identification with the Democratic Party (Stanley, Bianco, and Niemi 1986; Ra 1978).

The Data and the Dependent Variable

Using our statewide surveys of Ohio union members in the 1990, 1992, 1994, and 1996 elections, we can study voting loyalty to the union endorsements in four separate elections. Ohio is an excellent state in which to study union voting behavior. First, Ohio has a strong union presence with respect to numbers, activity, organization, and diversity of unions. Second, Ohio itself is a competitive two-party state at the state level even as it has solid Democratic and Republican regions within the state. Third, Ohio has an election calendar that separates its elections for governor and statewide administrative offices from the presidential race. That means that in all four elections that we study there was a highly visible office at the top of the ticket—the presidency in 1992 and 1996 and the governorship in 1990 and 1994—along with less visible statewide contests in all four years. Thus, we can study the impact of union endorsements in a variety of electoral settings.

Our dependent variable was simply the percentage of union-endorsed candidates on the statewide ballot that the voter supported. Obviously, different candidates and races were on the ballot each year, but our dependent variable for each year—the level of support for union-backed candidates—is identical. Thus, our dependent variable is somewhat unusual in voting behavior research since it is not vote choice in a single contest, but, instead, is a measure of vote preference across a set of election contests, thereby getting beyond the idiosyncrasies that might characterize any particular race for office. (A discussion of how variables were measured can be found in appendix C.)

A brief discussion of key races on the statewide ballot for each year will help the reader gain a better sense of the dependent variable. In 1990 and 1994, the statewide ballot included all of the state's top administrative officers—governor and lieutenant governor (who run as a single team), attorney general, auditor, secretary of state, and treasurer. Also on the statewide ballot in both years were two Ohio Supreme Court seats and, in 1994, a U.S. Senate seat. In 1992, the statewide contests were the presidential race, three Ohio Supreme Court seats, and one U.S. Senate seat, while in 1996 the only statewide contests were the presidential race and two Ohio Supreme Court seats. One interesting feature of Ohio Supreme Court contests is that although the court nominees are chosen in partisan primaries, the general election contest is *technically* nonpartisan in that the party labels of the court nominees do not appear on the ballot. In actuality, the supreme court elections are very partisan with both political parties working hard to elect their candidates, but Ohio voters do not have the party label on the ballot as an election day voting cue. Finally, the term of office for a supreme court judge is six years, while for governor and other statewide administrative offices the term is four years.

In all four elections, organized labor overwhelmingly endorsed Democratic candidates. In 1990, all three unions we studied endorsed all of the Democratic candidates with the important exception of one incumbent, Andy Douglas, a Republican supreme court justice who received strong and enthusiastic labor support. Thus, in 1990, total loyalty to the union-endorsed candidates required casting six Democratic votes and one Republican vote. In 1992, all three unions endorsed all five of the Democratic candidates; thus, complete loyalty to the union recommendations required casting five Democratic votes. The situation in 1994 was more complicated. The AFL-CIO endorsed the Democratic candidate in all eight of the statewide races. The Ohio Civil Service Employee Association (OCSEA) endorsed seven Democrats and one Republican (the Republican candidate for the state auditor's office). OEA endorsed in only four of the eight contests, recommending a Democratic vote in three races and a Republican vote in one of the supreme court contests. The OEA did not endorse in the contests for governor, treasurer, auditor, and secretary of state. In 1996, both the AFL-CIO and OEA endorsed the Democratic presidential nominee and the Democratic nominee for one of the supreme court posts. But in the other supreme court contest, both unions supported incumbent Republican Andy Douglas. (In 1996, we were unable to sample OCSEA members.)

Note that in 1992, the dependent variable "percentage support for union-endorsed candidates" is the same as "percentage support for Democratic candidates" since the three unions endorsed all the Democratic nominees. The 1990, 1994, and 1996 elections allow us to distinguish between support for Democrats and support for union-endorsed candidates. In the next section, we will take advantage of this opportunity by estimating multivariate models of support for Democrats and support for union-endorsed candidates. We expect very similar results since unions primarily endorsed Democrats, but some differences do arise.

One final methodological point must be noted. Not all voters complete their ballots even when they do show up at the polls. This raises the question of how we should treat a union member who failed to vote in a particular contest versus the union member who voted for the nonendorsed candidate. One possibility is to treat both behaviors identically—as a failure to support the union-endorsed candidate. But another possibility is to examine voting behavior for only those contests in which union members actually cast votes. For example, if the union endorsed six candidates in a particular election and the union member voted for four of the six and did not vote in the other two contests, one could argue that the level of support for union-endorsed candidates is 67 percent (four out of six). But if one examines only actual votes cast, the level of support would be 100 percent (four out of four). We decided to conduct our analyses using both measures to insure that the obtained results are robust. This methodological point does raise an important challenge for unions—it is not sufficient to simply get members to the polls. One also needs to engender loyalty to endorsed candidates and to encourage ballot completion.

The Determinants of Vote Choice for All Endorsed Candidates

Table 7.4 presents the levels of support for union-endorsed and Democratic candidates in our Ohio and union samples for all four elections using both measures of support. Note that in all years, the union samples did indeed support union-backed and Democratic candidates at a higher rate than did the Ohio samples. There were variations among the unions such that in 1990 and 1992, AFL-CIO members were much more supportive of union-backed candidates than were OEA members. One reason for this is that OEA members are less Democratic in their partisan affiliations than are AFL-CIO members and therefore less likely *ceteris paribus* to vote for union-endorsed Democratic candidates. In 1994, OEA members were more supportive of union-backed candidates, but this result is simply an artifact of the AFL-CIO's endorsement of the Democratic candidate in the gubernatorial contest; the OEA made no endorsement in this race. The Democratic nominee barely made a dent in the campaign and received only 25 percent of the total statewide vote.

In 1990, 1992, and 1994, there were minimal or no differences in levels of support for Democratic versus union-endorsed candidates. But in 1996 there were substantial differences with all groups providing greater support for union-backed candidates than for Democratic nominees. These differences arose because of union endorsement of Andy Douglas, the incumbent Republican supreme court justice. Labor union members, despite

TABLE 7.4

Percentage of Votes Cast for Union-Endorsed Candidates and Democratic Candidates in 1990, 1992, 1994, and 1996, Using Two Measures of Support

	1990		1992		1994		1996	
	Endorsed	Democrat	Endorsed	Democrat	Endorsed	Democrat	Endorsed	Democrat
First Support Measure—All Races in Which Unions Endorsed								
Ohio Sample	52	53	55		note 2	38	34	24
Union Sample	63	64	59		53	54	37	30
AFL-CIO	69	65	63		50	50	36	30
OCSEA	60	61	60		52	53	—	—
OEA	55	60	50		59	62	41	18
Second Support Measure—All Races in Which Respondents Voted								
Ohio Sample	54	48	58		38	38	52	44
Union Sample	64	58	58		49	49	59	46
AFL-CIO	66	60	63		52	52	59	47
OCSEA	61	56	61		54	54	—	—
OEA	58	52	49		40	41	60	45

Notes: 1) In 1992, the voting for endorsees and Democrats is the same; the unions endorsed all Democrats in statewide races in Ohio. 2) In 1994, since the unions endorsed different candidates in some races, only the percentage of votes cast for Democrats is presented for the Ohio sample. 3) In 1994, the percentage of votes for OEA members is based on only the four races in which OEA made an endorsement. 4) In 1996, OCSEA members were not surveyed. 5) The percentage in the top half of the table are based on all races in which unions endorsed regardless of whether citizens actually cast a vote in a particular contest. The percentages in the bottom half of the table are based on actual votes cast by the respondents.

their Democratic proclivities, overwhelmingly supported the Republican Douglas over his Democratic challenger. Indeed, Douglas ran better among union members than he did among our representative sample of all Ohioans. This contest clearly demonstrates the power of the union endorsement; organized labor conveyed its strong preference for Douglas and the rank-and-file members overwhelmingly followed that cue.

Which union members are most likely to follow the union endorsement? To answer this question, we constructed a model of vote choice that incorporates the many factors that can affect preferences for one candidate over another. Certainly, two key attitudinal variables are the party identification and the ideological identification of the union member. Democratic and more liberal union members would be more likely to support union-endorsed candidates who themselves are most often Democratic and on the liberal side of the political spectrum. There are also a number of standard demographic variables that have been associated with vote choice. The three that we consider are race, gender, and social class, the expectation being that female, minority, and working-class union members are more likely to support union-endorsed candidates. (Because of their prominence in the literature on voting behavior, we also examined the impact of income, education, and religion on vote choice. Each was consistently unrelated to vote preference and did not affect the overall regression estimations for our multivariate models. We do not show these results for simplicity of presentation.) The final cluster of variables we examine are four union-based measures: length of membership in the union, the perceived number of campaign activities in which the union engaged, an index of commitment to the union, and an index of the importance of union endorsements to the member. (These indices are defined in appendix C.) We expect that those union members with greater commitment to the union, who also believe that endorsements are important, who have been in the union for a longer time, and who see the union being active in campaigns will be more likely to support the union-endorsed candidates.

Table 7.5 indicates that the most consistent predictors of support for union-endorsed and Democratic candidates are party identification and ideology. Democratic and more liberal union members were more likely to vote for candidates backed by organized labor. This result fits very well with what we know historically about the labor vote in America. The demographic variables of gender, race, and class were inconsistent and weak in their effects, achieving statistical significance in only two of the four election years.

The union variables were also inconsistent in their impact on voting behavior. Members' views of the importance of union information and endorsements were significant in three of the four elections. Keep in mind

TABLE 7.5
Determinants of Support for Union-Endorsed and Democratic Candidates, 1990–1996

Explanatory Variables	1990 Endorsed	1990 Democrat	1992 Endorsed	1994 Endorsed	1994 Democrat	1996 Endorsed	1996 Democrat
Democratic Party ID	.47**	.47**	.46**	.48**	.48**	.38**	.48**
Liberal Ideology	.15**	.16**		.21**	.20**	.09	.12*
Gender (Male)				.08*	.09*	.10**	.09**
Working Class			.09*	.06	.06		
Race (Nonwhite)	.11**	.12**	.08*	-.06			
Tenure						.11*	
Union Political Activities						.11*	
Commitment	.16**	.16**	.09*				
Endorsement Index	.14**	.13**	.17**	.19**	.19**		
Constant	.65**	.66**	.55**	.76**	.79**	.64**	.65**
Adjusted R²	.47	.49	.38	.48	.49	.25	.37

Source: Ohio union surveys.
Note: Only variables significant at $p < .10$ are displayed; *$p < .05$; **$p < .01$ two-tailed test. Beta coefficients of OLS regression are presented in order to facilitate assessments of the magnitude of direct effects.

that this endorsement measure was an index composed of responses to
four items:

1. "Here is a list of sources from which people get information about
   government, public affairs, candidates and issues. For each of the
   sources, please tell me if it was very important, somewhat important, or not at all important in helping you decide how to vote: labor
   unions . . ."
2. "In general, do you think your labor union has an effect on how you
   vote? [if yes] Is this a big effect, a moderate effect, or a small effect?"
3. "If you knew that a candidate were endorsed by labor unions, would
   you be more likely or less likely to vote for that candidate, or would
   it make no difference"
4. "Is it OK or not OK for labor unions to try to affect their members by
   endorsing candidates and issues?"

Clearly, the union leadership needs to get the message to the rank and file,
but it also needs to convince members that political activities such as endorsements are legitimate and relevant cues for political behavior. The
union's agenda is advanced when it is able to inform members not only
about the endorsement per se, but also about the comparative record of
the opposing candidates that led up to the endorsement.

Commitment to the union was a significant predictor in 1990 and 1992,
but not in 1994 and 1996. The 1994 situation is readily explained by the fact
that the three items used to measure commitment and the four items in the
endorsement index all loaded on the same factor in a factor analysis that
we conducted. Thus, by including them as separate predictors, we have
entered two collinear independent variables into the regression analysis
and it is not surprising that one of them is insignificant. When the model
is rerun with a combined commitment/endorsement measure based on all
seven items, this single variable is highly significant. Likewise, when we
include commitment and exclude endorsements, commitment is highly
significant. For 1996, the commitment and endorsement indices are not
statistically significant, even when entered separately into the regression
equation. One speculative explanation for this result is that unions in 1996
shifted their message to focus on issue differences between candidates and
to downplay simple appeals to union loyalty (see chapter 5).

Thus, even though party identification is the most consistent predictor
of support for union-backed candidates, there are also some union-based
measures that affect vote choice including endorsements and commitment. How the union socializes its members and communicates with
them does make a difference. We conducted some additional analyses to
determine what factors made union members more likely to utilize union

endorsements and information as meaningful voting cues. Briefly, we found that three explanatory variables were consistently significant—party identification, union political activity, and commitment. Commitment had the strongest influence. This reinforces the importance of commitment and argues that one challenge facing the contemporary labor movement is the fostering of commitment to the union among the rank and file. Committed members are more likely to look to the union for cues and to follow those cues. But stimulating commitment in an era in which appeals to social class are often treated as illegitimate by the media and in which prosperity in many sectors has taken the edge off of union–business competition is a challenge. Focus groups that we conducted with union members as part of our research (see chapter 3) suggested that support for the union movement rested more on the contemporary performance of the union in improving the lives of its members than on any historical sense of class conflict and union/management strife.

Vote Choice in Races with Divided Union Endorsements

Until this point, we have been focusing on support for a set of union-endorsed and/or Democratic candidates in which the unions we studied agreed on the endorsed candidates. But in 1994, our Ohio unions disagreed on who the preferred candidate was in two specific races. Thus, we can test for the effect of specific union endorsements on their own members using the above model augmented by a series of dummy variables. In particular, in one supreme court race, the OEA endorsed Republican Deborah Cook, while the AFL-CIO and OCSEA endorsed Democrat J. Ross Haffey. In the auditor's race, OCSEA endorsed Republican James Petro, the AFL-CIO endorsed Democrat Randall Sweeney, and the OEA did not endorse at all. These union splits allow us to examine whether members follow the endorsement of their *own* union in a particular contest.

To determine whether union membership makes a difference in candidate support by members of that union, membership in OEA, AFL-CIO, and OCSEA was treated as a series of dummy variables and incorporated in the regression model presented in table 7.5. This then allowed us to estimate the effect of split union endorsements on a particular race while controlling for the other political, demographic, and union-based independent variables. In both estimations, the dependent variable was dichotomous—the vote for Haffey or Cook in the supreme court race and Sweeney or Petro in the auditor's contest—so Logit was used as the estimation procedure.

The results (not shown) support the proposition that union members do follow their own union's endorsement. In the Haffey/Cook race, both union affiliations are statistically significant predictors of the vote with

OCSEA members more likely to vote for Haffey and OEA members for Cook. Although the results for Petro/Sweeney do not quite reach statistical significance, the signs of the estimated coefficients are indeed in the right direction, meaning that AFL-CIO members were more likely to vote for Sweeney and OCSEA members more likely to support Petro. Hence, we have evidence that shows that even in relatively low-visibility elections such as for the auditor and supreme court justice seats, union endorsements make a difference, even when the effects of other explanatory variables are taken into account. Indeed, it may be exactly these kinds of contests where the potentiality for union influence is greatest. Where little information is available from other sources, then union cues may play a more substantial role. This of course assumes that there are union cues, that union members are aware of these cues, and that union members view these cues as legitimate guides to political behavior.

CONCLUSION

In this chapter, we have seen that organized labor remains important on election day. Union members register and vote at a rate higher than the overall population. This means that labor's share of the popular vote exceeds its proportion of the overall voting-age population. We have also seen that union members demonstrate substantial loyalty to union-endorsed candidates who are typically Democratic. Thus, while labor's presence as a share of the workforce may have diminished in recent decades, the labor vote on election day is still very significant. And that is separate from labor's overall involvement in the political campaign process, whether it be registration drives, phone banks, Get-Out-the-Vote drives, issue advocacy ads, or other activities, many of which reach broader audiences than simply union members. Moreover, labor's clout in any particular election contest will in part be a function of its density or penetration within that political jurisdiction. Even at the national level, organized labor tends to be strongest in those industrial states such as Ohio, Michigan, Illinois, and Pennsylvania that are often the key battlegrounds in presidential elections.

We have also seen that organized labor can generate even greater support for endorsed candidates from its members if it can generate a sense of commitment and support for the union movement among its rank-and-file-members. Certainly, this is one challenge facing the labor movement, particularly in an era of prosperity and diminished class conflict. Yet another challenge for the labor movement is to recruit new members in order to increase its absolute numbers and its share of the workforce. Achieving this goal will enhance labor's clout in elections. Whether labor becomes a more significant electoral force is not entirely within its control. Changes in the legal and political climate could either hinder or enhance labor's prospects, depending on the substance of these changes. Likewise, changes in the economic climate, particularly an economic downturn with greater perceptions among Americans of job insecurity, may enhance prospects for attracting new members. But whatever the legal or economic climate, it is clear that the leadership of organized labor will have to maintain a sustained and aggressive focus on strengthening labor's electoral clout.

8

Challenges and Opportunities for Organized Labor

As the twenty-first century opens, American labor unions are at a turning point in several senses. Since the election of John Sweeney as the AFL-CIO president in 1995, the top leadership of organized labor has been trying to revitalize unions both economically and politically. This chapter assesses core aspects of those efforts based both on recent general developments involving unions and our original empirical research reported in this book.

Economic and political power are not perfectly correlated, but the relationship is strong. Ultimately, if unions do not either increase their economic clout or at least stanch its decline they will lose political power. Sweeney's program, quite appropriately, is to address both the economic and political fronts simultaneously. In a sense, they feed off of each other. If economic strength increases, then electoral power increases. If electoral power increases then federal and state legislatures and executives become more friendly to labor's concerns. If legislatures and executives are more friendly to labor, then the legal context for labor to achieve more of its economic goals becomes more hospitable. Since, as we indicated in chapter 1, modern American unions are best considered as broad-gauged interest groups instead of as a social movement, there is a chicken-and-egg relationship between economic and political power, such as the one just sketched.

After setting both the economic and political context for assessing organized labor in the American electoral arena in chapters 1 and 2, we assessed the dynamics of union political mobilization efforts and electoral efforts in chapters 3 through 7. In doing so, we analyzed a great deal of data, including original data from our work in Ohio. In this final chapter, we will once again set a broader context for assessing the current state of union political influence, especially in the electoral arena and in terms of the effort of union leaders to mobilize members for political purposes.

155

Our general conclusions are that organized labor is showing signs of re-vivification on both the economic and political fronts. But there are still considerable challenges to overcome as well as considerable opportuni-ties for unions. Whether unions will continue to decline in economic strength, followed by a decline in political influence, whether they will in-crease in strength, or whether they will plateau at about the present level is unclear. It is certainly premature to proclaim a genuine resurgence of union economic and political power. It is also premature to proclaim that unionism has run its course in the American economy and polity and is doomed to a future of growing marginality and irrelevance. At present, the challenges outweigh the opportunities. But irrevocable continued de-cline is not inevitable.

In this concluding chapter, we first make a summary assessment of challenges. Second, we summarize some opportunities. In doing so, we recount a few leading contemporary examples of union activity that show both some successes and some failures. Third, we focus on some general-izations about the leader-member interaction we empirically analyzed in considerable detail in previous chapters. Finally, we address the question of what our research shows about how union leaders can improve their chances of delivering on their potential.

A CHALLENGING CLIMATE

The problems faced by organized labor in the United States at the begin-ning of the new century are serious and highly visible. Union member-ship has been going down steadily for four decades, both in absolute numbers and, even more dramatically, as a percentage of the workforce. The nature of the membership has also changed, which has presented new challenges to union leaders. Many union members are now white-collar workers, including a large proportion of government employees and teachers. Notions of "union solidarity" for these workers are likely to be quite different from the traditional views.

The legal climate for organized labor has also been getting pro-gressively worse for some decades. Both federal and state laws on a va-riety of matters important to unions—organizing, picketing, political fund-raising, and political spending—have become increasingly restric-tive. In the 1990s, more and more state legislatures and governorships moved into the Republican column, a party traditionally not close to or-ganized labor at best and often overtly hostile. Although a Democratic president won in both 1992 and 1996, the federal picture was not partic-ularly bright either. President Clinton was strongly wedded to free trade, a policy not to the liking of most leaders of organized labor and also unpopular with a majority of union members. Worst of all from the union point of view, the Democrats lost control of Congress after the 1994 election. And, even though the size of the Republican majority in the House shrank in the elections of 1996, 1998, and 2000, the Republicans still maintained control.

The challenges faced by organized labor are numerous. On the political front, organized labor does not have many friends in high places in the federal government or in many of the major states in which the union presence is substantial. The outcome of the national elections in 2000 produced a more hostile environment in which the Republican Party continues to control Congress and regained control of the White House.

The dominance of Republican governors, albeit moderate conservatives in many cases, along with Republican control of the state legislatures in many major states, means that organized labor will also face constant threat from the state level. For example, in Ohio, where the Republicans control the governorship, both chambers of the state legislature, the state supreme court, and all of the statewide elected administrative posts, organized labor—traditionally a significant force in state politics—is struggling. The Republican governor, who was newly elected in 1998, in early 1999 pledged not to support antilabor union legislation and started his administration with a good relationship with labor leaders. However, just a few months later the governor allowed a bill hostile to unions enacted by the state legislature to go into effect without his signature. The bill provided that employees of nonunion contractors could not be required to join a union or be forced to pay union dues in order to work on public projects. Moreover, a very conservative wing of the majority Republicans in the legislature were looking for additional opportunities to confront the unions.

As union membership has become more diverse in terms of demographics and occupations, the ability of union leaders to present a united front across a number of issues has become more difficult. In many unions, there is substantial diversity in the party affiliations and ideological preferences of the membership. For example, our surveys reveal that about one-third of the members of the Ohio Education Association (OEA), the largest teachers' union in the state, think of themselves as Democrat, another third identify themselves as Republican, and the remaining third see themselves as Independent. This fact, plus the reality of Republican dominance of elected offices, has pushed the leaders of the OEA to become increasingly supportive of Republican candidates, both in terms of formal endorsement and in terms of campaign contributions.

Another factor facing union leaders is the increased diversity of how union members perceive themselves in terms of social class. As more government workers and teachers have become union members, unions have taken on a more middle-class and professional coloration. If the union for publicly employed doctors that will be sponsored by the American Medical Association is actually created, even more class diversity will be injected into overall union membership. This increasing class diversification makes it virtually impossible for labor leaders to make successful broad class-based appeals in the old style and evoke the image of the noble working class fighting against the privileged classes. And few doctors are likely to engage in singing old union songs. Union leaders will increasingly have to segment their appeals to their members because the interests of members in different unions may well clash significantly.

In addition, even if unions wanted to use traditional appeals to class conflict, there is a substantial cultural bias in American politics and the media against such appeals. Often, political and media elites who are not sympathetic to unions successfully characterize class-based appeals as illegitimate, divisive, and even un-American because such appeals pit some citizens against other citizens. Appeals that can, accurately or inaccurately, be characterized as class-based also fly in the face of the myth that class does not exist in the United States. If union leaders are, in effect, denied the use of class-based appeals, their job is made even more difficult.

Organized labor also "suffers" from good as well as bad economic times. During a sustained period of general growth and prosperity—such as that in the United States since 1992—it is difficult for union leaders to arouse much passion for the plight of the workers and the health of unions, although a few deprived occupational sectors may be promising targets for union activity. Ironically, the continuing downsizing by many large companies may have made those holding jobs more timid about union activity since they do not want to upset a situation in which they remain employed. A study commissioned by the AFL-CIO also reported that "job growth is fastest in industries where unions are weakest while job losses are greatest in industries where unions are strongest" (quoted in Greenhouse 1999f). Unions, for example, have had no success in organizing workers in the booming technology sector. They are exploring nontraditional organizing techniques, but face an uphill fight (Greenhouse 1999g).

A number of companies also engage in practices, often called Continuous Quality Improvement or Total Quality Management, that make workers feel that they are a respected and valued part of the total corporate enterprise. This makes traditional union appeals ring less true to many potential members. Moreover, many companies are also providing profit-sharing and stock purchase plans for a wide range of employees. Such programs help reduce the perceived gap between management and labor and diminish an "us–them" mentality, again complicating the task of union leaders, especially organizers.

And yet the organizing challenge is a large one. As AFL-CIO organizing director Kirk Adams said recently:

> What Sweeney is saying is it can't be just five unions, or ten, that reshape themselves into organizing unions. Twenty or thirty have to move to this type of effort if we're going to grow. Last year, unions experienced a net growth of 100,000 members; this year it will go to 200,000. But we have to get to a net increase of 500,000 members to increase our density, what with the workforce growing at 2 million a year. That means we have to organize a million new members a year. We've got a ways to go yet. (Quoted in Meyerson 2000, 53)

The leaders of organized labor also receive low rankings from the American public in terms of trust. As indicated in chapter 1, labor leaders are among the least trusted in American society when compared to leaders in a number of other major institutions. Even though many new leaders have emerged in recent years, a large part of the public still adheres to negative stereotypes of union leaders as autocrats, often out of touch, and sometimes corrupt.

The ever-increasing mobility of the American population and changing notions of the meaning of "neighborhood" also limit the success that can be expected by union leaders. Solid union neighborhoods, with most of the males in one union at the same plant, have been in decline for many decades. At the beginning of the twenty-first century, they have virtually disappeared. The days when a lot of union members who shared religion, party affiliation, social class, occupation, and ethnicity and lived in the same neighborhood are long gone. Union members are as scattered as the population in general. Reinforcement for union values and union positions rarely comes after work hours. Most unions have also ceased to play a significant social role for their members and families.

Even if organized labor is successful in halting or even reversing declining membership, the leaders still face the challenge of inculcating union values and attitudes into the new members. New members typically do not come to unions because of agreement with political positions. Commitment by members to the union is an important factor in accounting for members' support of the union political agenda. But commitment is not something that union members automatically share simply because they are members. Indeed, many of the younger members have almost no knowledge of labor history or of the past successes of the union movement in general or even of the union to which they belong.

The ability of unions to increase their policy impact through working on and giving money to political campaigns has also been limited. Many

Republicans are particularly eager to limit the ability of unions to use members' dues for political purposes. At the same time, fewer limits inhibit the practices of corporate political action committees (PACs). Republican success at the polls has also shifted much of the corporate money that used to go to Democrats away from them to the majority Republicans. This shift was observable at the national level after the Republican capture of Congress in the 1994 election. It was also observable in Ohio after the Republicans took control of the state house of representatives in the 1994 elections after twenty-two years of Democratic control. These shifts by corporations have made labor dollars an even larger part of the financial support for Democratic candidates. But labor PACs are outspent by corporate PACs by a significant amount.

Those who focus only on these challenges facing unions come to the conclusion that unions have not only become weaker both economically and politically, but that they also seem fated to continue their downward spiral unabated. In this view, unions have become almost irrelevant to modern American reality—both economically and politically.

OPPORTUNITIES FOR UNION REVIVAL

Despite the bleak picture just summarized, there have also been some positive developments for organized labor. The mix of recent successes and failures suggests areas of opportunity for labor to make progress on both its economic and political aspirations.

Economic Activity

In one sense, unions are succeeding economically in that, even though real wages for American workers in general have been declining, the gap between union workers' wages and those of nonunion workers has increased. This suggests that unions do reasonably well in collective bargaining negotiations. However, the real test for unions comes in their ability to organize new workers, a challenge nicely summarized earlier in the statement by Adams. Also, when unions choose to strike they have an impact on public perceptions of organized labor and on the willingness of unorganized workers to support unionization. We summarize some recent developments on these fronts in the next two sections.

Organizing

In 1998, membership rose slightly compared to 1997, and was the first absolute membership gain for organized labor in several decades. However, union density (the proportion of the workforce that is unionized) continued to decline because the workforce expanded even faster than union membership. This success was even greater in 1999 (Greenhouse 2000b; Swoboda 2000b). The absolute increase in union membership—265,000—was the largest in two decades. Perhaps even more important, union density did not decline but remained stable at 13.9 percent of the total workforce and 9.4 percent of the private workforce.

The challenges of working with a more diverse union membership—diverse in terms of gender, ethnicity, education, occupation, income, and residence—also offers some opportunities that unions heretofore would not have had available. Unions have made major inroads in organizing teachers and government employees that would have been unthinkable three or four decades ago. And, in June 1999 an important symbol of new opportunities was presented to the union movement when the American Medical Association—one of the most staunchly conservative organizations in the country until very recently—voted to create a labor union for doctors who are salaried employees of organizations such as hospitals, public health institutions, and health maintenance organizations (Greenhouse 1999d).

In early 2000, a regional director for the National Labor Relations Board ruled that graduate associates at private universities could organize, thus according them the same status as graduate associates at public universities. In general, prounion activity on large campuses appeared to be increasing in 1999 and 2000. The UAW, for example, sought to organize graduate teaching assistants in California's university system.

At the same time as white-collar opportunities may be expanding, workers at the lower end of the economic ladder also present organizing opportunities. Early in 1999, organized labor was buoyed by victory on the part of the Service Employees International Union (SEIU) in its drive to organize seventy-four thousand home care workers who tend the elderly and disabled in Los Angeles County. These workers are usually paid at or close to the minimum wage. This was the single largest organizational accomplishment for organized labor since 1937, when 112,000 workers for General Motors (GM) joined the United Auto Workers (UAW) (Greenhouse 1999c; 1999d). This organizing effort by Sweeney's own union took eleven years and a union expenditure of $1 million.

Another notable organizing success came on the part of the Union of Needletrades, Industrial, and Textile Employees (UNITE) in June 1999. The union won an election at a major group of textile mills in North Carolina that had resisted unionization for over ninety years. The predecessor union to UNITE had lost elections at these mills in 1974 and 1985 and voting irregularities had led the National Labor Relations Board to declare elections in 1991 and 1997 to be null and void. The union won 52 percent of the vote before challenges were adjudicated and thereby won the right to represent fifty-two hundred workers at the mills. The size of the newly organized workforce is not trivial but, even more important from the union point of view, organized labor succeeded at specific mills in an industry in a state in which they had rarely tasted success. (Just over 4 percent of the workers in North Carolina belong to unions.)

The UAW also took on the challenge of organizing the Mercedes-Benz plant in Alabama after Daimler-Benz, a German company, bought Chrysler. Success was far from assured, but the union was willing to make a major effort (Meredith 1999).

Another dimension of some actual and more potential union success is the mobilization of new immigrants in unionized situations. An early example of union success in mobilizing a largely immigrant workforce in a strike situation occurred at a meatpacking plant in Washington state run by the largest meatpacker in the nation in mid-1999 (Verhovek 1999). The organizing success with home care workers in Los Angeles County, mentioned earlier, also involved a workforce with lots of new immigrants.

Recent Notable Strikes

Unions have grown increasingly reluctant to strike in recent years (Ball, Burkins, and White 1999). They realize that the probability of unfavorable media coverage and public reaction outweighs the likelihood of favorable coverage and reaction. Only a few strikes get much national media coverage and, therefore, only a few get much national attention. We refer to the most visible strikes in the last few years measured loosely by that standard.

Unusually, one of the few major strikes in recent years—that by the Teamsters against the United Parcel Service (UPS) in August 1997—elicited general public support. A survey conducted by the Cable News Network and *USA Today* during the strike found that 55 percent of those asked supported the Teamsters and 27 percent supported the management of UPS. Whether this support was idiosyncratic or really marked a more general change in attitudes toward unions is not certain, although claims that a new era of prounionism has descended upon us need to be viewed skeptically. Single events rarely mark major shifts in public opinion or interest. Likewise, it is unclear that this support for one limited (sixteen days) strike has any particular implications for the political power of organized labor. Perhaps, the lesson to be drawn is that the Teamsters were skillful in presenting their case to the public. It is also relevant that UPS delivery persons, who drive the same routes day after day, are known personally to millions of package recipients.

By contrast, in June 1998 the UAW struck at two GM plants in Flint, Michigan, which virtually halted all of GM's production in North America because those plants produce parts that are needed to assemble trucks and cars at all its other plants. The public seemed indifferent to the strike, which was settled in late July 1998.

Two strikes in early 2000 got considerable national publicity, although public reaction is not clear. The first was a forty-day strike at Boeing by engineers belonging to the Society of Professional Engineering Employees in Aerospace, a white-collar union independent of the AFL-CIO. About eighteen thousand engineers took part. The AFL-CIO was pleased that the strike took place and succeeded as it saw an indication that more white-collar workers might be more amenable to unionization in the future (Greenhouse 2000e; Cole 2000).

The second strike in early 2000 that got some national attention was by janitors in Los Angeles, who are at the opposite end of the economic scale from the engineers at Boeing. The janitors were represented by the SEIU. About eighty-five hundred workers, mostly new immigrants from Mexico and Central America, took part in the strike. After a strike of about three weeks, they ratified a contract that gave them significant gains, although from a very low base.

Political Influence

Unions seek political influence in two major ways. First, they attempt to influence policies directly. Second, they seek to help elect candidates to office who are supportive of their policy positions. The two efforts are, of course, related. Policy success is more likely if union-friendly candidates win office.

Policies

Some of organized labor's major policy successes since World War II came when they were allied with other major groups in support of issues broader than just employment-related ones. Civil rights expansion stands out as a success story. The creation of Medicare and some of the other liberal programs of the 1960s follow the same pattern (G. Wilson 1979). Even during that period, as noted earlier, organized labor had much less success in pushing federal legislation specifically supportive of unions and were also unable to prevent legislation they did not like, such as the Taft-Hartley Act in 1947 and the Landrum-Griffin Act in 1959.

Policy successes for organized labor at the federal level became less frequent after the Republicans recaptured the White House in the 1968 election and after the political mood of the nation became increasingly conservative.

In the 1990s, the failure of the unions to rally a Democratically controlled Congress and a Democratic president to prevent enactment of the

North American Free Trade Act is symbolic of the failure of organized labor to get much of what it wants legislatively. And, of course, once the Republicans captured both the House and Senate in the 1994 election and retained majorities in the 1996 and 1998 elections, despite major efforts by organized labor to regain control of the House, the legislative influence of organized labor was even further diluted.

Despite the handicap of the new Republican majority, in the 104th Congress (1995–1996) organized labor was on the winning side on increasing the minimum wage, providing health insurance that is portable from job to job, opposing budget cuts to Medicare, Medicaid, and student loans, and defeating a regulatory reform bill that would have undermined environmental and worker safety programs.

Organized labor also succeeded in helping push Congress to block "fast track" trade authority for the president in the autumn of 1997, thus furthering their protectionist (or "fair trade," as labor calls it) agenda. But, for the most part, legislation reflecting issue positions favored by organized labor went nowhere. In mid-1998, the AFL-CIO funded an ad campaign related to the national debate over reform of managed health care. The particular focus of this campaign was to support the Patients' Bill of Rights legislation introduced by the Democratic leader of the Senate and a senior House Democrat. The AFL-CIO had found that its members cared a great deal about this issue (McGinley and Burkins 1998). In late 1998, the AFL-CIO began preparing to participate in a major way in the debate over the future of social security (Burkins 1998). But, overall, the successes of organized labor on issues most specifically related to the welfare of unions were relatively few and far between.

In 1999 and 2000, organized labor became increasingly vigorous in opposing the expansion of international trade as part of "globalization" without what it considered appropriate safeguards, especially for American jobs and, to some extent, for workers' rights worldwide. Organized labor played a significant part in the November 1999 demonstrations in Seattle that disrupted a meeting of the World Trade Organization. In January 2000, at the World Economic Forum in Davos, Switzerland, where protests on a similar scale were not feasible, some of the leaders of the protests in Seattle were invited to participate. Sweeney, who attended for his third year, was particularly visible. In this setting Sweeney and his allies urged the kinds of safeguards they think necessary on corporate and political leaders from around the world. Organized labor, however, did not appear to play a major role in the demonstrations that sought to disrupt the annual meeting of the World Bank and International Monetary Fund in Washington in early spring 2000.

In early 2000, major attention of organized labor was focused on preventing Congress from granting permanent normal trade relations to

China. The poor human rights record of China was often used as an explanation for the opposition. Protection of American jobs was, of course, the primary motivation for the unions' position. Among other efforts, the AFL-CIO launched a week-long television ad campaign in fifteen congressional districts where the members, six Republicans and nine Democrats, were thought to be particularly vulnerable to the message. This struggle put the AFL-CIO in direct conflict with agricultural interests, which stood to gain major new exports, and with President Clinton and Vice President Albert Gore (Rogers 2000).

Labor lost this battle in the House of Representatives on May 24 by a vote of 237 to 197, with 73 Democrats joining the majority. For the most part, labor leaders did not seek to punish the Democrats who voted against their views or Vice President Gore, who endorsed President Clinton's position, although with little passion. Their paramount interest in 2000 was to help elect Gore as president and to restore a Democratic majority to the House of Representatives in the November election (Greenhouse 2000b; Eilperin and Broder 2000). But some individual union leaders remained more hostile to Gore and to defecting congressional Democrats.

Similar reductions in labor's legislative influence in the 1980s and 1990s took place in a number of states as more governorships were won by Republicans and as more state legislative bodies saw new Republican majorities. Ohio serves as a good example. A labor-friendly Democrat was elected governor for four-year terms in 1982 and 1986. A Republican not noted for close ties to organized labor won the elections in 1990 and 1994. Another Republican who fit that description won the governorship in the 1998 election, although a meeting of the state AFL-CIO with him early in 1999 went well as he pledged not to pursue an antilabor agenda. The state Senate was controlled by labor-friendly Democrats for parts of the 1970s and 1980s. But the Republicans regained it for the rest of the 1980s and all of the 1990s beginning with the 1984 election. The worst loss was the Ohio House of Representatives, which went Democratic in the 1972 election and returned to a Republican majority in the 1994 election. The Republican majority was reelected in both 1996 and 1998.

The same Democrat, Vern Riffe, was the powerful Speaker of the Ohio House of Representatives throughout the last twenty of the twenty-two years of the Democratic majority. He did not run for reelection in 1994 and was succeeded by a Republican Speaker in the House. Riffe and the Democratic caucus in the House—which he controlled—often worked closely with the leaders of organized labor in Ohio. His successor was not closely allied with labor.

In general, labor laws at both the federal and state levels have become less hospitable to organized labor in the last several decades. Labor has not been able to win battles alone on its core issues, whether it be congressional consideration of common situs picketing[1] in the 1970s or state-level consideration of workers' compensation reform in the 1990s.

Electoral Influence

Labor has had some modest electoral successes in recent years. And it has even more potential for additional successes. Some of its successes have been in supporting winning candidates, although it is not reasonable to claim that labor alone "won" the elections in which their favored candidates prevailed. But organized labor surely did play a helpful role in electing and reelecting President Clinton in 1992 and 1996. The AFL-CIO mounted a major campaign to recapture the U.S. House of Representatives in 1996 by allocating $35 million for independent expenditures. This supplemented $46 million contributed by union PACs to candidates. Unions also contributed $9.5 million in soft money. International unions spent an additional $6.7 million in independent expenditures. Labor fell short of achieving the goal of a Democratic majority in the House, but it is accurate to suggest that the Republicans saw their already modest majority after the 1994 election (235 seats of the 435 in the House) dwindle after the 1996 election to 226 seats in part because of the efforts and spending of organized labor. The efforts of organized labor helped the president and Democrats in general portray incumbent Republicans as unacceptably extremist in their conservatism. Concretely, prolabor House candidates won in forty-seven targeted races involving seventeen "at risk" incumbent Democrats, twelve open seats, and eighteen incumbent Republicans who were defeated. Likewise, some of the favorable outcomes for Democrats in the 1998 and 2000 congressional elections can be attributed to union political activity.

Labor remains important in helping to determine the identity of Democratic nominees for president. Even though Richard Gephardt, the Missouri Democrat serving as minority leader in the U.S. House of Representatives, withdrew from the race for the 2000 nomination despite his close ties to organized labor, it was clear that Vice President Gore, although challenged only by former senator Bill Bradley, continued vigorously to court organized labor. For example, he played a leading role in getting the Clinton administration to limit federal contracts for companies with poor records on issues about which labor was concerned (Simendinger 1999).

The AFL-CIO decided to endorse Gore very early in the process, in October 1999, while the Teamsters and UAW decided to endorse him many months later, the UAW in August 2000, and the Teamsters in September 2000. Although the AFL-CIO did not agree with Gore's support of the

Clinton administration's free trade positions, it felt he was better than the opposition, Bradley, and also felt that if they endorsed him early he would owe them enough that, if he were elected, they would be able to have some influence on his positions. Organized labor was very helpful to Gore during the caucus and primary season that led to Bradley's withdrawal in March 2000 after a string of Gore victories.

An article in the *Washington Post* summarized the key reasons for the continuing power of organized labor in Democratic presidential nomination politics:

> Despite sagging union membership, labor remains the one player in the Democratic coalition with the money, membership, staff and discipline to guarantee even a political long shot a presence in every presidential caucus and primary. Of the 4,320 delegates dancing the macarena at last year's [1996] Democratic National Convention, more than 800 were members of AFL-CIO affiliates. Throw in members of the National Education Association, and one-fourth of the convention carried union cards.
>
> Labor was expected to be even more visible in 2000. Since Sweeney's election as AFL-CIO president in 1995, organized labor's political apparatus—an operation that once seemed barely capable of cranking out a leaflet—has been staffed by skilled zealots who know how to spend what advertising people call "serious money" on TV, radio and direct mail. (Grossfeld 1997)

As noted several times, unions have also had some electoral successes, although not enough to displace Republican control of the U.S. House of Representatives, a primary goal of organized labor. Labor has also won some ballot issues at the state level. For example, in Ohio in 1997 organized labor successfully led the effort, through a referendum, to repeal parts of a workers' compensation law that labor felt was harmful to the interests of injured workers. In 1998, organized labor—minus the OEA—was on the winning side (which was opposed) of a school financing issue submitted to a referendum. Labor and its allies felt the proposal provided inadequate resources and the issue was defeated by an incredible four to one ratio even though it had the support of the Republican state political leadership, including the governor, most of the major newspapers in the state, and most of the business community. Some sizeable portion of the no vote also came from the conservative end of the electorate—that is, individuals who simply did not want new taxes for virtually any purpose, including education.

In California, organized labor successfully helped thwart an effort to restrict its ability to collect money from members for political use. The proposition that was defeated in June 1998 would have required unions annually to obtain written permission from each union member before spending money collected from dues for political purposes.

Organized labor has had enough successes to retain its reputation as a political force with which to be reckoned. This reputation can sometimes lead to accommodation even from political foes. For example, the Republican-controlled Ohio legislature will be wary of doing anything to change workers' compensation because of the recent success of organized labor in helping to get the electorate to overturn a decision in the legislature.

In recent years, organized labor has demonstrated heightened sophistication in addressing the changing nature of lobbying and campaigning. It has been aggressive in funding issue advocacy ads—a form of free speech protected by the U.S. Supreme Court. It recognizes that better coordination is needed among the constituent elements of the labor movement. It has become more nimble in telling its story through traditional media outlets as well as the newer modes of communication. And, it has modernized its lobbying and communication efforts. The current national leaders understand the changed political and media environment better than previous leaders.

But these communication efforts will have limited impact if organized labor fails to stop the decline in its own membership. And, even if the decline is stopped, or even reversed, labor leaders still face a major challenge in mobilizing the members for specific political efforts. Leaders need to demonstrate anew that they can deliver the goods—votes and workers—politically.

Unions can also point to some electoral successes in a generally bleak political landscape. We have previously summarized those successes. But the bottom line is that they have not been sufficient to produce a prounion political climate.

LEADER–MEMBER INTERACTION

A critical question for union leaders, as well as for outside observers interested in the future of organized labor, is what chance labor leaders have to mobilize members to pursue political ends favored by the leaders. Under what conditions are leaders more likely to succeed? What makes members more receptive to the mobilization efforts of leaders for political activity?

From the viewpoint of labor leaders at all levels—state and national AFL-CIO, state and national NEA, the leadership of individual international unions, leaders of central labor councils (CLCs) at the city/county level, and the leaders of individual locals—mobilizing members for desired political activity presents both a collective challenge and an individual challenge. Collectively, the challenge above the level of the local union is hierarchical: each layer in the federated structure needs to figure out how to motivate the leaders of the layers that are smaller than they are (although not "subordinate" in a truly hierarchical sense) to become interested in and then committed to pursuing designated political goals. The ultimate personal challenge is for the leaders of the locals, once they are committed, to figure out how to motivate individual members to join together to pursue the desired political ends. Much of the analysis in the preceding chapters focuses on both sides of this leader-member relationship at the local level.

Local union officers generally support political action. They have the most potential influence over members since they know them personally. Individual union members also generally support political action, although they make distinctions between types of political action and the strength of the support they give those various types. The Ohio data from 1990 through 1996 show that union member support for voter registration drives is very high, followed by candidate endorsements, lobbying for legislation, and collecting money for campaign contributions in that order.

Union leaders at all levels have to choose the issues on which to be active. At the local level, they clearly cannot be active on everything that is presented by more central union leadership and hope to succeed equally well on everything. They know that they must pick and choose among various issues, candidates, and elections on which to be most active. They can, of course, take positions on a wide variety of issues, candidates, and elections. But how to prioritize among them and how to choose major mobilization efforts remains a challenge. They need to consider the probability of success in approaching the membership about becoming active on any specific matter. And, of course, they need to develop strategies for enhancing their chances of success in mobilizing the members.

As the leaders of a local union seek support from the their members for a candidate or an issue, they need to decide which members are most likely to support them. A good local union leader knows his or her members well enough to know which members have been politically active and which ones are likely to be politically active again. Likewise, a good leader will be able to assess the preferences and agendas of individual members so that he or she can motivate them to undertake desired political activity by appealing to those preferences and agendas. Local union leaders tend to make these assessments informally and continuously. Some unions above the local level have commissioned formal surveys of their members in order to ascertain their preferences. Leaders also need to determine whether there is a payoff in building coalitions with other unions and the CLC in the area.

At the national level, the Sweeney-led AFL-CIO has switched to an outside strategy from an inside strategy for wielding political power. An inside strategy relies primarily on ties with officeholders and private lobbying to get legislative ends achieved. This had become the dominant AFL-CIO strategy nationally over several decades preceding the loss of Congress by the Democrats in the 1994 election. Organized labor in Washington calculated that maintaining close ties with Democratic members of the House and Senate, particularly senior members, would see them through vacillating political fortunes at the electoral level. Even in the days of a Republican Senate and president from 1981 through 1987, the national labor leaders felt they could make more headway—at least in blocking initiatives they did not like—by working with the senior members of the majority in the Democratically controlled House of Representatives. However, once that bastion of Democratic control fell into Republican hands after the 1994 elections the inside strategy looked barren. Even though the Democrats controlled the presidency, the incumbent, Clinton, and his administration were not particularly close to organized labor and were clearly at loggerheads on international trade policy.

Fortunately for Sweeney he launched his campaign for the presidency of the AFL-CIO just after the Republican electoral triumph of 1994. He articulated the necessity of moving to an outside strategy in which organized labor would not rely exclusively on inside ties with officials but would, instead, put much more reliance on creating a climate of public opinion and a formidable but targeted set of electoral activities. His general argument was that a dominant inside strategy led to complacency and, under the changed national political conditions following the 1994 election, failure. His argument might have prevailed in any event, but it was certainly given a major boost by election results of 1994.

Union leaders also constantly have to balance the amount of energy they spend and ask others to spend on political matters compared to the amount of energy used on economic goals, especially collective bargaining and, to a lesser extent, organizing new companies. Within the political realm, the leaders also have to decide what priority to place on fairly narrow goals (e.g., to elect Gwendolyn Cranch to Congress in 2000) versus broader goals (e.g., to mobilize union opinion on a major issue that affects labor in order to aid lobbying efforts with the state legislature or Congress).

In seeking to mobilize members to make desired voting choices, the evidence suggests that leaders enhance their chances of success by linking policy positions with individual candidates. Making this link can help underscore the importance of voting for a specific individual in terms of likely future policy outcomes. Union leaders have a slight advantage in magnifying their impact if they can increase the percentage of their members who make the desired choices because the turnout of union members tends to be a bit higher than the general population.

Personal appeals from local union leaders to individual members of that local for specific political activity are the most effective way of seeking support. Over time, a good leader of a union local will get to know his or her members very well and will develop a memory bank of who is reliable politically and also who is likely to respond positively to specific requests for political action of various kinds. Knowledge of which issues are most relevant to which members is also essential to producing the desired outcomes.

Leadership skills matter. Effective leaders do not simply ask for specific actions from members. They prepare the ground for those requests in several ways. First, they provide opportunities for political action through first identifying those opportunities and then publicizing them. As already indicated, a skillful leader will not present every opportunity to the members but will make judgments about the relative importance of those opportunities and the relative appeal of different opportunities to the membership.

Second, leaders need to provide training for members who want to engage in political activity so that they are maximally effective. Third, leaders, as already indicated, have to make choices about what requests to make of which specific members. Presumably, they want to enhance their chances of short-run success by approaching the members most likely to respond positively. At the same time, an adroit leader will also seek to expand his or her roster of approachable activists. Relying on the same core time after time eventually has diminishing returns as members leave for other employment, retire, or simply get tired of political action. New blood is always needed.

What members do leaders most often approach as they work at the task of political mobilization? Our data on Ohio provide a brief profile of such members. The most important predictor is level of education, which is a good surrogate for the possession of civic skills and civic interest. Level of interest itself is a major factor in predicting which members will respond most favorably to leadership requests. Level of commitment to the union is also a good predictor of positive responses. Those with a stronger commitment will be more likely to look to the union for some meaningful information on political matters. And, of course, individuals who agree most closely with union political positions are most likely to be responsive.

The modal most mobilizable union member for political purposes, then, is someone who

- is relatively highly educated,
- is interested in politics,

- is committed to the union and looks to it for political cues, and
- is in agreement with core union political positions.

Adept leaders have an image of their individual members on these dimensions and can accurately predict individual responses to requests. This accuracy of prediction also helps a skilled leader make judgments about which specific issues and candidates to choose for serious attention, which to endorse only nominally with no expenditure of real effort, and which simply to ignore. The issues and candidates are always more numerous than the chances for having genuine impact.

When a union, at any level, endorses a specific candidate, the members, of course, do not all agree on that choice. Nor do they turn out to vote the desired way. There is substantial evidence, however, that union endorsements—when targeted to races that are in doubt—can have the desired effect and can, in some cases, provide the margin of narrow victories. Gary C. Jacobson (1999) found that careful targeting by organized labor of freshmen Republicans in the U.S. House of Representatives resulted in Democratic victories in seven of the twelve targeted seats. Evidence from the Ohio elections we analyzed suggests some important marginal influence when unions engaged in similar targeting. Union leaders, if they are persuasive in getting additional marginal votes for endorsed candidates, do have the added advantage that union members turn out at a slightly higher rate than the population in general.

CONCLUSION

That American unions face an uphill battle in resuscitating their economic and political strength is hardly news. Much of the descriptive material in this book has documented the erosion of union strength, both economically and politically. However, is that strength foreordained to continue its decline? Is rejuvenation impossible? The answer to both of these questions is no. However, there is no doubt that if unions want at least to stabilize their importance, let alone increase it, they have a task ahead of them that will take great energy and commitment. Success is far from assured and the grade going up the hill may simply be too steep to allow success.

John Sweeney, as the national AFL-CIO president since 1995, has led unions in making some genuine change in the nature of union activity, both economically and politically. Sweeney, in his campaign for office, made it clear that he understood that unions were in danger of becoming artifacts from the past and irrelevant to modern American life. He does not intend to allow this to happen but instead is working with others in the labor movement to make unions increasingly relevant.

Most union leaders seem to understand that they have to be creative in seeking to regain some of their lost clout and importance, both economically and politically. Most also seem to understand that economic relevance and strength is the necessary prerequisite for political strength. Unions have money to offer in political campaigns to be sure. But, more important, they can offer numbers of people as voters and as workers in various capacities in campaigns for offices and in referenda. In short, organizational successes are a necessary prelude to increased political importance, particularly as unions pursue a strategy of outside influence, rather than relying primarily on inside contacts with officeholders.

Targets of opportunity for organizing previously unorganized workers, industries, and companies are present, although, particularly in a strong economy, they are neither numerous nor easy. Unions seem to be willing to find targets for organizing among immigrants, in dispersed industries such as home care, in companies with long-standing successful opposition to unionization, and in regions of the country traditionally not hospitable to unionization. Successes will be hard to come by and are certainly not guaranteed. But the effort will need to be made on many fronts unless unions simply accept continued decline in membership—or at least stability at a low level—as inevitable and irreversible.

Most union leaders have made the necessary adjustments to dealing with a much more diverse workforce than was the case several decades ago. The proportion of women, minorities, and immigrants in the workforce has increased. At the same time, more white-collar workers have been organized as the economy has moved away from a blue-collar base to a strongly white-collar base. As the number of traditional unionized workers (e.g., auto workers, steelworkers, and building trades workers) have dwindled, those remaining have also become solidly middle class economically. This fact also worked in favor of increased political conservatism on their part.

The achievement of middle-class status has also altered residential patterns for union members. These well-off workers have moved to a variety of suburbs, which has made it more difficult for union leaders to convene them for union meetings and various union-sponsored events. They interact with each other when not on the job less than would have been the case when they tended to live in the same neighborhood that was fairly close to the workplace. This also makes the job of union leaders in organized workplaces more difficult. The "boys in the bar near the factory after work" stereotype has been replaced by a picture of men and women living in scattered residential areas taking their kids to soccer after work rather than continuing to interact with each other.

One route to dealing with declining membership has been for unions to merge. In some cases merger efforts have gone well; in other cases problems have arisen. The proposed merger of three major industrial unions (the United Auto Workers, the United Steelworkers, and the International Association of Machinists), discussed in detail since 1995, did not take place in 2000 as initially announced. Different traditions and practices in the three unions have set back the planned merger, although the UAW and USWA may go ahead without the IAM (Greenhouse 1999e). Even though a single, large union would have more potential for new organizing drives, this merger would represent a setback for organized labor.

The evidence we have analyzed suggests that mobilization of union members by leaders for political purposes cannot be a haphazard matter. Careful planning of whom to ask for what contribution of time and energy appears to be a key to increased success in mobilizing members for political ends. This means that unions intent on converting whatever economic power they have into various forms of political power would be well advised to plan mobilization campaigns among their own members with considerable care. Unions should also pay attention to appropriate staffing of their offices to focus on political mobilization.

The evidence we have analyzed in this book suggests that, above all, union leaders have to worry about their basic economic strength. Their political strength and rate of political success will continue to dwindle if their membership continues to shrink. The evidence is also strong that unions have considerable political power left when effectively channeled and need to consider both how to use it best and most effectively in the short run and how to plan for the longer run.

In the political realm, labor leaders need to make requests of their members. But they also need to pay attention to the antecedents of getting favorable responses to those requests. They must especially be aware that programs to increase commitment to the union in general will also result in greater success in mobilizing their members for political purposes. Internal union education programs—both about the union itself and about the importance of the political context for union success in achieving core economic goals—are central as potential means for increasing member commitment to the union.

Some union leaders clearly understand the challenges they face. They know that the changed environment we have sketched—more diverse membership, declining membership, more conservative Republicans in power in more places throughout the nation, and an increasingly hostile legal environment—has to be faced and dealt with straightforwardly. The dual tasks of seeking to stem the hemorrhaging of membership and maintaining credibility as a political force at the same time are not for the faint of heart. But unless organized labor makes headway on both the economic and political fronts simultaneously, the future for unions does, indeed, look dim.

NOTE

1. If common situs picketing is legal, then construction trade unions with a grievance against a single contractor are allowed to picket and potentially shut down an entire building site since, presumably, other unions working at the site would refuse to cross picket lines. There was a major effort by unions to make common situs picketing legal in 1977 but Congress did not make the change and such picketing continued to be banned as a form of "secondary boycott," which is outlawed by the Taft-Hartley Act.

Appendix A

Research Design

We used data and information from many sources in constructing our analysis of some major union political activities and their influence. In assessing national developments, we use data from the American National Election Studies from their beginning in 1952 through the 1996 election. Naturally, we also rely on the literature on union political activity, much of which focuses on national activity. Also, one of the authors conducted interviews with national union officials.

We also focused considerable attention on Ohio, where we have developed our own data. Many of the data come from four statewide surveys taken just after the 1990, 1992, 1994, and 1996 elections. Details on these surveys are provided in appendix B. The authors also interviewed a number of Ohio union leaders over a number of years. Several focus groups were also held to supplement survey findings.

Ohio has much to commend it as a site for intensive examination of union political activity. Five points are relevant. First, unions in Ohio have a broad membership base and have a tradition of political activism. In 1995, there were almost nine hundred thousand union members in Ohio. This represented the fifth highest number of union members in the nation, exceeded only by California, New York, Illinois, and Michigan. This number also placed Ohio in the top ten states in terms of union density (percentage of the workforce unionized) (see Hirsch and Macpherson 1997, 26–7).

Second, organized labor in Ohio has the staff necessary to mount effective political mobilization efforts, including full-time political staff in the Ohio AFL-CIO central office and six county-level central labor councils with full-time officers, part of whose duties include political mobilization. National officials who commented in interviews were unanimous in stating their view that Ohio was one of the most active and innovative states in terms of union leaders seeking to mobilize members. Since we focus on mobilization as a key phenomenon, this presented us with a good laboratory in which to work.

Third, Ohio allows both compulsory union membership ("closed shops") and unionization of public employees. This situation helps produce a very diverse set of union members in the state. It also allows us to analyze the differences between union members who joined voluntarily and those who had no choice, and to compare the attitudes and behavior of three large, diverse groups of union members: those from traditional industrial and service unions, civil servants, and teachers.

Fourth, Ohio is a diverse state in several senses. It has major cities such as Cleveland, Cincinnati, Columbus, Toledo, Akron, and Dayton that also have several suburbs, while major portions of the state are small-town and rural. It has both a significant Appalachian population in the southeastern part of the state and a long-time traditional manufacturing population in the northeast. It has significant minority populations—especially African-American and, increasingly, Hispanic and Asian-American, with a sprinkling of Native American. Different parts of the state have quite different political traditions and habits that all have political impact. In short, although it would be foolish to claim that any single state is "representative" of the entire nation, it is quite appropriate to claim that Ohio is a microcosm of much of the variation—economic, demographic, political, and social—that characterizes the United States as a whole.

Fifth, Ohio is politically competitive. Both Democrats and Republicans win. Statewide races are usually competitive, as are presidential races. Party balance in the Ohio delegation in the U.S. House of Representatives and party control of the two chambers in the Ohio General Assembly fluctuate over time. As the new century opens, the Republicans are in solid control of both houses of the state legislature and all of the statewide elected administrative offices. Ohio is also an important state in political terms nationally and has the seventh largest number of U.S. Representatives and electoral votes in presidential elections.

Appendix B

The Ohio Union Surveys

The Ohio union surveys were telephone surveys conducted immediately following the 1990, 1992, 1994, and 1996 elections. The first three were conducted at Ohio State University by the Polimetrics Laboratory in the Department of Political Science. The 1996 survey was conducted at Ohio State by the Center for Survey Research in the College of Social and Behavioral Sciences. Funding for all four surveys came from Ohio State's Center for Labor Research.

There were two samples in each survey: one drawn from lists of union members in Ohio; the second was drawn from the entire adult population of Ohioans. The union sample was selected from three lists of members that were provided by the Ohio AFL-CIO, the Ohio Education Association (OEA), and the Ohio Civil Service Employees Association (OCSEA). The OCSEA declined to participate in the 1996 survey. Each list was systematically sampled proportional to its size in the total union population. This sampling design allowed us to compare, for example, the sample of the Ohio population and the union sample, nonunion Ohioans with union members, and AFL-CIO versus OCSEA versus OEA members.

In the 1990 survey, there were 750 respondents each in the union and Ohio samples for a total of 1500 respondents. In subsequent years, the number of respondents ranged from 613 to 617 in the union samples and from 410 to 422 in the Ohio samples.

The topics about which we asked, the question order, and most of the questions, were the same each year. The topics included: the member's attitudes towards unions, reasons for belonging to the union, problem agenda for the election, opinions on major economic and social issues, perceptions of union leaders' and coworkers' opinions on these same issues, party identification, ideology, vote turnout and choice in national and state elections that year, sources of political information, perception

179

of union electoral activities, participation in union electoral activities, attitudes toward the legitimacy of union political activities, and demographic characteristics. Nonunion members in the random sample of Ohioans were only asked demographic and election- and issue-related questions. Because we surveyed across four different elections, inevitably the precise wording of some questions varied according to the candidates and issues important in the election. We also added questions to address hypotheses regarding mobilization, participation, and voting that developed as the research progressed. Nevertheless, we have reasonably comparable surveys conducted across four distinct elections. Thus, we are able to replicate our analyses for multiple elections giving us greater confidence in our results when similar findings are obtained.

Appendix C

Variable Measurements: Ohio Union Surveys

Appropriateness. The number of political activities (out of three: making endorsements, registering voters, and donating money to candidates) the member thought it was "OK" for unions to perform.

Class. The respondent's self-described social class (1 = working class; 0 = middle class). Members who responded that they "did not think of [themselves] in those terms," were recoded at the mean.

Commitment. An index composed of three variables that measure the member's belief in the union movement, personal importance of union membership, and "polar affect" towards unions. These are based on the following: "I believe in the union movement and what it's done for workers in America" (1–5 agreement scale); "In general, how important is your labor union membership to you?" (very, somewhat, not important). The three categories were rescaled to be weighted equally to the other variables in the commitment index. Polar affect measures not only the liking of members of one's own group but also dislike of the members of an out-group (A. Miller et al. 1981, 496). It is measured by the difference between the feeling thermometer ratings of labor unions and big business. The polar affect score was divided into approximately equal quintiles by number of cases so that all three variables in the index would be weighted equally.

Coworkers' Support. The member's assessment of whether most of the people with whom he or she works closely strongly support the union. Response categories were: yes, mixed, or no.

Education. The measure for the respondent's level of education is a seven-point scale: grade school or less; nine to twelve years; high school diploma or general equivalency diploma; some college, nondegree; associate's degree; bachelor's degree; and postgraduate degree. In models of mobilization and participation, education acts as a proxy for the member's skills for political action.

Effective Representation. The member's evaluation of the extent to which his or her union represents his or her interests on the job effectively. The response categories were a four-point scale: very effective, somewhat effective, somewhat ineffective, and very ineffective.

Efficacy. An index based on respondent's level of agreement, on a 1–5 scale, with three standard American National Election Study efficacy statements: "Public officials don't care what people like me think"; "People like me don't have a say in what government does"; and "Politics and government seem so complicated."

Endorsement Index. Measures the extent to which a member is willing to use the union endorsement when making vote decisions. It is based on responses to the following questions: (1) "Here is a list of sources from which people get information about government, public affairs, candidates, and issues. For each of these sources, please tell me if it was very important, somewhat important, or not at all important in helping you decide how to vote: labor unions . . ."; (2) "In general, do you think your labor union has an effect on how you vote? [if yes] Is this a big effect, a moderate effect, or a small effect?"; (3) "If you knew that a candidate were endorsed by labor unions, would you be more likely or less likely to vote for that candidate, or would it make no difference?"; and (4) "Is it OK or not OK for labor unions to try to affect their members by endorsing candidates and issues?"

Friends' Support. The member's assessment of whether most of his or her friends support the union movement. Response categories were: yes, mixed, or no.

Gender. 1 = male; 0 = female.

Geographically Active. Scores are based on ratings given by the union international staff. The score is a dummy variable (1 = lives in a politically active region; 0 = lives in a less active region).

Helps with Wages and Benefits. The member's assessment of the union's assistance in gaining material benefits on the job. It is based on the member's strength of agreement, on a five-point scale, with the following statement: "Union membership helps me bargain with management for more money and benefits."

Income. Is measured based on the respondent's classification of his or her family's yearly income into one of seven categories: less than $10,000; $10,001–$20,000; $20,001–$30,000; $30,001–$40,000; $40,001–$50,000; $50,001–$60,000; more than $60,000.

Informational Dependence. "Here is a list of sources from which people get information about government, public affairs, candidates and issues. For each of the sources, please tell me if it was very important, somewhat important, or not at all important in helping you decide how to vote: labor unions . . ." (1–3 scale).

Number of Activities. The number of election campaign activities (out of a list of seven) the member perceived his or her union sponsored. The activities included: phone banks, literature distribution, placement of yard signs, voter registration, attendance at candidate meetings, solicitation of contributions for candidates or ballot issues, and work at party headquarters.

Opportunities. (*See Number of Activities.*)

Participation. Whether or not the member participated in any union sponsored campaign activity (1 = yes; 0 = no).

Participation in the Union. Whether or not the member claims to have ever taken part in union grievance procedures, strikes, picketing, or contract negotiations (1 = yes; 0 = no).

Percentage Support for Democratic Candidates. The proportion of votes cast for Democratic candidates in national and statewide races in a given election. These candidates included: U.S. president, U.S. senator, Ohio governor, Ohio auditor, Ohio secretary of state, Ohio treasurer, and justices of the Ohio Supreme Court.

Percentage of Support for Union-endorsed Candidates. The proportion of votes cast for candidates endorsed by the members' union (the Ohio AFL-CIO, the Ohio Civil Service Employee Association, and the Ohio Education Association) in national and statewide races in a given election. These candidates included: U.S. president, U.S. senator, Ohio governor, Ohio auditor, Ohio secretary of state, Ohio treasurer, and justices of the Ohio Supreme Court.

Political Agreement. The political agreement between the member and union leaders is calculated by summing the absolute values of the differences between the member's party identification and ideology and his or her perception of his or her union leaders' party identifications and ideologies.

Partisan proximity is the difference between the respondent's answer to two questions: "Generally speaking, do you usually think of yourself as a Republican, a Democrat, an Independent, or what?" and "Generally speaking, do you usually think of leaders of labor unions as Republican, Democrat, Independent, or what?" Ideological proximity is the difference between the respondent's answer to: "We hear a lot of talk these days about liberals and conservatives. What would you call yourself, very liberal, somewhat liberal, middle of the road, somewhat conservative, very conservative, or don't you think of yourself in these terms?" and to "And how about labor union leaders?" (same five options).

The party and ideological proximity scales were then added together into a single scale and inverted so that the higher the member's level of political agreement with union leaders, the more likely he or she will be contacted to participate in union political activities. A number of members did not know the party and/or ideology of their leaders. To avoid losing these cases for the statistical models, those who answered "don't know" to any of the leader questions were recoded as distant from leaders because they are not participating in politics based on agreement if they do not know what the union positions are. Members who answered "don't know" or who refused to answer any question on their own partisanship or ideology retained missing values.

Political Interest. The member's estimate of how much attention he or she pays to politics (1–5 scale).

Politically Active Union. Each international's score on the active union scale is the total points the union received based on nominations by union international officers during interviews. One point was given to an international for each respondent who named it as one of the most active unions; one-half point was given for each respondent who named the international as moderately active. Survey respondents received the score of the international of which they are a member.

Race. The respondent's racial identity (1 = nonwhite; 0 = white).

Receiving a Request to Participate. Whether or not the union asked the member to participate in any union sponsored campaign activity (1 = yes; 0 = no).

Religion. The respondent's religious preference (1 = nonprotestant; 0 = protestant).

Responsiveness to Mobilization Appeals. A member's responsiveness to union mobilization appeals is measured by the total number of mobilized activities in which the member claims to have participated. Mobilized participation occurs when the member claimed the union asked him or her to engage in a political activity *and* he or she complied with that request.

Targeted District. Whether or not the member resides within a congressional district targeted by their union. A computer program classified members into Ohio congressional districts based on their phone numbers (1 = lives in targeted district; 0 = does not live in targeted district).

Tenure. The respondent's estimate of the total years he or she has belonged to a labor union. In the "response to mobilization appeals" equation, both the linear and the logarithmic terms are entered in order to capture the diminishing marginal impact of organizational experience on activism (see Rothenberg 1992, 110–11).

Turnout. Whether the respondent claims to have voted in the election (1 = voted; 0 = did not vote).

Union Family. Whether or not anyone in the individual's immediate family was a union member when he or she was a child living at home (1 = yes; 0 = no).

Union Political Activities. (See *Number of Activities.*)

Voluntary Membership. Whether the member joined voluntarily or was "coerced" by a closed shop (1 = voluntary membership; 0 = required membership).

References

Abramson, Jill, and Steven Greenhouse. 1997. "Labor's Victory on 'Fast Track' Show Its Power." *New York Times*, 12 November, A1, A16.

AFL-CIO. 1996. *Building to Win, Building to Last: 1996 Election Results*. Washington: AFL-CIO.

———. 2000. "Labor 2000: Working Families Vote." Available at: www.aflcio.org/labor2000/election.htm. Last accessed: November 9, 2000.

AFL-CIO Committee on Political Education. N.d. "Checkoff Yes, Union Yes: A Step-by-step Guide to Collecting Political Funds!" Washington, D.C.: AFL-CIO COPE.

Alexander, Herbert E. 1992. *Financing Politics*. 4th ed. Washington: Congressional Quarterly Press.

American National Election Studies. 1952–98. Available at: www.unich.edu/~nes. Last accessed: November 14, 2000.

Baer, Denise L., and Martha Bailey. 1994. "The Nationalization of Education Politics: The National Education Association PAC and the 1992 Elections." In *Risky Business?: PAC Decisionmaking in Congressional Elections*. Ed. Robert Biersack, Paul S. Herrnson, and Clyde Wilcox. Armonk, N.Y.: Sharpe.

Ball, Jeffrey, Glenn Burkins, and Gregory L. White. 1999. "Why Labor Unions Have Grown Reluctant to Use the 'S' Word." *Wall Street Journal*, 16 December.

Balz, Dan, and David S. Broder. 1998. "Shaken Republicans Count Losses, Debate Blame." *Washington Post*, 5 November, A1, A34.

Barling, Julian, Clive Fullagar, and E. Kevin Kelloway. 1992. *The Union and Its Members: A Psychological Approach*. New York: Oxford University Press.

Baumgartner, Frank R., and Beth L. Leech. 1998. *Basic Interests: The Importance of Groups in Politics and Political Science*. Princeton, N.J.: Princeton University Press.

Biersack, Robert, Paul S. Herrnson, and Clyde Wilcox, eds. 1999. *After the Revolution: PACs, Lobbies, and the Republican Congress*. Boston: Allyn and Bacon.

Bok, Derek C., and John T. Dunlop. 1970. *Labor and the American Community*. New York, N.Y.: Simon and Schuster.

Brady, Henry E., Kay Lehman Schlozman, and Sidney Verba. 1999. "Prospecting for Participants: Rational Expectations and the Recruitment of Political Activists." *American Political Science Review* 93:153–68.

Brehm, John, and Scott Gates. 1996. *Working, Shirking, and Sabotage: Bureaucratic Response to a Democratic Public.* Ann Arbor: University of Michigan Press.

Broder, David S. 2000. "Voters' Views Sharply Divided." *Washington Post,* 8 November, A1.

Buckley v. Valeo, 424 U.S. 1 (1976).

Bureau of Labor Statistics. 1999. "Current Population Survey, Union Members Technical Notes." Available at: stats.bls.gov/bishome.htm. Last accessed: July 7, 2000.

Bureau of National Affairs. 1999. "Statistical Abstracts, Union Membership and Earnings Data Book, Compilations from the Current Population Survey." Washington: Bureau of National Affairs.

Burkins, Glenn. 1998. "Labor Gears up Now for '99 Debate on Social Security." *Wall Street Journal,* 28 September.

———. 1999. "Labor Unions See Membership Rise Slightly." *Wall Street Journal,* 26 January.

Burns, Peter F., Peter L. Francia, and Paul S. Hernnson. 2000. "Labor at Work: Union Campaign Activities and Legislative Payoffs in the U.S. House of Representatives." *Social Science Quarterly* 81:507–22.

Burstein, Paul. 1998. "Interest Organizations, Political Parties, and the Study of Democratic Politics." In *Social Movements and American Political Institutions.* Ed. Anne N. Costain and Andrew S. McFarland. Lanham, Md.: Rowman and Littlefield.

Campbell, Angus, Philip E. Converse, Warren E. Miller, and Donald E. Stokes. 1960. *The American Voter.* New York: Wiley.

Cassata, Donna. 1998. "Independent Groups' Ads Increasingly Steer Campaigns." *CQ Weekly Reports,* 2 May, 1108–14.

Center for Responsive Politics. 2000. Available at: www.opensecrets.org/pubs. Last accessed: April 19, 2000.

Clark, Hugh M. 1982. *A Study of the Political Campaign Activities of Officers of Local Unions Affiliated with the Ohio AFL-CIO.* Columbus, Ohio: Decision Research Corporation.

Clark, Peter B., and James Q. Wilson. 1961. "Incentive Systems: A Theory of Organizations." *Administrative Science Quarterly* 6:129–66.

Clawson, Don, and Mary Ann Clawson. 1999. "What Has Happened to the US Labor Movement?" In *Annual Review of Sociology.* Vol. 25. Ed. Karen S. Cook and John Hagan. Palo Alto, Calif.: Annual Reviews.

Cole, Jeff. 2000. "Labor Says a White-collar Walkout at Boeing Boosts Change for Organizing." *Wall Street Journal,* 28 February.

Communication Workers of America (CWA) v. Beck, 487 U.S. 735 (1988).

Conover, Pamela Johnston. 1984. "The Influence of Group Identification on Political Perception and Evaluation." *Journal of Politics* 46:760–85.

Converse, Philip E., and A. Angus Campbell. 1968. "Political Standards in Secondary Groups." In *Group Dynamics.* 2nd ed. Ed. Dorwin Cartwright and Alvin Zander. New York: Harper and Row.

Cook, Constance E. 1998. "The Washington Higher Education Community: Moving Beyond Lobbying 101." In *Interest Group Politics.* 5th ed. Ed. Allan J. Cigler and Burdett A. Loomis. Washington: Congressional Quarterly Press.

Cornfield, Daniel B. 1999. "Shifts in Public Approval of Labor Unions in the United States, 1936–1999." Available at: www.gallup.com/poll/gs990902.asp. Last accessed: November 14, 2000.

Corrado, Anthony. 1997. "Financing the 1996 Election." In *The Election of 1996*. Ed. Gerald M. Pomper. Chatham, N.J.: Chatham House.

Craver, Charles B. 1993. *Can Unions Survive? The Rejuvenation of the American Labor Movement*. New York: New York University Press.

Dark, Taylor E. 1996. "Organized Labor and the Congressional Democrats: Reconsidering the 1980s." *Political Science Quarterly* 111:83–104.

———. 1999. *The Unions and the Democrats: An Enduring Alliance*. Ithaca, N.Y.: ILR Press.

Delaney, John Thomas. 1991. "The Future of Unions as Political Organization." *Journal of Labor Research* 12:373–87.

Delaney, John Thomas, Jack Fiorito, and Marick F. Masters. 1988. "The Effects of Union Organizational and Environmental Characteristics on Union Political Action." *American Journal of Political Science* 42:616–43.

Delaney, John Thomas, and Marick F. Masters. 1991. "Unions and Political Action." In *The State of the Unions*. Ed. George Strauss, Daniel G. Gallagher, and Jack Fiorito. Madison, Wisc.: Industrial Relations Research Association.

Delaney, John Thomas, Marick F. Masters, and Susan Schwochau. 1990. "Union Membership and Voting for COPE–endorsed Candidates." *Industrial and Labor Relations Review* 43:621–35.

Eilperin, Juliet. 2000. "Battle for the House: Labor on the Front Lines." *Washington Post*, 29 August, A1.

Eilperin, Juliet, and David S. Broder. 2000. "Despite UAW Threat, Low Risk Seen in China Vote." *Washington Post*, 24 May.

Epstein, Edwin M. 1980. "Business and Labor under the Federal Election Campaign Act of 1971." In *Parties, Interest Groups, and Campaign Finance Laws*. Ed. Michael Malbin. Washington: American Enterprise Institute.

Federal Election Commission. 2000. Available at: www.fec.gov. Last accessed: April 26, 2000.

Federal Election Commission (FEC) v. Massachusetts Citizens for Life, Inc., 479 U.S. 248 (1986).

Fields, Mitchell W., Marick F. Masters, and James W. Thacker. 1987. "Union Commitment and Membership Support for Political Action: An Exploratory Analysis." *Journal of Labor Research* 8:143–57.

Fink, Gary M. 1998. "Labor Law Revision and the End of the Postwar Labor Accord." In *Organized Labor and American Politics, 1894–1994: The Labor-Liberal Alliance*. Ed. Kevin Boyle. Albany: SUNY Press.

Foerstel, Karen. 1998. "Interest Groups Seek Best Value for Copious Campaign Dollars." *CQ Weekly Reports*, 12 December, 3295–8.

Form, William. 1995. *Segmented Labor, Fractured Politics: Labor Politics in American Life*. New York: Plenum.

———. 2000. *Can Social Movement Theory Explain Societal Change?* Ohio State University. Typescript.

Freeman, Jo. 1999. "Introduction." In *Waves of Protest: Social Movements since the Sixties*. Ed. Jo Freeman and Victoria Johnson. Lanham, Md.: Rowman and Littlefield.

Fullagar, Clive, and Julian Barling. 1989. "A Longitudinal Test of a Model of the Antecedents and Consequences of Union Loyalty." *Journal of Applied Psychology* 74:213–27.

Gais, Thomas L., and Jack L. Walker Jr. 1991. "Pathways to Influence in American Politics." In *Mobilizing Interest Groups in America*. Ed. Jack L. Walker Jr. Ann Arbor: University of Michigan Press.

Gerber, Elisabeth R. 1999. *The Populist Paradox*. Princeton, N.J.: Princeton University Press.

Gerber, Robin. 1999. "Building to Win, Building to Last: AFL-CIO COPE Takes on the Republican Congress." In *After the Revolution*. Ed. Robert Biersack, Paul S. Herrnson, Clyde Wilcox. Boston: Allyn and Bacon.

Gimpel, James G. 1998. "Grassroots Organizations and Equilibrium Cycles in Group Mobilization and Access." In *The Interest Group Connection*. Ed. Paul S. Herrnson, Ronald G. Shaiko, and Clyde Wilcox. Chatham, N.J.: Chatham House.

Goldfield, Michael. 1987. *The Decline of Organized Labor in the United States*. Chicago: University of Chicago Press.

Goldstein, Kenneth M. 1997. "Public Opinion Polls and Public Opinion in the 1996 Election." In *America's Choice*. Ed. William Crotty and Jerome M. Mileur. Guilford, Conn.: Dushkin.

———. 1999. *Interest Groups, Lobbying, and Participation in America*. New York: Cambridge University Press.

Gordon, Michael E., John W. Philpot, Robert E. Burt, Cynthia A. Thompson, and William E. Spiller. 1980. "Commitment to the Union: Development of a Measure and an Examination of Its Correlates." *Journal of Applied Psychology* 65:479–99.

Greenblatt, Alan. 1998. "Labor Wants out of the Limelight after Glare of Probes, Backlash." *CQ Weekly Reports*, 28 March, 787–91.

Greenhouse, Steven. 1997. "AFL-CIO Puts Recruiting at Top of Its Agenda." *New York Times*, 17 February, A8.

———. 1999a. "Activism Surges at Campuses Nationwide, and Labor Is at Issue." *New York Times*, 29 March.

———. 1999b. "A.M.A.'s Delegates Vote to Unionize." *New York Times*, 24 June.

———. 1999c. "In Biggest Drive since 1937, Union Gains a Victory." *New York Times*, 24 February, A1, A15.

———. 1999d. "The Labor Movement's Eager Risk-taker Hits Another Jackpot." *New York Times*, 27 February.

———. 1999e. "Three Unions Say Conflicts Will Delay Merger." *New York Times*, 25 June.

———. 1999f. "Union Leaders See Grim News in Labor Study." *New York Times*, 13 October.

———. 1999g. "Unions Need Not Apply: High-technology Sector Still Unmoved by Labor's Song." *New York Times*, 26 July.

———. 2000a. "A.F.L.–C.I.O. Votes to Spend More Than Ever before on Candidates." *New York Times*, 16 February.

———. 2000b. "China Trade Vote Splits Labor Movement: Backlash in Elections Threatened, but A.F.L.–C.I.O. Seeks Unity." *New York Times*, 28 May.

———. 2000c. "Despite Defeat on China Bill, Labor Is on Rise." *New York Times*, 30 May.

———. 2000d. "Growth in Unions' Membership in 1999 Was the Best in Two Decades." *New York Times*, 20 January.

———. 2000e. "Unions Predict Gain from Boeing Strike." *New York Times*, 21 March.

Greenstone, J. David. 1969. *Labor in American Politics*. Chicago: University of Chicago Press. Reprint, New York: Knopf, 1977.

Grossfeld, Jim. 1997. "Lobbying for the Union Label." *Washington Post National Weekly Edition*, 1 September.

Grossinger, Ken. 1998. "How Labor Defeated California's Proposition 226." *WorkingUSA* September/October, 84–90.

Grunwald, Juliana, and Robert Marshal Wells. 1996. "At Odds with Some Workers, AFL-CIO Takes Aim at GOP." *CQ Weekly Reports*, 16 April, 993–8.

Heberlig, Eric S. 1997. "Sprouting at the Grassroots: Organized Labor's Political Mobilization and Member's Political Activism." Ph.D. diss., Ohio State University.

———. 2000. "Coordinating Issues and Elections: Organized Labor in the Republican Era." *American Review of Politics* 20:163–80.

Heinz, John, Edward O. Laumann, Robert L. Nelson, and Robert H. Salisbury. 1993. *The Hollow Core: Private Interests in National Policy Making*. Cambridge, Mass.: Harvard University Press.

Heldman, Dan C., and Deborah L. Knight. 1980. *Unions and Lobbying: The Representation Function*. Arlington, Va.: Foundation for the Advancement of the Public Trust.

Herrnson, Paul S. 1995. *Congressional Elections*. Washington: Congressional Quarterly Press.

———. 1998a. *Congressional Elections*. 2nd ed. Washington: Congressional Quarterly Press.

———. 1998b. "Parties and Interest Groups in Postreform Congressional Elections." In *Interest Group Politics*. 5th ed. Ed. Allan J. Cigler and Burdett A. Loomis. Washington: Congressional Quarterly Press.

Herrnson, Paul S., and Clyde Wilcox. 1994. "Not So Risky Business: PAC Activity in 1992." In *Risky Business? PAC Decisionmaking in Congressional Elections*. Ed. Robert Biersack, Paul S. Herrnson, and Clyde Wilcox. Armonk, N.Y.: Sharpe.

Hirsch, Barry T., and David A. Macpherson. 1997. *Union Membership and Earnings Data Book*. Washington: Bureau of National Affairs.

Hojnacki, Marie. 1997. "Interest Groups' Decisions to Join Alliances or Work Alone." *American Journal of Political Science* 41:61–87.

Hojnacki, Marie, and Lawrence Baum. 1992. " 'New-style' Judicial Campaigns and the Voters: Economic Issues and Union Members in Ohio." *Western Political Quarterly*, 45:921–48.

Hojnacki, Marie, and David Kimball. 1999. "The Who and How of Organizations' Lobbying Strategies in Committee." *Journal of Politics* 61:999–1024.

Huckfeldt, Robert, and John Sprague. 1993. "Citizens, Contexts, and Politics." In *Political Science: The State of the Discipline II*. Washington: American Political Science Association.

Hula, Kevin. 1995. "Rounding up the Usual Suspects: Forging Interest Group Coalitions in Washington." In *Interest Group Politics*. 4th ed. Ed. Allan J. Cigler and Burdett A. Loomis. Washington: Congressional Quarterly Press.

Jacobson, Gary C. 1999. "The Effect of the AFL-CIO's 'Voter Education' Campaigns on the 1996 House Elections." *Journal of Politics* 61:185–94.

Jenkins, J. Craig, and William Form. 1999. "Do Social Movements Bring about Change?" Ohio State University. Typescript.

Johnson, Alan. 1998. "Ohio Police Union Supports Taft for Governor." *Columbus Dispatch*, 15 July, 5C.

Johnson, Haynes, and David S. Broder. 1996. *The System: The American Way of Politics at the Breaking Point.* Boston: Little, Brown.

Johnson, Paul Edward. 1991. "Organized Labor in an Era of Blue-collar Decline." In *Interest Group Politics.* 3rd ed. Ed. Allan J. Cigler and Burdett A. Loomis. Washington: Congressional Quarterly Press.

Johnston, David Cay. 1997. "On Payday, Union Jobs Stack up Very Well," *New York Times*, 31 August.

Juravich, Tom, and Peter R. Shergold. 1988. "The Impact of Unions on the Voting Behavior of Their Members." *Industrial and Labor Relations Review* 41:374–85.

Kelloway, E. Kevin, and Julian Barling. 1993. "Member Participation in Local Union Activities: Measurement, Prediction, and Replication." *Journal of Applied Psychology* 78:262–79.

Kelly, Caroline. 1993. "Group Identity, Intergroup Perceptions, and Collective Action." *European Review of Social Psychology.* Vol. 4. Ed. Wolfgang Stroebe and Miles Hewstone. New York: Wiley.

Kilborn, Peter T. 1996. "Republicans Are up in Arms at Labor's Political Rebirth." *New York Times*, 3 April, A1, A13.

King, Gary. 1989. *Unifying Political Methodology: The Likelihood Model of Statistical Inference.* New York: Cambridge University Press.

Kirchmeyer, Catherine. 1992. "Nonwork Participation and Work Attitudes: A Test of Scarcity vs. Expansion Models of Personal Resources." *Human Relations* 45:775–95.

Knoke, David. 1990. *Organizing for Collective Action: The Political Economies of Associations.* New York: Aldine de Gruyter.

Kollman, Ken. 1998. *Outside Lobbying: Public Opinion and Interest Group Strategies.* Princeton, N.J.: Princeton University Press.

Kornhauser, Arthur, Harold L. Sheppard, and Albert J. Mayer. 1956. *When Labor Votes: A Study of Auto Workers.* New York: University Books.

Kosterlitz, Julie. 1996. "Laboring Uphill." *National Journal* (March): 474–8.

———. 1999. "Searching for New Labor." *National Journal*, 1 September, 2470–7.

Leighley, Jan E. 1995. "Attitudes, Opportunities, and Incentives: A Field Essay on Political Participation." *Political Research Quarterly* 48:181–209.

Levi, Margaret. 1988. *Of Rule and Revenue.* Berkeley: University of California Press.

Lowi, Theodore J. 1971. *The Politics of Disorder.* New York: Basic.

Masters, Marick F., Robert S. Atkin, and John Thomas Delaney. 1989–90. "Unions, Political Action, and Public Policies: A Review of the Past Decade." *Policy Studies Journal* 18:471–9.

Masters, Marick F., and John Thomas Delaney. 1987a. "Union Legislative Records during President Reagan's First Term." *Journal of Labor Research* 8:1–18.

Masters, Marick F., and John Thomas Delaney. 1987b. "Union Political Activities: A Review of the Empirical Literature." *Industrial and Labor Relations Review* 10:336–53.

McGinley, Laurie, and Glenn Burkins. 1998. "AFL-CIO Ad Blitz on Revamp of Managed Care Has Warning on the Political Cost of Opposition." *Wall Street Journal*, 15 July.

Meredith, Robyn. 1999. "A Union March on Alabama." *New York Times*, 29 June.

Meyerson, Harold. 2000. "Rolling the Union On." *Dissent*, Winter, 47–55.

Michels, Robert. 1915/1958. *Political Parties*. New York: Free Press.

Miller, Arthur H., Patricia Gurin, Gerald Gurin, and Oksana Malanchuk. 1981. "Group Consciousness and Political Participation." *American Journal of Political Science* 25:494–511.

Miller, Warren E., and J. Merrill Shanks. 1996. *The New American Voter*. Cambridge, Mass.: Harvard University Press.

Miller, Warren E., and Donald E. Stokes. 1963. "Constituency Influence in Congress." *American Political Science Review* 57:45–57.

Moe, Terry M. 1980. *The Organization of Interests*. Chicago: University of Chicago Press.

Moody, Kim. 1988. *An Injury to All: The Decline of American Unionism*. Chelsea, Mich.: Verso.

Morehouse, Macon. 1988. "For Lobbyists, Wage Fight Is 'a Holy War.' " *CQ Weekly Reports*, 4 June, 1519–20.

Mowday, Richard T., Lyman W. Porter, and Richard M. Steers. 1982. *Employee-organization Linkages: The Psychology of Commitment, Absenteeism, and Turnover*. New York: Academic.

Mundo, Philip A. 1992. *Interest Groups: Cases and Characteristics*. Chicago: Nelson-Hall.

Nie, Norman H., Jane Junn, and Kenneth Stehlik-Barry. 1996. *Education and Democratic Citizenship*. Chicago: University of Chicago Press.

O'Donnell, Norah M., and John Bresnahan. 1998. "House GOPers, Blue Dogs Seek New Labor Relations." *Roll Call*, 30 July, 15, 20.

O'Reilly, Charles, III, and Jennifer Chatman. 1986. "Organizational Commitment and Psychological Attachment: The Effects of Compliance, Identification, and Internalization of Prosocial Behavior." *Journal of Applied Psychology* 71:492–9.

Ohio AFL-CIO Committee on Political Education. 1994a. "1994 COPE Manual." Columbus: Ohio AFL-CIO.

———. 1994b. "1994 Telephone Bank Manual." Columbus: Ohio AFL-CIO COPE.

Olson, Mancur. 1965. *The Logic of Collective Action*. Cambridge, Mass.: Harvard University Press.

Orren, Karen. 1986. "Union Politics and Postwar Liberalism in the United States, 1946–1979." *Studies in American Political Development* 1:215–52.

Page, Benjamin I., and Robert Y. Shapiro. 1992. *The Rational Public: Fifty Years of Trends in Americans' Policy Preferences*. Chicago: University of Chicago Press.

Piven, Frances Fox, and Richard Cloward. 1978. *Poor People's Movements*. New York: Pantheon.

Powell, G. Bingham, Jr. 1980. "Voting Turnout in Thirty Democracies." In *Electoral Participation*. Ed. Richard Rose. Beverly Hills, Calif.: Sage.

———. 1986. "American Turnout in Comparative Perspective." *American Political Science Review* 80:17–43.

Public Perspective. 1997a. "The NORC Series on Confidence in Leaders of National Institutions." *Public Perspective* 8 (2): 2–5.

Public Perspective. 1997b. "Labor Unions: A Roper Data Couter Review." *Public Perspective* July/August.

Ra, Jong Oh. 1978. *Labor at the Polls*. Amherst: University of Massachusetts Press.

Radcliff, Benjamin, and Patricia Davis. 2000. "Labor Organization and Electoral Participation in Industrial Democracies." *American Journal of Political Science* 44:132–41.

Rapoport, Ronald, Walter J. Stone, and Alan I. Abramowitz. 1991. "Do Endorsements Matter? Group Influence in the 1984 Democratic Caucuses." *American Political Science Review* 85:193–203.

Robertson, Peter J., and Shui-Yan Tang. 1995. "The Role of Commitment in Collective Action: Comparing Organizational Behavior and Rational Choice Perspectives." *Public Administration Review* 55:67–80.

Rogers, David. 2000. "U.S. Farm Shipments to Beijing Bolster the Push for Normalizing Trade Relations with China." *Wall Street Journal*, 26 April.

Rosenau, James N. 1974. *Citizenship between Elections*. New York: Free Press.

Rosenstone, Steven J., and John Mark Hansen. 1993. *Mobilization, Participation, and Democracy in America*. New York: Macmillan.

Rothenberg, Lawrence S. 1992. *Linking Citizens to Government*. New York: Cambridge University Press.

Rozell, Mark J., and Clyde Wilcox. 1999. *Interest Groups in American Campaigns: The New Face of Electioneering*. Washington: Congressional Quarterly Press.

Rudolph, Thomas J. 1999. "Corporate and Labor PAC Contributions in House Elections: Measuring the Effects of Majority Party Status." *Journal of Politics* 61:195–206.

Sabatier, Paul A. 1992. "Interest Group Membership and Organization: Multiple Theories." In *The Politics of Interests: Interest Groups Transformed*. Ed. Mark P. Petracca. Boulder, Colo.: Westview.

Sabatier, Paul A., and Susan McLaughlin. 1990. "Belief Congruence between Interest Group Leaders and Members: An Empirical Analysis of Three Theories and a Suggested Synthesis." *Journal of Politics* 52:914–35.

Sabato, Larry J. 1990. *PAC Power: Inside the World of Political Action Committees*. New York: Norton.

Salisbury, Robert H. 1969. "An Exchange Theory of Interest Groups." *Midwest Journal of Political Science* 13:1–32.

———. 1984. "Interest Representation: The Dominance of Institutions." *American Political Science Review* 78:64–76.

Schattschneider, E. E. 1960. *The Semisovereign People*. New York: Holt, Reinhart, and Winston.

Schaubroeck, John, and Daniel C. Ganster. 1991. "Beyond the Call of Duty: A Field Study of Extra-role Behavior in Voluntary Organizations." *Human Relations* 44:569–82.

Schier, Steven E. 2000. *By Invitation Only: The Rise of Exclusive Politics in the United States*. Pittsburgh: University of Pittsburgh Press.

Schlozman, Kay Lehman, and John T. Tierney. 1986. *Organized Interests and American Democracy*. New York: Harper and Row.

Simendinger, Alexis. 1999. "Gore's Contract with Labor." *National Journal*, 12 June, 1596.

Sinclair, Barbara. 1982. *Congressional Realignment*. Austin: University of Texas Press.

Skocpol, Theda. 1997. *Boomerang: Health Care Reform and the Turn against Government*. New York: Norton.

Sorauf, Frank J. 1984–5. "Accountability in Political Action Committees." *Political Science Quarterly* 99:591–614.

———. 1992. *Inside Campaign Finance*. New Haven, Conn.: Yale University Press.

Sousa, David J. 1993. "Organized Labor in the Electorate, 1960–1988." *Political Research Quarterly*, 46:741–58.

———. 1998. "No Balance in Equities: Union Power and the Foundations of the Modern Campaign Finance Reform Regime." Paper presented at the annual meeting of the Midwest Political Science Association, Chicago, Illinois, March.

Stanley, Harold W., William T. Bianco, and Richard G. Niemi. 1986. "Partisanship and Group Support over Time: A Multivariate Analysis." *American Political Science Review* 80:969–76.

Stanley, Harold W., and Richard G. Niemi. 1990. *Vital Statistics on American Politics*. 2nd ed. Washington: Congressional Quarterly Press.

———. 1998. *Vital Statistics on American Politics, 1997–1998*. Washington: Congressional Quarterly Press.

Stimson, James A. 1991. *Public Opinion in America: Moods, Cycles, and Swings*. Boulder, Colo.: Westview.

Stimson, James A., Michael B. MacKuen, and Robert S. Erikson. 1995. "Dynamic Representation." *American Political Science Review* 89:543–65.

Sweeney, John J. 1996. *America Needs a Raise*. Boston: Houghton Mifflin.

Swoboda, Frank. 1999a. "AFL-CIO Plots a Push for Democratic House." *Washington Post*, 18 February.

———. 1999b. "Membership Trends Are Mixed for Unions." *Washington Post*, 26 January.

———. 2000a. "Labor Targets 71 House Districts in 'Watershed Year.'" *Washington Post*, 16 February, A14.

———. 2000b. "Labor Unions See Membership Gains." *Washington Post*, 20 January.

———. 2000c. "Unions Reverse on Illegal Immigration." *Washington Post*, 17 February, A1.

Thacker, James W., Mitchell W. Fields, and Lizabeth Barclay. 1990. "Union Commitment: An Examination of Antecedent and Outcome Factors." *Journal of Occupational Psychology* 63:33–48.

Uhlaner, Carole J. 1989. "Rational Turnout: The Neglected Role of Groups." *American Journal of Political Science* 33:390–422.

U.S. Census Bureau. 1999. *Statistical Abstracts of the United States, Current Population Report*. Washington: Government Printing Office.

Verba, Sidney, and Norman H. Nie. 1972. *Participation in America*. New York: Harper and Row.

Verba, Sidney, Kay Lehman Schlozman, and Henry E. Brady. 1995. *Voice and Equality: Civic Voluntarism in American Politics*. Cambridge, Mass.: Harvard University Press.

Verhovek, Sam Howe. 1999. "The New Language of American Labor." *New York Times*, 26 June.

Victor, Kirk. 1995a. "High Noon in the House of Labor." *National Journal*, 15 July, 1852.

———. 1995b. "Labor's New Look." *National Journal*, 14 October, 2522–7.

Wahlke, John C., Heinz Eulau, William Buchanan, and LeRoy C. Ferguson. 1962. *The Legislative System*. New York: Wiley.

Walker, Jack L., Jr. 1991. *Mobilizing Interest Groups in America*. Ann Arbor: University of Michigan Press.

Waltenberg, Eric. 2001. *Choosing Where to Fight: Forum Selecting in the Modern Regulatory State*. Albany: SUNY Press.

West, Darrell M., and Burdett A. Loomis. 1999. *The Sound of Money: How Political Interests Get What They Want*. New York: Norton.

Wilcox, Clyde. 1994. "Coping with Increasing Business Influence: The AFL-CIO's Committee on Political Education." In *Risky Business?: PAC Decisionmaking in Congressional Elections*. Ed. Robert Biersack, Paul S. Herrnson, and Clyde Wilcox. Armonk, N.Y.: Sharpe.

Wilson, Graham K. 1979. *Unions in American National Politics*. London: Macmillan.

Wilson, James Q. 1973. *Political Organizations*. New York: Basic.

Wright, John R. 1996. *Interest Groups and Congress: Lobbying, Contributions, and Influence*. Boston: Allyn and Bacon.

Wright, Samuel F. 1982. "Clipping the Political Wings of Labor Unions: An Examination of Existing Law and Proposals for Change." *Harvard Journal of Law and Public Policy* 5:1–36.

Index

abortion, 57, 58, 138
Abraham, Spencer, 103
Adams, Kirk, 159, 160
advertising: generic, 78; issues based, 91–92, 97, 98–99, 101, 103, 105n5, 168; membership mobilization and, 101; Republican candidates, 102
affiliate unions: collective goals, 66; congressional elections and, 99; and contributions to 1996 races, 97–98, 105n1; issues of, 81; Labor '96 and, 100; marginal committees, 87n2; targeting decisions, 75, 87n2
AFGE (American Federation of Government Employees), 73
AFL (American Federation of Labor), 10, 11
AFL-CIO. See American Federation of Labor–Congress of Industrial Organizations (AFL-CIO)
AFL-CIO PAC. See Committee on Political Education (COPE)
AFSCME. See American Federation of State, County, and Municipal Employees (AFSCME)
AFT (American Federation of Teachers), 9, 28
agency fees, 77
agendas, 66–68; international unions, 81; issue ads and, 98; liberal issues, 84; set by Sweeney, 89–92
age of union workforce, 37–38, 45
air traffic controllers, 16
Alinsky, Saul, 94

America Needs a Raise, 98, 101
American Federation of Government Employees (AFGE), 73
American Federation of Labor (AFL), 10, 11
American Federation of Labor–Congress of Industrial Organizations (AFL-CIO): achieving collective goals, 66; candidate endorsements, 69, 72–73, 145–47; election of president, 2, 21, 29, 67, 89, 129, 155; Gore endorsement, 166–67; influence of, 21; issues' successes, 164–65; membership, 1–2, 18; members' support of, 49; party identification of members, 55–56; post-1955 mobilization, 90–92; reunification of, 10; structure of, 8–10; unions' alignment with, 81. See also central labor councils (CLCs)
American Federation of State, County, and Municipal Employees (AFSCME), 9, 28, 83, 97, 101
American Federation of Teachers (AFT), 9, 28
American Medical Association, 158, 161
American National Election Study (ANES), 24, 27
antiunion employers, 16
apprenticeship programs, 121
attitudes of union members, 39–45, 148–50, 151
automobile industry, 161, 162–63

bargaining to organize, 95
Bensinger, Richard, 94

big business, 43–45

Blacks, 57; earnings, 37; union membership and, 35–37, 45; voter turnout rate, 138

blue-collar workers, 28–29, 45; gender of, 31–33; union membership decline, 173

Bok, Derek C., 107

Bradley, Bill, 166, 167

Brady, Henry E., 131n2

Brehm, John, 119

budgets, organizing funding increase, 96

building trades councils, 9, 121

bureaucracies, 5

Bush, George, 128

businesses: campaign contributions, 78–79; political action committees, 76, 80, 98, 160

Cable News Network, 162

campaign contributions, 75–80, 91; 1996 elections, 97–102; to Democratic Party, 12; PACs and, 75–80, 87n7; recommendations for, 72; to Republican Party, 160; union's role in elections and, 166; weighted preference to contributors, 73

campaign finance reform, 77–78

campaign literature, 11, 110–11

candidate endorsements. *See* endorsements

Center for Responsive Politics (2000), 78

central labor councils (CLCs), 9; candidate endorsements, 69–70; phone calls to members, 140

check cards, 95

China, trade relations with, 164–65

churches, political activism of, 131n2

CIO (Congress of Industrial Organizations), 10, 11

CIO-PAC, 11, 87n3

Citizens Action, 97

civil rights, 13

civil servants, 56

Clark, Peter B., 119

Clawson, Don, 4

Clawson, Mary Ann, 4

CLCs. *See* central labor councils (CLCs)

cleavage groups, 134

Clinton, Bill, 86, 105n6, 128, 165; 1996 election, 99, 105n4; health care reform, 58; labor's role in election of, 166; move to center on issues, 12; support for, 102; trade policy, 156–57, 170

closed shops, 178

coalitions, 92, 94, 97, 100

collective action, 41; benefits of, 109–10; political activities, 108; union members' commitment to, 48–53

collective bargaining, 64, 65; payroll deductions, 120; political activism and, 6–7

commitment to union, 48–53, 126, 130, 159, 181; approval of political activities and, 60–62, 63; definition, 64n1; education level and, 171; free ride and, 82, 126; participation in political activities and, 122–24, 171; as predictor of member's actions, 171; voting behavior and, 148–51

Committee on Political Education (COPE), 11–12, 69, 87n3; candidate endorsements, 72–73; Checkoff Yes Pamphlet, 113; contributions to Democratic candidates, 79; mobilization activities, 115; phone calls to members, 140; polling, 141; targeting decisions, 74–75

communications: with members, 91–92; political, 76–77, 87n6, 139–40. *See also* Committee on Political Education (COPE)

Communication Workers of America (CWA), 112

Communication Workers of America (CWA) v. Beck, 77–78

congressional elections, 99; candidate endorsements, 69–70, 72–73, 102; PACs contributions to, 76–77, 79–80; political strategy used for, 97; support of Democratic candidates, 141–43; unions' contributions to, 19–20, 79; voter turnout rates, 136

Congress of Industrial Organizations (CIO), 10, 11

conservatives, 55–57

Continuous Quality Improvement, 158

Contract with America, 98

conventions, 67, 68

Cook, Deborah, 151–52

COPE. *See* Committee on Political Education (COPE)

coworkers' support, 181

craft unions, 10

cultural bias, 158

Dark, Taylor E., 84
Davis, Patricia, 134
decentralization of unions, 109
decertification elections, 6
Delaney, John Thomas, 7, 68
Democratic Leadership Council, 99
Democratic Party: campaign finance
    reform, 77–78; candidate endorsements
    in Ohio, 145–53; candidates support,
    141–43, 183; contributions to
    candidates, 78–80; feeling thermometer
    ratings, 43–45; labor contacts with,
    84–85; liberal agenda of, 40; union
    legislation and, 11–13; union
    membership and, 53–55; union support
    of, 12–13, 134 demographics of
    membership, 23; appropriateness of
    union political activities and, 61, 62,
    63; challenges for leaders, 38–39;
    changes in (1952–1999), 26–38, 45;
    commitment to union and, 51, 52;
    earnings and, 37; lifestyle changes and,
    39; voting behavior and, 148
demonstrations, 164
Denny's, 94
Donahue, Thomas R., 1–2, 67
Douglas, Andy, 145, 146–48
dues, 76–78
Dunlop, John T., 107

earnings, 33; categories of, 182;
    commitment to union and, 51, 52;
    minorities, 35–36; political participation
    and, 132n10; union's assistance in gains
    in, 182
economics, 160; government role in, 57, 58;
    as labor unions' core interest, 6;
    members control of, 67; political
    activism and, 6–8; role in union
    membership, 16
education accounts, 87n6
education associations, 9
education level, 181; appropriateness of
    union activity and, 61, 62, 63;
    commitment to union and, 51, 52, 171;
    political activism and, 124, 129–30;
    relationship to request for
    participation, 117, 118, 131n5; of
    workforce, 33–34, 45
education of members, 6, 112; difficulty of,
    82–84; ineffectiveness of unions' issues

education, 58–59; political education, 11,
    18, 136, 139–40
Educators' PAC (EPAC), Ohio, 71, 75
elections, 6; 1990, 135, 136–37, 144–53; 1992,
    79, 98, 128, 135, 136–37, 144–53; 1994,
    19–20, 79, 89, 135, 136–37, 144–53, 166,
    170; 1996, 19–20, 79–80, 86, 97–102, 128,
    135, 136–37, 139, 144–53, 166; 1998
    midterm, 19–20, 78, 102–3, 128, 137;
    2000, 20, 103; AFL-CIO president, 1–2,
    29, 67, 89, 129, 155; contested, 67; labor's
    impact on in Ohio, 143–52; multiplier
    effect in, 25; national results, 141–43;
    unions' participation in, 59–60; voter
    turnout rate, 133–38
employer–employee relations. *See*
    labor–management relations
endorsements, 60; AFL-CIO CLCs, 69–70;
    campaign literature and, 110–11;
    decisions by labor, 68–69; divided
    between parties, 151; effect of on
    members, 172; federal races, 72–73; of
    Gore, 166–67; index, 182; international
    unions, 73–74; members' participation
    in, 115; members' vote choice and,
    138–41; NEA, 69, 70–72; state races,
    72–73; success of in 1996 elections, 102;
    support for union-endorsed candidates,
    183; targeting decisions, 74–75; voting
    behavior and, 144–53, 148
engineers, 163
environmental groups, 97
EPAC. *See* Educators' PAC (EPAC), Ohio
Epstein, Edwin M., 87n5
equal rights, 13
evolution of union structure, 10

Federal Election Commission, 87n5, 105n2
federal races: candidate endorsements,
    72–73; targeting decisions, 74–75
Federation of Organized Trades and Labor
    Unions (FOTLU), 10
feeling thermometers, 43–45
females: earnings, 37; support for Clinton,
    102; union membership, 30–33, 45;
    voting behavior and, 148
Fiorito, Jack, 68
Form, William, 3
FOTLU (Federation of Organized Trades
    and Labor Unions), 10
Fraternal Order of Police (FOP), 73

free riders, 82, 109–10, 126
free trade, 156
Freeman, Jo, 3
fund-raising, 120

Gates, Scott, 119
gender patterns, 30–33, 182;
    appropriateness of union political
    activity and, 61, 62, 63; changes in, 45;
    commitment to union and, 51, 52;
    earnings and, 37
General Motors (GM), 161, 162–63
General Social Survey, 24
Gephardt, Richard, 166
Get-Out-the-Vote drives, 78, 103, 110, 111,
    121, 126
Gingrich, Newt, 104
globalization, 164
Gompers, Samuel, 10
Gordon, Michael E., 48
Gore, Al, 103, 165, 166
government workers, 31, 82, 161
governors, 157
graduate assistants, 95–96, 161
Greenberg, Stanley B., 85
gun control, 138

Haffey, J. Ross, 151–52
Hall, Tony, 84
health care, 57, 58, 164
health care workers, 95
Herrnson, Paul, 105n2
Hispanics, 35–37, 45
history of labor unions, 4
home care workers, 161
Hotel Employees and Restaurant
    Employees, 95
households, decline in size of, 27
housewives, 32, 38

IAM (International Association of
    Machinists), 14, 74
ideology, 55–57; campaign contributions
    and, 79; participation in political
    activities and, 119–20, 123–24, 131–32n8;
    party identification and, 56–57, 148–50,
    151 immigrants, 94, 163 income. *See*
    earnings
incumbent president, midterm elections
    and, 103, 105n6
incumbents: campaign contributions to,
    78–80, 87n7, 98, 105n3; endorsement of,

72, 73; Project '96 and, 98, 105n3;
    protection of, 105n6; targeting, 75
Independent Party, 42, 54
industrial unions, 10, 28–30; growth of, 11;
    membership, 14, 15; mobilization of
    members, 83. *See also names of specific
    unions*
information, 112–13, 182
inside strategies, 21, 84–85, 170
interest groups, 1–2; compared to unions,
    82; promotion of organization's
    interests, 5–8; vs. social movements, 3–6
International Association of Machinists and
    Aerospace Workers, 114
International Association of Machinists
    (IAM), 14, 174
International Brotherhood of Electrical
    Workers, 28
International Brotherhood of Teamsters
    (Teamsters), 2; endorsement of Gore,
    166–67; membership, 14; support for
    Sweeney, 90; UPS strike, 162
International Monetary Fund, 164
international trade, 13
international unions, 8–9; candidate
    endorsements, 73–74; collective goals,
    66; contributions to Project '96, 98;
    diversity of, 81–82; issues of, 81–82,
    108–9; PACs and, 11–12, 76; phone calls
    to members, 140; political agendas, 81;
    targeting decisions, 75
issue advocacy ads, 91–92, 168;
    ineffectiveness of, 103; member
    mobilization and, 101; used against
    incumbents, 105n5; as way to set
    election agenda, 98–99
issue education, 58
issues, 57–59, 80–82; determination of, 97;
    electoral success of, 167–68; failures of,
    163–64; liberals, 84; members' support of,
    169; member vote choice and, 138–41;
    successes of, 163–64; targeting and,
    139–40; workers' compensation, 167, 168
IUE (Union of Electrical, Radio, and
    Machine Workers), 121

Jacobson, Gary C., 19, 102, 172
janitors, 163
Johnson, Lyndon B., 84
judicial decisions, unions and, 7

Kirkland, Lane, 1, 90

Labor '96, 99–102, 128
Laborers International Union of North
America (Laborers), 2, 90
labor–management relations, 43–45, 94–95,
158–59
labor movement vs. union, 4
labor policy, 81
Labor Political Training Center, 100
labor relations consultants, 71
Labor's League for Political Education
(LLPE), 11, 87n3
Landrum-Griffin Act of 1959, 16, 163
laws and legislation: campaign
contributions, 76, 87n4; climate for, 15–16;
common situs picketing, 175n1; hiring of
illegal immigrants, 94; importance to
unions, 7–8; labor's influence on, 12,
165–66; legal climate for labor unions,
156–57; political parties and, 11–13;
regulation of unions, 7; staff contacts,
131n1. *See also* National Labor Relations
Board; Taft-Hartley Act of 1947
leadership of unions: access to membership,
18–19; agenda setting, 66–68; challenges
for, 174; concentric circles of influence
and, 25–26; delegates vs. trustees for
members, 61, 63, 64n6; demographic
changes and, 38–39; effectiveness of, 171;
issues agreement with members, 57–59;
members' perception of ideology of,
55–57; mobilization efforts, 83, 109–10,
114, 117, 171; party identification and,
53–55; personal contacts by, 113; political
activities of, 114–15, 116–17, 171–72;
political issues and, 8; providing of
information to members, 112–13; public
confidence in, 17; relationship with
members, 168–72, 183–84; reliance on
inside strategies, 84–85; requests of
members for political activism, 116–17,
171–72; training sessions, 112; union
objectives and, 65
Levi, Margaret, 119
Lewinsky, Monica, 105n6
liberals: appropriateness of union political
activism, 61; ideology, 55–57; issue
agreement between union members and
leaders, 57–58
LLPE (Labor's League for Political
Education), 11, 87n3
lobbying, 6, 64n5, 80–82, 97, 130; candidate
endorsements and, 73; inside strategies,
84–85; Labor '96, 100–101; organizing
strategy and, 94–95
local races, candidate endorsements, 70–72
local unions, 8–9; leadership and members
relationship, 169–71; mobilization and,
114; voter registration and, 140–41
lower class, 134
low-wage workers, 95

males: commitment to union, 51, 52;
earnings, 37; support for Clinton, 102;
union membership, 30–33, 45
marginal committees, 74, 87n2
Masters, Marick F., 7, 68
McEntee, Gerald W., 96–97
McGovern, George, 12
McLaughlin, Susan, 64n1
Meany, George, 1
media, 91, 162
membership, 6; access of leaders to, 18–19;
AFL, 11; AFL-CIO affiliations, 18; age of,
37–38, 45; agreement with leaders'
positions on issues, 57–59; attitudinal
changes of, 39–45; beliefs of, 48;
broadening appeal for, 92–93; campaign
contributions, 76, 87n4, 120–21; CIO, 11;
commitment and, 48–53, 123–24, 159;
compliance with requests for activism,
118–20; coworkers' support, 181; decline
of, 15–17, 26–28, 93; democratic
involvement of, 66–68; demographics
of, 23, 30–33, 45; diversity of, 35–37, 45,
81–83, 157, 161; economics and, 158;
effectiveness of issue education, 58–59;
effectiveness of representation, 182;
expansion strategy, 90; friends' support,
182; gender of, 30–33, 45; government
workers, 31; ideology of, 55–57;
incentives for PAC contributions, 120–21;
increase in, 161; in industrial unions, 14;
information needs, 110, 112–13; issue ads
and, 101; mobilization of, 82–84, 108–9,
118; nature of relationship with union,
50–51; occupations of, 26–38, 45;
opportunities for involvement, 110–12;
organizing strategy, 92–96, 173; overview,
13–15; participation in union activities,
110–12, 115–18; party identification and,
53–55; peaks in, 26–28; political activities,
4, 59–62, 122–23; reasons for, 65, 108;
regional differences in, 16; relationship
with leaders, 168–72, 183–84; relationship

with union, 60–61, 63; residence patterns, 34–35, 36, 45; social class identification, 40–41, 45; summary of changes in, 45; support for Democratic candidates, 141–43; technology sector, 29, 158; tenure, 51, 53, 61, 123–24, 125, 132n9, 143; union density and, 161; voluntary, 185; voter choice, 138–41, 148; voter turnout rates, 133–38. *See also* nonunion households; union households

mergers, 9, 173–74

middle class, 45, 158; commitment to union, 52; identification with, 40–41; ideology, 134; political activism and, 62; residences, 173

Miller, Warren E., 141

minimum wage, 8, 101, 161

minorities, earnings, 35–36

mobilization, 6, 22; 1998 midterm elections, 102–3; 2000 elections, 103; coordination efforts, 100–101; definition, 131n3; difficulty of, 82–84; leaders' role in, 109–10, 113, 117, 174; limits to, 113–15; local activities, 99–100; members' awareness of, 118; NEA, 112; overview, 108–9; personal contacts by leaders and, 113; political activism and, 118–20, 122–26, 132n12, 174; post-1995 strategy, 90–91; vote choice and, 170–71; voter turnout rates and, 134

moderates, 55–57

Morris, Dick, 99

National Abortion Rights League, 5

National Association of Manufacturers, 81

National Council of Senior Citizens, 97

National Education Association (NEA), 9, 28; 1996 elections, 105n4; Association Days, 122; candidate endorsements, 69, 70–72; members' support of, 49; mobilization of members, 110, 112; partisan endorsements, 101; use of persuasion and, 113

National Federation of Independent Business, 102

national federations, 100, 102

National Labor Relations Board, 7, 95; creation, 14; disputes before, 8; ruling on graduate associates, 161; UNITE elections, 161–62

National Rifle Association, 5

NEA. *See* National Education Association (NEA)

NEA-PAC, 71–72; contributions to, 87n7; targeting decisions, 75

neighborhood of union members, 159

Nonpartisan League, 11

nonpolitical union activities, 114

nonunion households; housewives in, 32; political party identification, 41–42; voter turnout, 135–37

nonunion workers, 15, 24–25; appropriateness of union political activities, 60; earnings, 37; education level of, 33–34; endorsement communication, 131n1; feeling thermometer ratings, 43–45; ideology of, 56; opportunity for organizing, 173; political activism compared to union member activism, 126–28; residence patterns, 35; social class identification, 40–41; support for Clinton, 102; support of Democratic candidates, 141–43

North American Free Trade, 164

occupations: gender and, 31–33; shifts in, 28–30, 45

OCSEA. *See* Ohio Civil Service Employee Association (OCSEA)

Ohio: election results, 143–52; research design, 177–78; research surveys, 179–80. *See also* Ohio AFL-CIO; Ohio Civil Service Employees Association (OCSEA); OhioEducation Association (OEA)

Ohio AFL-CIO, 177, 179; candidate endorsements, 70; ideology of members, 56; Phone Bank Manual, 113, 115; support for political activities, 59

Ohio Building Trades Council, 74, 114

Ohio Civil Service Employees Association (OCSEA), 179; candidate endorsements, 145, 147; ideology of members, 56; mobilization of members, 83; party identification of members, 55–56

Ohio Education Association (OEA), 70, 179; candidate endorsements, 139, 145–47; diversity of, 157; education issues, 82–83; ideology of members, 56; party identification of members, 55–56; targeting decisions, 75

Ohio State University, 179

open-seat races, 74, 75, 79–80, 98
organization of unions: current structure, 8–10; for political activities, 10–13; strategy for, 92–93
Organizing Institute, 94
Orren, Karen, 7
outside strategies, 21, 84, 170

Packwood, Bob, 97
PACs. *See* political action committees (PACs)
party-building activities, 78
party identification, 41–42, 45, 53–55; ideology distinctions and, 56–57, 148–50, 151; voting behavior and, 148–50, 151
Patients' Bill of Rights, 164
Paycheck Protection Act, 77–78
payroll deductions, 120
peak association, 5
persuasion, 112, 113
Petro, James, 151–52
picketing, 166, 175n1
Plumbers and Pipefitters, 121
Poisson regression model, 125–26, 132n13
political action committees (PACs), 11–12; campaign contributions by, 98, 120–22; characteristics of, 19; education associations, 9; election spending and, 75–80; independent expenditures, 91; NEA, 71–72; spending limits, 160; voluntary contributions to, 91; weighted preference to contributors, 73. *See also* Committee on Political Education (COPE)
political activism, 183; appropriateness of, 59–62, 181; categories of, 6; churches, 131n2; collective bargaining and, 6–7; compared to public activism, 126–28; compliance with requests for, 118–20, 131nn7–8, 184; economics and, 6–8; heterogeneity of unions and, 81–83; leaders of unions, 114–15; level of participation in, 4, 110–12, 122–23, 183; limits on, 159–60; as means to further organization's goals, 5–6; mobilization efforts, 86, 108, 113–15; number of activities, 61, 62, 183; organization of labor for, 10–13; participation efforts, 117–18; participation request for, 115–18; payment for, 122; policy successes, 163–64; power of organized labor in,

167; reasons for participation in, 122–26; recruitment techniques and incentives, 120–22; relationship to education level, 117, 118, 131n3; resources for, 18–20; staffing and, 174; support of, 169; vote choice and, 139; voter turnout rates, 133–38; voting behavior and, 148–51. *See also* endorsements
political education, 11, 18, 136, 139–40. *See also* Committee on Political Education (COPE)
political influence, concentric circles of, 25–26
political parties: Congressional races and, 19–20; divided endorsements, 151; labor-based relationship to voter turnout, 134; linkage to cleavage groups, 134; membership identification with, 41–42; Ohio, 178; realignment of, 42; union membership and, 53–55. *See also* Democratic Party; Independent Party; Republican Party
political strategies: inside strategies, 21, 84–85, 170; outside strategies, 21, 84, 170; Sweeney's, 20–21, 22, 85, 96–97
polling, 21; by COPE, 141; used to evaluate races, 74–75
population, union membership in proportion to, 27–28
Powell, G. Bingham, Jr., 134
presidential elections: labor's endorsement of Gore, 166–67; political activism and, 127–28; support of Democratic candidates, 141–43
private-sector workers, 14, 15, 28
Professional Air Traffic Controllers Organization, 16
Project '95, 97
Project '96, 97–98, 100
Proposition 226, 78
public employees' unions, 90
public opinions, 91; about leaders of unions, 17; about unions, 17–18; use of, 21
public-sector workers, 14, 28

Ra, Jong Oh, 143
race, 184; commitment to union and, 51, 52, 63; political activism and, 61, 62; racial diversity of union members, 35–37, 45; voting behavior and, 148

Radcliff, Benjamin, 134
Reagan, Ronald, 16
Republican Party: campaign contributions to, 79, 160; campaign finance reform, 77–78; as challenge to organized labor, 156–57; feeling thermometer ratings, 43–45; union legislation and, 11–13
research: design of, 177–78; Ohio surveys, 179–80
residence patterns: neighborhood of union members, 159; relationship to political activism, 125; union members, 34–35, 36, 45, 173
resources: for political activities, 18–20; targeting decisions and, 74–75
Reuther, Walter, 68
Riffe, Verne, 85, 165
Roosevelt, Franklin D., 40
Rosenau, James N., 118, 131n3
Rosenthal, Steve, 139
Rothenberg, Lawrence S., 132n9

Sabatier, Paul A., 64n1
scanning committees, 69–70, 87n1
Schlozman, Kay Lehman, 67, 131n2
school boards, 70
screening committees, 70–72, 73
secondary boycott, 175n1
SEIU. *See* Service Employees International Union (SEIU)
Service Employees International Union (SEIU), 95, 161, 163
service industries, 95, 163
service sector unions, 90, 94, 95, 161, 163
Shanks, J. Merrill, 141
Smith, Gordon, 97
Smith-Connally Act of 1943, 87n4
social class, 62, 181; identification of by union members, 40–41, 45; political activism and, 130; union members and, 157–58; voting behavior and, 148
social movements: definition, 3–5; image of, 93
Society of Professional Engineering Employees in Aerospace, 163
soft money contributions, 78–79; Project '96, 98; use of instead of voluntary contributions, 91
Sorauf, Frank J., 19, 80, 131n7
Sousa, David J., 87n5, 137–38
spending, 91; on Congressional races,

19–20; limits to, 160; PACs and, 75–80. *See also* campaign contributions
Stabenow, Debbie, 103
staff, 109; activist work, 115; contact with members, 131n1; information to members, 112; mobilization and, 114, 174
state federations, 100
state races, 70; candidate endorsements, 72–73, 74; targeting decisions, 74–75
state workers, union membership and, 83
strategies: Sweeney's focus, 20–21, 22, 85, 96–97. *See also* political strategies
strikes, 162–63
structure of unions, mobilization and, 108–9
suburban areas, union members in, 35, 36, 45
surveys: Ohio unions, 179–80; Teamsters strike against UPS, 162
Sweeney, John J.: AFL-CIO presidential elections, 1–2, 29, 67, 89, 129, 155; agenda setting, 89–92; effectiveness as leader, 172; labor agenda, 155; on labor union dichotomy, 3–5; organizing strategy, 92–96; political strategies, 20–21, 22, 85, 96–97, 107; on status of unions, 39
Sweeney, Randall, 151–52

Taft, Bob, 73
Taft-Hartley Act of 1947, 108, 163; contributions to candidates, 87n4; passage of, 11, 16; secondary boycotts, 175n1
targeting decisions, 74–75, 92, 184; campaign contributions for Project '96, 98; of members of Congress, 172; industries for organizing, 93–94; issues and, 139–40; the South, 94
Taylor, Peggy, 94–95
teachers, 9; ideology of, 56–57; organizing of, 161; party identification, 55
teaching assistants, 96
Teamsters. *See* International Brotherhood of Teamsters (Teamsters)
technology sector, 29, 158
tenure, 61, 123–24, 125, 184; activism and, 132n9; commitment and, 51, 53; Democratic support and, 143; voting behavior and, 148

textile workers, 161–62
Tierney, John T., 67
Total Quality Management, 158
trade policy, 156–57, 164, 170
trade relations, China, 164–65
training sessions, 112, 171
turnout rates, 92, 133–38, 184

UAW. *See* United Auto Workers (UAW)
UMWA (United Mine Workers of America), 2, 14
union certification elections, 95
Union of Electrical, Radio, and Machine Workers, (IUE), 121
union households, 24, 184; decline in, 27; earnings, 37; education level of, 33–34; feeling thermometer ratings, 43–45; housewives in, 32; political activism and, 61, 127–28; political party identification, 41–42; residence patterns, 35; social class identification, 40–41; voter turnout, 135. *See also* membership
union members. *See* membership
Union of Needletrades, Industrial, and Textile Employees (UNITE), 161–62
Union Summer programs, 96
UNITE (Union of Needletrades, Industrial, and Textile Employees), 161–62
United Auto Workers (UAW), 2, 8, 9, 103; composition of, 28; endorsement of Gore, 166–67; GM workers and, 161; issues, 109; membership, 14; mobilization of members, 83; organizing challenges, 162; proposed merger, 174; Reuther's agenda, 68; support for Sweeney, 90
United Food and Commercial Workers, 8
United Mine Workers of America (UMWA), 2, 14
United Parcel Service (UPS), 162
United Steelworkers of America (USWA), 2, 90; member education, 112; occupational changes and, 28; proposed merger, 174
University of Chicago, 24
University of Michigan, 24
Unruh, Jesse, 91
urban areas, union members in, 35, 36, 45

USA Today, 162
U.S. Chamber of Commerce, 5, 81, 102
USWA (United Steelworkers of America), 2, 90

Verba, Sidney, 131n2
voluntarism, 10, 121–22, 131n7
volunteers: commitment to union and, 123–24; coordinators of, 99; recruitment of, 115, 121–22
vote choice, 138–41, 148, 170–71
voter guides, 99
voter registration, 140–41; as appropriate activity, 60; Ohio, 135; union spending on, 78
voting behavior, 199; factors involved in, 148–53; influence of endorsements and, 144

Wagner Act of 1935, 14
Washington Post, 167
white collarization of unions, 29, 31
white-collar workers, 28–29, 45, 95–96, 156; education level, 34; engineers, 163; gender of, 31–33; organization of, 173; union membership, 28–29, 31, 156; voter turnout rates, 137
whites: commitment to union, 51, 52; union membership and, 35–37, 45; voter turnout rates, 138
Wilson, John Q., 119
workers' compensation, 167, 168
workers' rights, 164
workforce: age of, 37–38, 45; diversity of, 173; earnings, 37; education level of, 33–34, 45; suburbanization of, 35, 36; union membership and, 26–27
working class, 40–41; commitment to union, 51, 52; ideology, 134; voting behavior and, 148
workplace, benefits of, 65
World Bank, 164
World Economic Forum, Davos, Switzerland, 164
World Trade Organization, 164
Wright, James E., 84
Wyden, Ron, 97

About the Authors

Herbert B. Asher is Professor Emeritus of Political Science at the Ohio State University and serves as counselor to the university president.

Eric S. Heberlig is Assistant Professor of Political Science at the University of North Carolina at Charlotte.

Randall B. Ripley is Dean of the College of Social and Behavioral Sciences and Professor of Political Science at the Ohio State University.

Karen Snyder is the President of The Strategy Team, Ltd., a public opinion research firm.